York County Virginia

DEEDS, ORDERS, WILLS, ETC.

1720–1722

Kathleen Carrow Ingram

HERITAGE BOOKS
2023

HERITAGE BOOKS

AN IMPRINT OF HERITAGE BOOKS, INC.

Books, CDs, and more—Worldwide

For our listing of thousands of titles see our website
at
www.HeritageBooks.com

Published 2023 by
HERITAGE BOOKS, INC.
Publishing Division
5810 Ruatan Street
Berwyn Heights, MD 20740

Heritage Books by the author:

York County, Virginia Deeds, Orders, Wills, Etc., 1720–1722

York County, Virginia Deeds, Orders, Wills, Etc., 1722–1725

York County, Virginia Deeds, Orders, Wills, Etc., 1725–1728

International Standard Book Number
Paperbound: 978-1-68034-829-3

INTRODUCTION

This book contains abstracts of deeds of lease and release, wills, inventories and court orders from Liber 16, pages 1 through 187. Items in the inventory are generally described but not in detail, in order to save space. The names of all slaves are shown here.

The original page numbers are given in the text.

Limited punctuation has been added in some instances for clarity.

The original liber is in extremely poor condition and difficult to read. Portions of pages are missing throughout. The handwriting is hard to read compounded by the clerk's use of his own creative and inconsistent abbreviations along with legal terms long out of use. In the following page we attempt to interpret his use of legal terms and abbreviations. The author deserves much credit for her painstaking conversion of these records into readable print.

<u>Earlier works</u>

Between 1938 and 1949 Beverley Fleet created 34 volumes of Virginia Colonial Abstracts covering the earliest vital records of birth, marriage and death; tax lists; court orders; militia lists; wills; and deeds. These volumes were merged into three volumes by and published by Genealogical Publishing Co., Baltimore. Volume three has records of York, Charles City, Henrico, Lower Norfolk and Washington counties.

Abstracts by Benjamin B. Weisiger III have been published by New Papyrus Publishing Co., Inc., Athens Georgia. These include York County Virginia Records 1665-1672; York County Virginia Records 1672-1676, and York County Virginia Records, 1672-1676.

John Frederick Dorman has abstracted and published 7 volumes of York County Deeds, Orders, Wills, for the period 1687-1697.

Work is proceeding to complete the abstraction of York County records prior to 1760 including deeds, court orders and probate.

F. Edward Wright
Lewes, Delaware
2005

LEGAL TERMS & ABBREVIATIONS USED BY THE COURT CLERK

accn - account
accon - action
accs - accounts
acct. - account
ackn - acknowledged
Ad - Adam
admon - administration
admr - administrator
aforsd - aforesaid
agst - against
agt - against
als - also
als exo - also execution (?)
Andw - Andrew
Anth. - Anthony
Arcgibd. - Archibald
Archbd - Archibald
Arth - Arthur
ass, - assault
att - attorney
atta - attachment
auts - accounts (?)
balla. - balance
battry - battery
Benj. - Benjamin
Benja. - Benjamin
chattles - chattels. Personal property (as opposed to real property or land and whatever is growing on the land)
cl cur - clerk of the court
complt - complainant
cont - continued
covenent (covenant) - an agreement, convention, or promise of two or more parties, by deed in writing. In its broadest usage, it means any contract.
currt - current
Danl - Daniel
decd - deceased
dec't. - decedent
dedireus, dedirus, dedinius - probably meant for dedimus potestatem which refers to an old English practice, a writ or commission issuing out of changer, empowering the persons named to perform certain acts, as to administer oaths to defendants in chancery and take their answers...
deft - defendant
detinue - a form of action which lies for the recovery in specie of personal chattels from one who acquired possession of them lawfully, but retains it without right, together with damages for the detention. Possessory action for recovery of personal chattels unjustly detained.
dismt - dismissed
Do or do - ditto
Edwd - Edward
Elia - Elizabeth

Eliz - Elizabeth
enulling - annulling
est - estate
execr - executor
execrx - executrix
Exectr. - executor
exo - execution?
demurrer - an objection by the defense
feoffors - persons making a feoffment
feoffment - a gift of a freehold interest in land accompanied by livery of seisin
genl - general
gentl - gentleman
Geo - George
imparlance - time given to either of the parties to an action to answer the pleading of the other.
imprs - imprimis - in the first place, first of all
indemnify - to secure against loss or damage; to give security for the reimbursement of a person (or entity) in case of an anticipated loss falling to the person or entity.
inv - inventory
inventus - found
invry - inventory
Jms - James
Jno - John
Jos - Joseph
Lawr - Lawrence
Lawre - Lawrence
livery of seisen - the appropriate ceremony for transferring the corporal possession of land or tenements by a grantor to his grantee
Margt - Margaret
Math - Mathew
Merch - merchant
Mich. - Michael
mon - motion
Nath - Nathaniel
Nihil dicit - the defendant says nothing in the face of the plaintiff's declaration; omits to plead
non est inventus - (he) is not found
nonsuit - termination of an action which did not adjudicate issues on the merits, a judgment rendered against a party on his inability to maintain his cause in court
ordry - ordinary, meant here for a public house where food, drink, and lodging were furnished to the traveler and his beast, at fixed rates.
pet - petition
petiton - petition
petr - petitioner
plt - plaintiff
presentment - an accusation usually initiated by the grand jury
pson - person
Querum fidem -

Richd - Richard
rejt - rejected
replevin - an action whereby the
owner or person entitled to
repossession of goods or chattels
may recover those goods or
chattels form one who has
wrongfully detains such goods or
chattels.
respondt - respondent
retnd - returned
Ro - Robert
Rob - Robert
Robt - Robert
Saml - Samuel
Susa - Susanna
sd - said
Tho: Thomas
Thos - Thomas
tob - tobacco
tobo - tobacco
vendue - a sale usually at public
auction under authority of law
vert - verdict
vizt. - videlicet, to wit, namely, that is
to say
WmBurgh - Williamsburg(h)
wth - with

York County, Virginia
Deeds, Orders, Wills, Etc.
Book 16

1720-1722

YORK COUNTY COURT 16 Jan 1720

The last will and testament of John Thebo Dec'd was presented in court by Elinore Thebo the execr. therein named who made oath to it being proved by the Oath of Alexr. McDonald, one of the witnessed thereto is admitted to Record. May County/Court 1721
This Will was furthur proved by the Oath Test Phi: Lightfoot Co. Cur. of . . . Hansford which is ordered to be. . . Phi. Lightfoot Co Cur. (probably for Co-executor)

Know all me by these presents that we Elinor Thebo, Saml. Hyde and David Holloway of the County of York are held & firmly bound unto the Worshipfull the justices of the County aforesaid in the sum of one hundred pounds sterling payable to the sd Justices their heirs or Sucessors or some of them to which the payment well & truly to be made. We bind ourselves & every one of us & every of our heirs execrs & admsnrs joyntly & Severally firmly by these presents Sealed with our Seals & dated this 16th day of January 1720.

The condition of this obligation is such that if the above bounden Elinor Thebo Executor of the last Will & Testament of Jno. Thebo, Dec. do make or cause to be made a true & perfect inventory of all & singular the Goods Chattles & Credits of the said John Thebo, Dec. , which have or shall make come to the hands, possession or knowledge of her the said Elinor Thebo or into the hand of any other person or persons for her & the same to made to exhibite or cause to be exhibited in to the County Court of York at such time as she shall be therunto required by the Court of the Same Goods Chattels & Credits & all other of the Goods Chattels & Credits of the sd. Jno. Thebo Dec'd at the time of his death which at anytime after shall come to the hand or the possession of her the sd. Elinor Thebo or into the hand or possession of any other person or persons for her to well & Truly Admin or according to law & further do make a true and just accounting of her accots & doings therin when hereto required by the Ad (aforesaid) Court & also pay & deliver all her legacys contained & specified within A (aforesaid) Testament as far as the sd. Goods & Chattles & Credits will therunto extend according to the value thereof and the law shall charge her. Then this obligation to be void & of none effect otherwise to remain in full force & vertue. Elinor (her mark) Thebo. Wit. Sam. Hyde, David Holloway.

At a Court held for York County January the 16th 1720
This bond was presented & acknowledged in Court by the parts therto & admitted to record.

Appraisement of the est of Samuel Burkhead. Barkhead Jno and C. Valued at £16. 16. 6. Wit. Thos X Cox, Edmd. Sweny, Robt. Shield, X . Johnson's

At a Court held for York County Jany. 16th 1720. This inventory of the state of Samuel Barkhead dec'd was presented by Jno. Johnson the Adm & Admitted Record (?) by sd Test & Phi. Lightfoot. Co. Cur

Page 8
Oliver from Porteus.
I do by these presents appoint John Oliver my Special Attorney, Factor and Overseer to appear & proseintes as my Attorney & in my name any persons indebted to me on any Aus. t whatsoever also to dispose of Goods, Cattle and hoggs & other moveable things belonging to the estate of me the Subscriber, only to my proper use & Advantage. I also by these presents give unto the Ad John Oliver the charge of all my Plantations and Negroes-- & Stock. Except my upper plantation in King & Queen . . over which Mr. George More has the Charge & I also give him power to disperse of the Stock, Corn & Any other produce of sd. plantation for my use and advantage. Except Tobacco which is to be shipt home for England on my proper Ausp. Hereby giving & Granting unto my A Attorney Factor & Overseer full power in the premises. In witness have herunto set my hand & Seal the Sixth day of May 1720. Robt Porteus. Wit. Thos. Nelson.

At a Court held for York County Feb 20th 1720
This power of Att. from Robert Porteus Esq to John Oliver
J Walker was presented in Court by the Sd Oliver & proved
By the oaths of Thomas Nelson & Joseph Walker-
Tho. s Wyatt Witnessed therto & admitted To Record.
Eliza. Powers Test. Phi. Lightfoot Cl. Cou.

H. Hayward

At a Court held for York County February 20, 1720. Present: John Holloway, Thos Nelson, Hen. Tyler, Graves Park, Lawre. - Genl. Justices

Holloway from trustees
Deeds act- John Clayton Esq & Wm. Robertson Genl.
of the Feoffors or Trustees for the Land appropriated for the building & creating of the City of Wm. Burgh presented & acknowledged their

Deeds of Lease & release for 2 Lotts of the Ad will be Rec'd thereon to John Holloway Gentl. at whose môn they are admitted to record.

Holland from Trustees
Deeds ack.
John Clayton Esq. & Wm. Robertson Gentl. two of the feoffors or Trustees for the land appropriated for the building and creating the City of WmBurgh presented & acknowledged their deeds of lease & release with a receipt thereon for eight Lotts of the Ad. Land to Lewis Holland which Deeds & rec. on the Ad. Hollands môn. are admitted to record.

Cobbs from Trustees Deed Ack.
John Clayton Esquire & Wm. Robertson Gentl. Two of the feoffors or trustees for the land appropriated for the building & creating of the City of WmBurgh presented & acknowledged their Deeds of Lease & Release with Receipt thereon for one Lott of the Ad. Land to Saml. Cobbs which Deeds & Rec. & on the Cobbs môn. are admitted to Record.

Digger's Accd. agt.
Baylors estate proved

Cole Digges Esq made oath to an Acct. agt. the estate of Jno. Baylor Dec'd the ball. whereof amounting to five hundred & five pounds Sixteen Shillings & three pence & Three farthings which is ordered to be paid.

Page 9
Cole Digges Esq made oath to an acctng against the estate of Matthew Bollan, dec. the ball[ance] whereof amounting to One Hundred & ten Pounds two shillings and 0 pence which is ordered to be certified.

An inventory of the estate of David Cuningham Decd. was presented in court By Saml. Cobbs the Exec & admitted to record.

An Invry. & C. of the estate of John Thebo Decd. was Presented by Elinor Thebo Exec. r & admitted to Record.

A power of Attorney from Robt. Porteus Esq. to Jno. Oliver was proved by the Oaths of Thomas Nelson & Joseph Walker Gentl witnesses thereto & admitted to record.

Sam a Negroe boy belonging to Wm. Lee is adjudged to be fourteen years old.

Jenny a negro girl belonging to Sarah Barry is Adjudged to be thirteen years old.

Francis Tyler presented & Acknowledged his Deeds of lease and release for four Lotts of ground in the City of WmBurgh in this County to Gavin Corbin on whose Môn they are Admitted to record.

Wm. Robertson & Sam. Cobbs presented & acknowledged their deeds of lease & release for one Lott of ground lying in the City of WmBurgh in this County to Nathl. Newton on whose motion they are admitted to record

Wm. Robertson & Sam. Cobbs presented & acknowledged their deeds of lease & release for one Lott of ground lying in the City of WmBurgh in this County to George Newton on whose motion they are admitted to record

Stephen Fuller presented & Acknowledged his Deeds of Lease & Release for one Lott of ground Lying in YorkTown sd. Land for performance of Covenenants to John Gibbons. & also appeared Eliza. wife of the sd. Stephen & relinquished her Rights & Title of Dower - in the sd. Lott being privately examined by the sd. John Gibbons which Deed bond & relinquishment on the sd. Gibbons mon. are admitted to record.

On the petition of Armiger Parsons praying to have a share in the estate of James Hay who dyed an infant , having intermarried with the Sister of the sd. James Decd. . it is therupon ordered that the Sheriff summon John Hay in whose hands the estate of the sd. James was in to answer the sd. Petition at the next court.

On the petition of Uriah Hudson & Thomas Cripps ,Setting forth that they being security for Sam Millingtons sd. Motion on the estate of Jno. Morris and praying to be released from the said securityship the sd Millington appeared & agreed to give them security at the next court or surrender the estate of the sd. Morris to the pett. rs it is thereby ordered be continued until the next Court.

Matthew Pierce, Robt. Cobbs,Rich. Page& John Daniel or any three of them having been sworn before a Justice of the County are appointed to appraise the estate of John Layton dec'd & Make report thereof to the next Court.

On the petition of Francis Kendall orphan of Richd. Kendall dec'd . Richard Stewart is appointed her Guardian & he having entered into Bond together with Saml. Timson & Jno. Davis his securitys for the purpose of which being deeds of Dec'd , bond is admitted to record. It is ordered that the sd. Stewart take care of the sd. Infant & her estate. -

An inventory of the estate of John Potlin (Pollin?) Decd. was presented in Court and admitted to Record.

An Inventory of the estate of Henry Hayward Decd. was presented in Court by Eliza. Hayward & Edward Tabb Exec. rs & Admitted to record.

On the petition of Edwd. Sweny & Jno. Robinson Church Wardens of Cha. parish setting forth that Henry Hayward Decd. desired that fifteen pounds might be given to the poor of the sd. Parish , more than was specified by his the sd. Hayward Will. Which appears by the dep. on of Edw. Tabb one of the Exec. rs of the sd. Will being admitted to Record. The sd. Tabb appeared & Acknowledged the Same to be true. It is thereupon Ordered that the Exec. rs of the Sd. will pay the sd. Sum out of the Decd. Estate to the pet. trs to be applied to the uses. Declared by the Testator. -

On the petition of Wm. Livingston agt. his servant maid Mary Ansell for the trouble of his house in the time of her lying in having been delivered of a bastard child. It is thereupon ordered that the Sd. Ansell serve her Sd. Master One whole year in consideration thereof after her time by / indenture custom or former order is expired according to law.

On the petition of Benj. Weldon agt. Jeremiah Hill for four pounds Eight shillings & eight pence halfpenny proved by the plt. oath on his môn. Indgn. is granted him for the Tot. Sum & costs. An Att. for the Indgn being returned executed by the Sherif in the hands of James Roscow Esq. It is ordered that the said Roscow be summoned to render an Act. of the Sd. Hills effects in his hands at the next Court.

The difference between Wm. Henry plt. & Godfrey Pole def. is dismt being agreed

The action upon the Case between Joseph Thomas & Jno. Avery deft. is dsmt. Neither party appearing.

Page 10
On the petition of Wm. Livingston agt. His Servant maid Mary Ansell for absens, time & charges taking her up on her confession. It appearing that she had been absent from her Sd. Masters Service the space of Seven weeks. -& that he had expended Ten shillings in pursuit of her, It is thereupon Ordered that she serve her Sd. Master Seventeen weeks and four days after her time by Indenture is done or former order is expired. -

In the suit in Chancery brought by John Hay & Mary his wife complrs agt. Thomas Tomer Surviving Execr &c, of John Tomer, Decd. Resondnt. & the sd. respndr. failing to appear and answer the sd. Suit. It is ordered that an Att. Find agt. The Respondg. Body for his appearance at the next Court.

In the action of Detinue between Thos. Tomer plt. & Sam. Tomkins deft. For one hundred pounds Sterling damage an Imparlance is granted the deft. Until the next court.

The difference between Wm. Gordon plt. & Wm. Ratliff def. neither party appearing is dismissed.

The difference between Thomas Delany plt. & Cha. s Rowan Deft. is dismt.

The action of Debt between Saml. Ramsden plt. & Saml. Sweny deft. Neither party appearing is dismt.

The Difference between John Shaife plt. & Thos. Wyatt deft, is dsmt.

The petition of Justinian Love agt. Dennis White is dsmt.

The difference between Lewis Delony plt. & Jeremiah Hill deft. is dsmt.

The difference between Thomas Jones plt. Archibd. Blair & Jno. Blair Execrs. &c. of Mongo Ingles Decd. . deft. is dismt.

The difference between Susannah Tavernor plt. & Wm Tavernor deft. Neither party appearing is dsmt.

In the action upon the Case between Joseph Stacy plt. & Robt. Ross deft. For-fifteen shillings Current money. issue being implied the Cause is referred For tryal untill the next Court

Indentures between John Holdworth & John Selby were presented & acknowledged in Court to be Certifyed.

The presentment of the Church Wardens of Bruton Parish agt. Margaret Torrance for having a bastard child is dismt.

The action upon the Case between Wm. Fleming plt. & Lawre Smith deft. for Seven hundred pounds of Tob. & Cash . the Cause is continued to try the issue & demurrer until the next Court. -

Rich. Ambler made Oath to an Acct. Agt. The Estate of John Baylor Decd. which is ordered to be certified.

The Ejections For in and Brought by Robert Westlake plt. agt. Ann Worley deft. For Ten pounds current money is continued at sd. Deft. Môn. and charged until the next Court. -

Page 11
I do order give & dispose the (blurred. . .) form following inpt. I give and bequeath unto my loving wife Elizabeth Hayward Negroes Viz: Andrew ,Kate Bess, George, Tony, Jenny, Mingo old Sarah & Nanny, which sd. Negroes I give unto my loving wife to enjoy her natural life & After her decease all that Shall be left of the sd. Ten Negroes & their increase my will & Desire is & I do hereby give unto the Children of my loving sister Margaret Tabb to be equally divided amongst them, to them and their heirs for ever. Item, my will is that a share that I expect in by the first fleet of ships from London with theWhip & harness I give unto my loving wife. Item my will that I give unto my Kinsman John Tabb son of Thomas Tabb as a Legacy of twenty-five pounds Sterling. Item I give unto my nephew John Tabb afore sd. All the acct. that he stands indebted to me by book as a Legacy. Item I give unto my NephewJohn Tabb my Silver hilted Sword & Cane. Item I give unto my Nephew John Tabb my Shirt buttons that I ware. Item I give unto my Nephew Henry Wyth my watch & a p. of new Gold shirt buttons that now is by me & my two Rings that I frequently ware as a Legacy. Item I give unto my Nephew John Tabb one Negroe man named Ralph to him & his heirs for ever. Item I give unto my Nephew Thomas Tabb the son of Thomas Tabb a Negroe man named Cafan to him & His heirs forever. Item I give unto my Nephew Henry Tabb son of Thomas Tabb a Negroe man named In'peter (?) to him and his heirs for ever. Item I give unto my Niece Mary Tabb the daughter of Thomas Tabb a Negroe man named Peter as a Legacy for her & her heirs for ever. Item I give unto my Niece Rachel Tabb the daughter of Thomas Tabb a negroe boy named James as a legacy to her and her heirs forever. Item I give unto John Chisman the son of John Chisman one Negroe named Roger as a legacy to him & His heirs Forever. Item I give unto my Nephew Henry Chisman son of John Chisman a Negroe boy named Oliver as a Legacy to him and his heirs forever. Item I give unto my niece Diana Chisman the daughter of John Chisman a Negro girl named Hannah to her & her heirs for ever. Item I give unto my niece Elinor Chisman daughter of John Chisman a Negroe girl to her & her heirs for ever. Item I give unto my Nephew Benjamin Moss the son of Benja. Moss a Negroe girl named Nancy to him & his heirs forever. Item I give unto my nephew Francis Moss the son of Bena. Moss a Negroe girl named Penny to him & His heirs forever- Item I give unto my Nephew John Moss son of Bena. Moss a Negroe girle named Dinah to him & his heirs forever. Item my will is that five Negroes left as a Dowry in the Last Will of my deceased father Henry Hayward Viz. Jack, Nancy, Tom Peter & old Black Betty that was not given away by the will of my dec'd father with all their increase after the death of my Mother-in-law Eliza. Tabb I do give & bequeath my four Nephews & Nieces the sons & daughters of John Chisman & my four Nephews & Nieces before mentioned the Children of Benjamin Moss the sd. Five Negroes & their Increase to be

appraised and equally divided among the Eight Children of Jno. Chisman & Ben. Moss share & share alike. Item all the rest of my estate be it of what notice (?) Served (Bottom line mostly illeg.) I am Vir. . . . . . household Goods, White Se. . (*missing*)
Page 12
Merchandise, Corn, Tobo. ,Hoggs , Cattle, horses, Sheep, Book Debts & other debts, bills, bonds & every thing in right appertains & belongs to me being I wholly valued & appraised out of which my Just Debts & Legacys before exprest, being first paid & discharged, I Give the full half of the residue of my personal estate to my loving wife Eliza. Hayward for ever, out of the other half of the estate it is my desire my Execx. & Exec. rs hereafter named shall pay & diver of the Goods of my Store to the poor of Charles parish Twenty five ppounds in Such Sorts of Goods as Shall Suit their wants best, The other hald of my Estate when the Legacy of the Poor is taken out I give to be equally divided among my Kinfolks hereafter named, John Tabb, Dianah Robinson, Thomas Tabb,Henry Tabb - Mary Tabb, Rachel Tabb the Children of Thomas Tabb dec'd, John Chisman, Henry Chisman, , Diana Chisman & Elinor Chisman Children of Jno. Chisman, Benja. Moss,Francis Moss, John Moss & Edward Moss the Children of Benjamin Moss Share & share alike. I nominate my loving wife Elizabeth Hayward Executrix, Bena. Moss, Edward Tabb & John Chisman Joynt Executors with my wife of this my last will and Testament to see it performed according to the true intent & meaning there of . My desire is that my Exerx. & Execrs. Shall give my Servant Boy Robert Fue (Tue?) two years Schooling to read & Write, Acknowledging this my Last will & Testament revoking all other wills heretofore made by me as Witness my hand & Seal the day & year find above written. H. Hayward. Wit. John Slater.

At a Court held for York County Jany. The 16th 1720
Robt Philipson. Bernard Cowdert

This last Will & Testament of Henry Hayward Decd. was presented in Court by Elizabeth Hayward & Edward Tabb Two of the Execrs. therein named who made Oath to it, The other Exectrs. Having relinquished their right to Exershp. & being proved by the Oaths of all the Witnesses, Therto is admitted to Record. Test Phi. Lightfoot Cl Cur

Edward Tabb maketh Oath that Cattee a Negroe Girle not being disposed of in the will of Henry Hayward Decd. further sd. Henry Hayward desired that the sd. Negroe Girle should be given to his wife Elizabeth Hayward during her natural life & after her decease to Edward Moss son of Benj. Moss by Dianah his wife to him & His heirs forever & furthur- desired that Fifteen Should be given to the Poor in Charles parish more than what is mentioned in his will. Edward Tabb

At a Court held for York County Jany. the 16th 1720.
This depon of Edward Tabb relating to a Codicil to the last Will & Testament of Henry Hayward Decd. being Sworn by the sd. Tabb is admitted to record.
Test Phi. Lightfoot Cl. Cour.

Page 13
For the Judgement M... (?)
Security or Surrender the sd. . . (*missing*) estate to the pet. r. before the next Court. The petition of Saml. Millington agt. Ralph Graves neither appearing is dismst.

In the petition of Francis Sharp agt. James Netter for Fifteen Shillings & Sis pence current money due by Note the Cause is continued & Morris Walker to appear pursuant to a former order to give an acctg. of sd. Netters effects in his hands at the next court.

The difference between Saml Millington plt. & Wm. Bigges deft. is dismst.

In the action in the Case between Jno. Abbott plt. & Jno. Ness (Neff?) deft. For ten pound, Ten Shillings and ten pence curr. Money due by Acct. in the deft. Motion Oyer is granted him until the next Court.

The petition of Jas. Bates for ad min` in the estate of Mary Brewer dec'd is s referred until the next Court.

Joseph Freeman is appointed Constable for the City of Williamsburg that lyes in this County. Ordered that he repair to some Justice of the county and take the usual Oath.

The last Will and Testament of John Layton dec'd was presented in Court by the Attorney of Mary Layton the execx therein named together with a Certificate under the hand of Henry Tyler gentl. of her having under oath therto & the same being proved by the Oaths of the witnesses is admitted to record. On the motion of the Sd. Execr. She having entered with bond security. . (*missing*) acknowledged is admitted to record of certificate is granted her for obtaining probate thereof in due form.

It appearing for Certificate returned to this Court under the hands of Thomas Nelson & Graves Park Gent. ,trustees that they have suspended Katherine Craig and ordinary Keeper in the City of Williamsburgh on a complaint made to them by the Governor for interefering in divers of his servants, the Sd. Caraig hath time until next Court to answer thereto till then (when) She Stands further Suppressed.

In the petition of Joseph Freeman agt. Thomas Pinkett his apprentice praying that he might be repaid the time which the Sd. Pinkett hath been absent during his apprenticeship which appears to be two years ordered that he serve his Sd. Master two years compleat after his time by indentures is expired.

Peter Brewer of the County of James City on evidence for John Bates the petition of such (find Ad. Brewer having made oath that he attended four days & Traveled Eighteen miles coming & going each time that the Sd. Bates pay him for the Same according to Law & Costs als. Exo

In the Accus. of trespass between Wm Gordon pet. & Lawrence Smith Deft. One hundred Pounds damage by means of the Deft. Obstructing a survey of certain lands lying in York County in the parish of Yorkhampton (?) duly entered forewith the survey for Court assessing by estimation at two Hundred acres to. . (*missing*) the defendant having pleaded Not guilty. It is thereupon ordered that the Surveyor of the County with an able jury of the Antient freeholders of the vicinage who are in no way concerned by affinity or consanguinity to either of the partys of interest to the Land in Controversie nor liable to any other just exception to be summoned by the Sheriff & Sworn before a Justice of the Peace of the County go upon the land in Difference on the 15th day of March next if fair , if not the next fair day & survey & lay out the Same according to the most Antient known & reputed pounds thereof having regard to all patent Evidences that shall be produced by either party & if they find the deft. A trespasser that they value the damages & make report of their proceedings to the next court.

In the action of the trespass on the Case between the Hon. Alexander Spotswood Esq . Plt. & John Holloway deft. For One Hundred pounds current money damage by means of the deft. Refusing to pay unto the Plt. The sum of Ninety Nine pounds due to him from one Rich. Fitz Wilkams & the WI. The def. by
Page 14
notes or isnstrum under hand & Seal and assume upon himself & faithfully to pay al as the declaration is more fully expressed. The makers of Law arising from the Express verdict given and received in this Cause being this day fully argued & heard the Court of Indigence. For the Plt. Whereupon it is considered that the Plt. Recover Agt. The def. The Sum of Seventy Nine Pounds Seven Shill. Being the damages by the Jurors adjudged with Costs also. Exo. From wth. Judgement: The def. prayed and appeal to the Seventh day of the Next General court wh. is granted he having together with Nathl. Burwell Atg (. illeg.) his Security entered into Court the Plt. In the Sum of Four Hundred & Fifty Pounds for his own prosecution of the sd. appeal according to Law is. Oath being acknowledged is admitted in to record Ordered that the Court be Adjourned until the Court in Course. Lawr. Smith. Truly Entered by Phi. Lighfoot ClCur

In the Name of God Amen, I John Laton of Bruton Parish in York County being at that time in Good health & perfect memory, Praise be given to God, Do make & order this my Last Will & testament , revoking & hereby Dismissing all former Wills whatever by me made. First of all I bequeath my Soul to Almighty God the (illeg) in hopes of p. . (*missing*) of my sins through the merits of Blessd Lord & Savior Christ Jesus & my body to the ground to be decently buried in Christian fashion & for all such estate hath it pleased God to Bless me with . After my debts are& funeral charges paid , I do dispose of in manner following Item I Give & Bequeath to my loving daughter Martha Bloxom about Six years old. Item I give unto my loving son Thomas Laton my Plantation whereon Francis Dursson & Mullinin (?) Laton now live & One half of all my Lands to him & His heirs forever. Item I give unto my loving son David Laton My Manor planta. tion where I now live & the other half of my lands to him & His heirs forever. It is my will & Desire that all my lands be equally divided between them both. Item I Give & bequeath unto my loving wife Mary Laton my Negroe man named Dick for her lifetime and after her decease then to my sd. Sons Thomas Laton & David Laton forever. Item I give & bequeath unto my wife Mary & my Two Sons Thomas Laton & David Laton my personal estate as Cattle Horses Mares & household stuff to be equally divided among them. Item I give unto my two sd. sons Thomas Laton & David Laton the land I gave to my daughter Martha Bloxom for her lifetime and after her decease to be equally divided between my two sd. Sons. Lastly I do bequeath my loving wife Mary Laton & Cosin John Green Execr. of this my last will & Testament. In witness of the truth hereof I have hereunto put my hand & Seal this 30th day of July 1719. (Mary Laton identified before signed) John X Laton. Wit. George White. Thos. Laton for (?) Laton. Her mark

Page 15
Know all men by these presents that we Elizabeth Hayward, Edward Tabb, Benj Moss & Jno. Chisman of the County of York are held & firmly bound unto the Worshipfull the Justices of the County Aforesaid in the Sum of two thousand pounds Sterling payable to the Sd. Justices their heirs and successors. Some of them to this which payment well & Truly to be made. We bind ourselves & every of our heirs. Execurs. Adminors. Joyntly & Severally firmly by these presents Sealed with our Seal & Dated this 16th Day of January 1720.
The Condition of this Obligation is Such that if the above bounden Eliza. Hayward & Edward Tabb Execrs. of the last Will & testament of Henry Hayward dec'd to make or cause to be made a true & perfect inventory of all & Singular the Goods Chattels & Credits of the Sd. Henry Hayward dec'd which have or shall come to the Hands possessions or Knowledge of them the Sd Eliza. Hayward or Edw. Tabb or into the hands or possessions of any other person or persons for them & the same do make . . . do exhibite or cause to be exhibited into the County Court of York at such time as they shall be thereunto required by

the Sd. Court & the same Goods Chattles & Credits & all other the Goods Chattles & Credits of the Sd. Henry Hayward dec'd at the time of his death which at anytime after shall come to the hands & Possessions of them the Sd. Elizabeth Hayward & Edward Tabb or into the hands or possessions of any other person or persons for them to well & Truly administer according to & further do make a true & Just Acct. of their Actings & doings therein when thereto required by the Sd. court & also pay & Deliver all the Legacys contained & specified in the Sd. Testament as far as the Sd. Goods Chattles & Credits will thereunto extend According to the value thereof & Law shall charge them then this Obligation to be void & of None effect. Otherwise remain in full force & Vertue.

At a Court held for York County Jan'y the 16th 1720

Eliza Hayward, Edw. Tabb, Benjamin Moss, John Chisman
This Bond was presented & acknowledged in Court
By the Partys thereto & admitted to Record . Test Phi. Lightfoot Cl. Curr

In the name of God Amen, I Samuel Barnard of the parish of Yorkhampton in the County of York, Clerk, being weak of body but of perfect Sense & Memory praised be Almighty God for the Same do make make & ordain this my last will & Testament in manner & form flowing Revoking all former & other wills by me heretofore made. Do hereby declare this My last Will & testament as followeth. First my soul I Committ to the hands of Almighty God, my Creator & my body is to be decently buried at the discret. of my Execr. Hereafter named. And as to what worldly possessions it hath pleased God to bless me with I give & bequeath as follows after my just debts be paid. I give and bequeath unto my Beloved wife Martha all my estates both real & personal under denomination SW& to her heirs for ever & do hereby nominate & appoint my said wife. Sole Exectrx. Hereunto Sett my hand & Seal the Fourteenth Day of November One Thousand Seven Hundred Twenty. . Sam. Barnard
Wit. J. Walker, Eliza. . Moody's (mark)

At a Court for York County January 16th 1720
This last Will & testament for Sam Barnard dec't was presented in Court by Martha Barnard the Exectr. Therin named who mad Oath to being proved by the Oaths by the Witnesses thereto is admitted to Record. Test. Phi. Lightfoot Cl. Cur.

Know all men by these presents that we Joseph Walker, Lawr. Smith & Thomas Nelson of the County of York Gentl. Asked & firmly bound unto the Worshipfull the Justices of the County aforesaid. In the Summ of three Hundred Pounds Sterling to the which payment well & Truly be made to the Justices their heirs & successors or some of them. We find ourselves & every of us our &

Every of our heirs Excetrs. & Adminrs. Jointly & Severally firmly by these presents Sealed with our Seals & Dated this 16th Day of January 1720.
The Condition of this Obligation is Such that if the above bounden Joseph Walker Adminr. With the Will payment of all the Goods Chattels & Credits of Saml. Barnard dec'd to make or cause to be made a true & perfect Inventory of all & Singular the Goods, chattels & Credits of the sd. Sam. Barnard Decd. which have or shall come to the hands & Possessions of him the Sd. Joseph Walker or into the hands or possessions of any other persons or persons for him & the Same to make do Exhibite or cause to be exhibited into the County of York as such time as he shall be ther unto required by the sd. Court & the same Goods Chattels & Credits & all other & all other the Goods, Chattels & Credits of him the Sd. Sam Barnard dec'd at the time of his death which at anytime after shall come to the hands or possessions of him the sd. Joseph Walker or into the hands or possessions of any other person or persons for him. In well & Truly Admin. According to Law & Furthur do make a true & Just Acctg. of his Actings & Doings therein when thereto required by the sd. Court & Also to well & truly pay & Deliver all the legacys contained & specified in the sd. Will & testament as far as the Sd. Goods Chattels & Credits will thereunto extend according to the value thereof & The Law Shall charge him. Then this obligation to be void or else to remain in full force & Vendue. J. Walker, Lawr. Smith, Tho. Nelson

At a Court held for York County January the 16th 1720.
The Bond was presented & acknowledged in Court by the partys thereto & Admitted to record. Test. Phi. Lightfoot Cl. Cur.

The name of God Amen, I John Thebo of Yorkhampton parish is York County being sick & weak of body but of perfect Sense & Memory do make this my Last will & Testament. Item I give & bequeath to my wife Elinor Thebo all my land to her & her heirs forever. Item I likewise give to my wife Elinor- after all my just debts are paid- all the rest of my Personal estate & further I do Constitute & appoint her the sd. Elinor whole & Sole Exec. of this my last Will & Testament. In Witness whereof I have hereunto sett my hand & Seal this 7th day of April 1720. Wit. Chas. Hansford, Alexander Markemole Jno. Thebo.

Page 17
The petition of John Ballard agt. Phi. Lightfoot is dismist.

The petition of Sackfield Brewer for Adm. of Mary Brewer's estate is dismist.

In the action in the case between Marjory Creed plt. & James Harman deft. For two Pounds Seven Shillings and Seven pence half penny due by Act both partys having submitted the Tryal to the Court who on hearing the evidence Judgement is granted the plt. for the aforesaid Sum of Two Pounds Seven Shillings Seven pence half penny Current money. Twenty shillings for a Lawyers fee & its ordered that the dft. Payeth same to the Plt. With Costs als Exo.

John Davis presented & Acknowledged his Deeds of lease & release for one Lott of ground lying in WmBurgh in this County to Christo. DeGraffenreid on whose Mon. they are admitted to Record.

An inventory of the Estate of Sam. Barnard dec'd was presented in Court & admitted to record.

Wm Marshall being summoned on evidence of Marjory Creed agt James Hardman having attended five days. It is ordered that he be paid by the Plt Two Hundred pounds of Tob. For the Same with Costs als/Exc.

Sarah Matthews on Evidence for Marjory Creed agt. James Hardman having attended five days, It is ordered that the plt. Pay her two Hundred Pounds of Tob. For the Same with Cost & Exec.

In the Suit in Chancery depending between Lawr. Smith and Mildred his wife late Mildred Goodwin Complts & John Goodwin Execr. &c of James Goodwin dec'd Respond. of the partys Thos Nelson , Joseph Walker & Richd. Ambler or any two of them are appointed & desired to and State & Settle the Aud. In difference & That each party have liberty to produce Such Evidences as are necessary in the sd. suit & Make report thereof to the next Court.

The action of Debt between David Morse (Morce?) plt & Joseph Frith deft. For £10. 2. 11 Current money due by note is Continued at the deft. Mon. & Charge until the next Court.

The action of Debt between George Winter plt & John Cooks deft. is dismist.

In the action of the case between Philip Lightfoot & Mary his wife Execrs. in the Last Will & Testament of James Burwell dec'd plt & Timo. Sullivant & Ann his wife Execr. of the last Will & Testament of John Merott Decd. deft. For Seventy Two Pounds Thirteen Shillings & One penny Half penny Current money due by Acctg. It appearing by a Settlement produces that the Sum of Twenty Three pounds & Three Shillings & Four pence half-penny Current money is due to the plts whereupon it is considered that the plt recover agt the deft the Sum of twenty Three pounds & Three Shillings & Four pence half-penny out of the sd. Estate with Costs als Exc.

Wm Robertson & Thos. Jones Execrs. of Susanna Allen hath further time allowed them to bring in an Ivry. of the sd. Estate until the next Court.

In the Petition of Ann Frith agt Wm Gray for Four Pounds Ten Shillings & Two pence farthing Current money due by Act George Ridley being summoned , according to a former order appeared & Acknowledged that he had four Pounds of the Gray's money in his custody. It is thereupon ordered that he pay the same to the petitioners als Exc.

The action upon the Case between Henry Borrodale & Judith his wife late Judith Hynton on behalf of the legatees of Mary Moory dec'd & Wm Tucker Exec &c of John Merry dec'd who was Execr. of Thos Merry dec'd who was Execr. &c of the aforesd Mary Moory Decd. deft. For Nine Hundred & Eleven pounds of Tobacco due by Aut issue being Joyned the Cause is Referred for Tryall the next Court.

The difference between Jno. Bates plt & Saml. Millington deft. Neither party appearing is dismist.

Page 18
The difference between Nicho. Morphey plt & Jane Bennet deft is Dismt.

The Difference between Lockay Myhill plt. & Nick. Manuel deft. is Dismt.

The difference between Harwood and Eliz. his wife Execr. of John Roberts Decd. plt. & Thos. Robbins & Mary his wife Admin &c of Wm. Davis dec'd defts is dismst.

The difference between John Abbott plt. & Jere. Hill deft. is dismist.

The difference between Jere Hill plt & Jno. Abott deft. is dismist.

In the action on the Case between Thomas Bell plt. & Chas. Rowan deft. For Two pounds Ten shillings due by Acct. Issue being Joyned the Cause is referred for Tryall until the next Court.

The action upon the Case between John Holloway Esq. plt. & Wm Alexander deft. For Five pounds current money damages is dismist. & ordered that the deft. Pay costs.

The action upon the case between Archib. Blair plt & Wm. Alexander deft. is dismist.

The difference Between the Reverend James Blair plt. & Wm. Alexander deft is dismist & it's ordered that the deft. Pay Costs & a Lawyors fee als. Ex.

The difference between John Cooke plt. & George Thomas deft. is dismist.

In the action in the case between Ann Wakefield plt & Francis Sharp deft. For twenty Pounds damage issue being Joyned the Case is referred for Tryal until the next Court

The difference between Thomas Robins plt & Richd. Turner deft. is dismist

The difference between Thomas Robins plt & Benj. Mann deft is dismist.

The action of Debt between Peter Beverley plt. & James Rickets deft. is dismst.

The difference between Joseph Soward plt. & Richd. Baker def is dismist

The difference between Wm Ford plt & Edw. Friend deft. is dismist.

The action upon the Case between Nath. Hooke plt & Mary Cary deft. is dismt.

The difference between Wm Shrine plt & Jno. Matlock deft, is dismist.

The difference between Saml. Tomison plt. & Jno. Abbott deft. is dismist.

In the action in the case between Thos. Nelson Gentl. & Thos. Robins & Mary his wife deft & the defts. Failing to appear & no Security being returned for them- Judgement is granted to the plt. For the sd. Sum & Costs agt. The sd. defts. Joseph Walker gent. Sherif unless the deft. Appear at the next Court & answer the plt action.

The difference between Chas. Rowan plt & Tim. Bryant deft. is dismist.

In the action upon the Case between John Eyre plt & Jos. Freeman deft for For Three Pounds, Eighteen shillings & Eight pence half penny Current money due by Acctg. On the deft. Motion and Imparlence is granted him until the next Court.

In the Action on the Case between Jno. Walsh plt & Thomas Robins deft for two pounds Current money due by acct. the deft, failing to appear and no Security being returned for him Judgement is granted ythe plt for the sd. sum & Costs agt the deft. & John Walker gentl. Sherif unless the deft. Appears at the next Court and answer the Action.

The difference between Wm Dalton plt & Math. Pope deft is dismist.

The difference between Edw Tabb plt & Timo. Bryant is dismist

The difference between Thos. Bell plt. & Heny Ward is dismist.

The difference between Jno. Crowley plt & John Filbetts deft. is dismist.

Difference between Jno. Butterworth plt & Jno. Lankford def is dismist.

The difference between Robt Russell plt & Roger Barkley deft is dismist.

In the action in the case between Jno. Wooden plt & Jno. Abbott deft for six pounds Twelve Shillings due by Agt the plt failing to prosecute it is ordered that he be non suited & That he pay thedeft. Damages according to Law & Costs als. Exec.

In the petition of Richd. King agt Wm Bigges Setting forth that he being bound as a Security for the estate of Thos Pinkethman (??) therein the proceeds for the estate of Jno. Braithwaite who is now dec'd& his widow being married to Wm Bigges (illeg) . To be released (illeg) . Widow (illeg.) Def.

Page 19
An Inventory & Appraisement of the estate of David Cunningham Dec'd. Total £311. 19. 8

In Obedience an Order of the Court oF York County dated the 15th day of February 1719. We the Subscribers being sec & Sworn have appraised Such estate of David Cunningham as was produced to us by the Exectr. Amounting as above to Three Hundred Eleven Pounds & Nineteen Shillings and Eight pence halfpenny current money which we report under our hands this 19th Day of December 1720. Saml. Cobbs Survg [surviving] Execr, Joseph Davenport, Jean Pasteur. Louis Deloney

At a Court held for York County February the 20th 1720

This inventory & Appraisement of the estate of David Cunningham decd. Was presented in Court by Samuel Cobbs the Surviving Executor & Admitted to a record. Phi Lightfoot Cl. Cur

Pages 20, 21,22 are as follows
An order of York County Court bearing date January 16th 1720. We the Subscribers being full sworn before Capt. Thomas Chisman one of His Majestys

Justices of Peace for the County have appraised the estate of Henry Hayward dec'd So far as have been laid before us by the Exctx & Exectr. Viz.
Page 23. £694. 10. 7 ¾. Jno. Slater, Thos. Curtis, Robt Shields Jr.
At a Court held for York County February the 20th 1720.
This Inventory &c of the estate of Henry Hayward dec'd is presented in Court by Eliza. Hayward & Edw Tabb the Execrs. & Admitted to Record. Test Phi/ Lightfoot ClCur

At a Court held for York County March 11th 7120.
Present: Rob Holloway, Thos Nelson , Law. Smith, Wm Sheldon. . Thos Chisman Genl Trustees

Michael Butterly & Wm Shrine committed to the Gaol of this County on suspicion of them breaking into the Store house of Thomas Nelson Gentl. And taking thence about Two Hundred pounds in Gold & Silver together with Severall Rings & other things of considerable value & they being before the Court, the Examination of Witnesses & the Confession of the sd. Michl. Butterly are of opinion that the sd. Michl Butterly & Wm Shrine be remanded to the prison of the County under the Custody of the Sheriff from thence to be conveyed to the Publick Gaol in Williamsburgh
In order for a Tryal at the general Court as the Law in Such cases Directs.

Page 25
Elinor Aringer, Wm. Gordon, Wm Lindsay, Jno. Ballard, Jno. Gomer, & Jos. Chapman in open Court before His. Mag. tyes Justices acknowledged themselves indebted to Our Sovereign Lord the King , his heirs & Successors with the Sum of Twenty pounds Sterling each to be levied on their Goods & Chattels with Condition that if Elinor Aringer, Wm Gordon, Wm Lindsey,Jn Ballard, Jno. Gomer & Jos. Chapman Shall appear before the genl Court on the 4th day thereof and attend from Time to Time then & There to give Evidence for our sd. Lord the King agt. Michl. Butterly & Wm Shrine who stand Committed to the Gaol of this County on Suspicion & Felony then the above Recognizance to be void or else to remain in full force.

Thos. Nelson genl. In Open Court acknowledged himself indebted to Our Sovereign Lord the Kind, his heirs & Successors with the Sum of Fourty Pounds Sterling to be levied on his Goods & Chattles with Condition that if he appear at the next Genl. Court on the 4th Day thereof & and attend from Time to time attend & Prosecute Michael Butterly & Wm Shrine this day examined & Committed on Suspicion of Burglary & Felony then the above Recognizance to be void or else to remain in full force.

At a Court held for York County March 20, 1720. Present: Jno. Holloway, Thos

Nelson, Henry Tyler, Lews. Smith, Wm Sheldon. Genl. Justices

Scipio a Negroe boy belonging to Wm . Rogers is adjudged to be twelve years old.

An inventory of the estate of Jane Allen dec'd was presented in Court by the Executor & Admitted to Record.

An Iventory of the estate of Susa. Allen dec'd was presented in Court by the Executor & admitted to record.

The action of trespass between Philip Lightfoot plt & Robt Ballard deft. For Twenty Pounds damages in dismist.

The Sheriff hath further time allowed him to bring in an Act & Settlement on the Estate of John Mely dec'd till the next Court.

In the petition of Rich King agt Wm Bigges Stating forth that he being Bound as Security for the Estate of Thos. Pinkethman there in the hands of Jno. Brathwaite dec'd & Mary the wife of Jno. Braithwaite being married to the sd. Wm Bigges & praying to be released from the Security the defts. Failing to deliver up to the sd. Rich . King the estate of the Sd. Thomas Pinkethman Decd. for which the petitioner was bound / according to the order of the last Court . Wherefore it is the Opinion of the Court that the Ex go agt the defs. For the sd Pinkethmans estate.

The Court on Consideration of the petiton of Kathn. Craig on order in Ordinary Keeper in Williamsburg praying that her Suspension from retailing Liquors might be taken off. , on her promise of Keeping more Regular order in her sd ordinary than hitherto She hath Done, It is Ordered that she Have leave to retail Liquors during the tyme expressed on her Lycence.

On the petition of Thomas Crips Guardian of Sarah Pinkethman Orphan of Thomas Pinkethman dec'd Setting forth that the estate of the sd Orphan being in the hands of Wm Bigges & praying that the Estate may be committed to the Pettrs. care. It is thereupon ordered that the sd Wm Bigges & Richd. King apy & Deliver the sd. orphans estate in their hands to the petr. & the sd Bigges refunding to the ad. King all such Costs as he hath been at in obtaining the sd estate from the sd Bigges.

The difference between Thos Delany plt. & Timothy Bryant deft is dismist being agreed.

In the action in the case between Philip Lightfoot plt & Timothy Bryant deft for Nine Pounds Two Shillings & Eight pence farthing due by actg the deft. Being in Custody of the Sherif confessed Judgement for the Ad. Sum that he pay the aforesaid sum of Nine pounds Two Shillings & Eight pence farthing to the plt with Costs.

Page 26
The difference between Ann Frith plt. & Wm Alexander def. neither party appearing is dismist.

John Dowsing in Open Court presented & acknowledged his Deed of Gift to his Son Robert Dowsing for half of a Lott of Ground in York Town On Whose motion it is admitted to record.
George Gilbert presented & Acknowledged his deeds of Lease & release for Land Lying in the County to Graves Pack genl. On whose motion they are admitted into record.

The action of debt between Robt. Philipson plt & Tim Bryant deft neither party appearing is dismist.

The difference between Francis Elinor plt & Thos. Wray deft. neither party appearing is dismist.

The difference between Charles Stagg plt & Wm Livingston deft. Neither party appearing is dismist.

The difference between Benja. Weldon plt & Jno. Mandell deft neither party appearing is dismist.

In the action is the Case between Benj Weldon plt & Wm Blaikley deft for Eleven pounds Seven Shillings & & Six pence half penny Current money due by Acct. the deft. Failing to appear judgement is granted the plt. Agt the deft & Francis Tyler his Security for the Sd Sum & Costs unless the deft. Appear at the next Court & answer the plt action.

The Action upon the case between Phillip Lightfoot plt & Daniel Thomson deft for twenty pounds one shilling & three pence Current money due by Actg is continued until the next Court.

The petition of Walter Butler agt Mary Joby & Jane Morland Execr of John Young dec'd neither part appearing is dismist

On the petition of Benj Moss & John Chisman for their proportion of the estate of Wm Hayward dec. in right of their Wives, Sisters to the sd. Wm & children of Henry Hayward dec. . it is thereupon ordered that the Sherif Summon Eliz Tabb Surviving Exectr of the sd Henry Hayward to appear & answer the Ad. Petition at the next Court.

The action of Trespass upon the Case between Kathr. Edwards plt & Jane Morland Exectr & def of Elis. Babb who was Execr & of Wm Babb dec. deft. Is dismist.

In the Action upon the case between George Winer plt. & John Cooke deft for Sixteen Pounds Current money due by Acc the deft being in the Custody of the Sheriff The matter being submitted by both partys to the court upon hearing the evidence and an Allowance of the defts discount. Judgement is granted the Plaintiff for Nine pounds ten Shillings & four Pence half penny & its ordered that the deft pay the same to the plt. The plt paying the deft costs Als Ex.

William Wise presented & acknowledged his Deed of Gift for land lying in this County to his Son Robert Wise on whose Motion it is admitted to record.

The difference between Saml. Gaile plt. & . . (*missing*) Greenock deft. Neither party appearing is dismist.

In the Action upon the Case between Baldwin Matthews plt & John Abbott deft for two pounds Ten Shillings Current money due on ball. of Acct. the deft being in the custody of the Sheriff confessed Judgement to the plt for the Ad. Sum Whereupon it is ordered that the deft pay the same to the plt with Costs.

In the Action upon the Case between Saml. Timson plt & John Abbott deft for Four Pounds Current money due by act. The deft being in the Custody of the Sheriff confessed Judgement to the Plaintiff for the sd sum whereupon it is ordered that the deft pay the same to the plt with Costs.

Page 27
Phillis a Negroe Girle belonging to Robert Peters is judged to be ten Years Old

Robert Laughlin on his petition hath an order granted him for a Lycence to keep an ordinary in WmBurgh in this County he having together with Robert Ballard & Thos Cripps his Securitys entered into & acknowledge their bond to the county for that purpose which bond is admitted to record.

An Inventory of the estate of Jno. Layton decd. Was presented in Court by the Excr & Admitted to record.

Wm Robertson Att of George Winter acknowledged Satisfaction of the sd. Winter Judgement this day obtained against John Cooke which is ordered to be entered.

The difference between Lewis Holland plt & Wm Bigges deft. is dismist.

In the action of debt between Thomas Jones plt & Jno. Battles for Eight Pounds fifteen Shillings Current money due by note Note the deft. Confessed Judgement for the sd Sum Whereupon its ordered that the def pay the sd Sum to the plt. If Fourty Shillings thereof is not already paid to the plt by Sarah Atkinson with Costs als. Ex.

The difference between Lewis Holland plt & Wm Bigges deft is dismist.

In the Action of Debt between Richard Pepper Assignee of Richd. Cooke plt& John Abbott deft for two pounds & eight shillings current money due by Note the deft being in Custody of the Sheriff confessed Judgement to the plt for the sd Sum, and it is thereupon ordered that the def pay the sd Sum to the plt with Costs.

In the Action upon the Case between Eliza/ Moody Execx of Philip Moody decd plt & Thos Barbar deft for three pounds Nine Shillings & Six pence Current money due by Acct the deft failing to appear Judgement is granted to the plt for the sd Sum & agt the deft & Francis Tyler his Security unless the deft appears at the next Court & answers the plt action.

In the action upon the case between Eliza Moody Execr &c of Philip Moody decd plt. & Thos Barbar Adminr. &c of Wm Barbar decd deft for three pounds Six Shillings current money due bt the Acct the deft failing to appear Judgement is granted against the plt for the sd Sum & Costs agt the deft & Frans. Tyler his Security unless the deft appears at the next Court & answers the plt action.

The difference between Saml. Cobbs plt & Jno. Mundell deft neither party appearing is dismist.

The difference between George Luke Esq & Jno. Nichols is dismist.

The difference between Benj. Weldon plt & Jno. Mundell deft is dismist.

The difference between Benj Weldon plt & Francis Sharp deft is dismist.

The difference between Uriah Hutson plt & John Holdsworth deft is dismist.

Present: Graves Park, genl.

In the motion between on the case between Henry Powers plt & jn Jas Lewis deft for Ten Pounds eighteen Shillings & four pence Current money due by acctg the deft failing to appear plt motion is granted him for the sum and costs agt the deft & Francis Tyler his Security unless the deft appears at the next Court & answers to the plt. Action.

Page 28
The difference between Benj Weldon plt & Jos Freeman deft is dismist.

The last Will & testament of Margaret Kendall dec together with the Codicil not presented in Court & Robert Clark & Mary Mackerly. Witnesses thereto declared that they Saw the Same executed by the ad. Decd as her will which is at Mr. Graves Park's motion is admitted to Record.

On the motion of John Gibbons against his servant man Lewis Davis for Charges in taking him up & absent time the deft confessed the petitioners demands were just. It is thereupon ordered that the sd Lewis Davis serve his sd Master Nineteen months after his time by Indenture or Custom is expired according to Law.

The action upon the Case between John Pratt plt & Lewis Delony deft is dismist.

In the Action of debt between Mary Barbar & Same. Timson Execrs &c of Thomas Barbar decd. plt & Thos Barbar def. is dismist neither party appearing.

On the pettion of David Sebrell praying that Andrew Laprade may be appointed his Guardian he having together with George Gilbert & Richard Harrison his Securitys entered into & acknowledged their bond to the Court which it is admitted to Record, it is ordered that the sd Laprade take care of the ad. Orphan & His estate.

On the Action upon the Case between Same. Timson & Mary Barbar Execrs. &c of Thos Barbar decd. Plt & Anna Maria Timson Execr &c of Wm. Timson dec'd deft for Twelve Pounds Thirteen shillings & Seven pence due by accg after an allowance of the discount the deft confessed judgement to the plt for Eleven pounds Eight Shillings & eleven pence halfpenny , It is ordered that the deft pay the sd Sum to the plt out of the decds estate with Costs als Exo.

In the Jure facias brought by John Brooke agt John Brush for two Hundred Fourty Seven Pounds of Tobo. The deft offering no discount or Objection why Exa. Should not go agt him the sd deft for the Sum, Therefore it is ordered that

Exec issue agt the sd deft for the sd Sum & costs together with Fifteen Shillings for lawyers fees.

The difference between Joseph Walker plt & Eliza Hansford deft is dismist.

The petition of Armiger Parson agt John Hay is dismist.

The petition of Uriah Hutson & Thos Cripps agt Sam Millington praying to be relieved of their Securityship for the sd Millingtons admin. of the estate of Jno. Morris dec'd by the consent of the partys it is continued until the next Court.

The petition of Benj. Weldon against Jeremiah Hill for Four pounds eight shillings & eight pence Current money is continued for the appearance of James Rosion Esq to give an Acctg of the sd Hill effects in his hands.

Of the suit in Chancery brought by Jon Hay & Mary his wife complt agt. Thos Tomer surviving Execr of Jno. Tomer decd Respondth the respondt. Appeared & hath further time allowed him to answer thereto until the next Court.

In the Action of detinue between Thomas Tomer plt & Saml. Tompkins deft. For one hundred pounds damage the defendant having had time to plead & Now called & failing to do the same on the plt motion Judgement is granted him agst the sd deft for the sd Sum & Costs Nihil Dicit confirmable at the next Court on the like Default.

In the Action upon the Case between Joseph Stacy plt & Robt Ross deft for Five pounds damages issue being Joyned a Jury{to Witt} Robt Peters, Rob Ballard, Robt Shields, Walter Butler, Richd Stewart, Richd Harrison, Thos Cripps, John Davis, Jno. Goodwin, Jno. Chisman, Giles Moody & Benj Moss were

Page 29

Sworn & they having heard the evidence received a Spect verdt drawn up by both partys retired & afterwards Returned again into Court & delivered the Same in these Words (to witt) We find that a certain discourse was moved between the plt & the deft & That upon that discourse the plt did promise to the deft / if one Simon Stacy who was at that time dangerously Sick Should he died before the deft Should depart his Colony that the Plt would pay him five pounds for the sd Saddle & That the deft in consideration thereof did promise to the plt if the sd Simon was living at the time of his departure of the Country that the deft. would deliver the plt the sd Sadlle for nothing. We find that Sometime after the sd deft did depart this Colony & that at the time of his departure the sd Simon was living. We find that Simon Stacy died before the 28th day of May 1720 . law in the plt Declon. And if the Law be for the plt. We find for him £2. 10 damages if not we find for the deft Robert Peters which Verdn at the plt motion is recorded & the matters of Law arising therefrom is refered by the Consent of both partys to be argued till the next Court.

The petiton & forma brought by Robt Westlake plt agt Ann Worley deft is dismist.

The difference between Henry Borrodale plt & Wm Tucker deft is dismist.

In the action upon the Case between Thomas Bell plt & Chas Rowan deft for Two Pounds Ten Shillings Current money due bt acctg both partys submitting the Tryall to the Court who upon having the evidence & the plts Path to thereupon order the the deft pay the sd Sum of two pounds Ten Shillings to the plt with Cost als Ex.

Charles Rowan & Lydia his wife presented their Deeds of Lease & Release of Lands lying in this County & Bonds for performance of Covenants to Beaufort Pleasant the sd Lydia being also presently examined relinquished her Right of Dower in the sd Lands to the sd Beaufort which sd Deeds Bond & Relinquishment of the sd Beaufort's motion is admitted to Record.

In the Action upon the Case between Wm Fleming plt & Lawr. Smith deft for Seven Hundred pounds of tobo. & Cash the Court on Arguing the demurrer were of Judgement for the plt the issue on the plt mon & Costs is refered till the next Court.

In the action of Debt between David Morse plt & Jos Frith def for ten pounds Two shillings & eleven pence Current money due by note under hand, issue being joined A Jury (to witt) Robt Peters &c were Sworn & they having heard the evidence & recd as Pere. Verde. drawn up by both partys agreed thereto & delivered the Same in these words (to witt) We find that the bill declared on was delivered by the plt to Martin Goodwin in part of the probate estate of the sd Martin and other Orphans of Robt Goodwin decd . We find that the Will of the sd Martin Goodwin hereto annexed & that he therein did devise all his personall estate to his mother then the wife of the deft & made her execr. We find that after the death of the sd Martin the sd bill was Delivered to Abraham Cole by the sd Exectr in order to Satisfy a debt due by the Testator. We find that after the delivery of the sd bill as aforesaid & being returned by Abraham Cole the defts wife ordered the Same to be delivered to the plt. & if the Law be with the plt. We find the sd Ten pounds Two Shillings & eleven pence due on balla . for the plt & if the law be with the deft for the deft. We find the bill given by the deft to the plt & That Ten pounds Two Shillings & eleven pence is due on blla. & yet unpaid. We find for the plt if the law be for him. Robt Petters. , Which verdc. At the plt motion is recorded & the matter of law arising therefrom to be argued till the next Court.

In the Suit in Chancery depending between Lawrence Smith & Mildred his wife complts & Jno. Goodwin Execr. &c of James Goodwin decd. Respondt theAudrs Rept. Exhibited in this Suit is on the Compl motion recorded & appearing therby that the Sum of Sixty Seven Pounds Twelve pounds & four pence farthing is due to the Complt wherefore it is adjudged ordered & Decreed that the Respond. pay the Sum of Fourty Five pounds in Current money & The Sum of Twenty Two pounds twelve shillings & Four pence farthing to the Complt out of the Goods appraised to be Sett apart by Thos. Nelson & Wm Sheldon.

Page 30
In the action upon the Case between Thos Nelson Gentl plt & Thos Robins & Mary his wife deft for five pounds damage for dealing with plts negroe Slaves It appearing by the confession of one of the defts that she the Ad Mary did receive of ye Ad negroe Slave Sixteen pounds and a half of Tallow of the value of Eight Shillings & Three pence It is therefore ordered that the ad Mary be imprisoned for the Space of one Kalender month without bail or Mainprise & then to be continued in prison untill She gives Security in the Sum of ten pounds for her good behavior for one year & moreover that the deft pay unto the Plt the Sum of Thirty three Shillings being four times the value of the Goods recd with costs als Exo

John Bond on Evidence for Joseph Sharp agt Robt Ross having attended one day It is ordered that the Sd Joseph pay him fourty pounds of Tobo. for the same according to Law with costs als Exo

Jno Welsh on Evidence for Thos Bell agt Chas Rowan having attended Six days it is ordered that the sd Thomas pay him two hundred pounds of Tobaccoit being for five of the sd days attendence & that the sd Chas Rowan pay him fourty pounds for the other days attendence according to Law with costs als Exo

Tim Bryant on evidence for Chas Rowan at the suit of Thos Bell having attended one day ordered that the Ad Chas pay him fourty pounds of Tobo. for the same according to law with Cost als Exo.

Wm Palmer on Evidence for Chas Rowan at the suit of Thos Bell having attended one day ordered that the Ad Charles pay him fourty pounds of Tobo. for the Same according to law with costs als Exo

In the action of trespass on the Case between Ann Wakefield plt & Fran Sharp deft for twenty pounds damage the cause is continued at the plts mon & Charge untill the next Court

In the action upon the Case between John Eyre plt & Joseph Freeman deft for three pounds fourteen Shillings & Eight pence half penny Current money by Acct the defts having had time to plead & being now called and failed to do the Same on the plts mon Judgement is granted him for the Sd Sum by Nihil Dicit confirmable at the next Court on the like default

Nath Hooke is appointed Constable in York Town in the room of Wm Trotter It is ordered that he immediately Repair to some Justice of the peace for this County & take the usual Oath.

Mary White came into Court & made Oath that Dennis White departed this life without making any will So far as She knows or believes & She having together with Wm Wise her Security entered into & Acknowledged their bond to the Court for her just & faithfull admon on the sd Dennis's estate & which bond is admitted To record. On her mon Certificate is granted her fore her obtaining a Comission of admon on the sd estate in due form

Robert Kerby Thos Kerby & Bennit Tompkins or any two of them being Sworn before a Justice of the County are appointed to appraise the estate of Dennis White decd & make report thereof to the next Court

Ordered that the Court be Adjourned untill the next Court in Course, Lawr Smith. Truly Entered Phi Lightfoot ClCur

Know all me by these presents that We Mary White & William
Wise of the County of York are held and firmly bound unto the Worshipful
the Justices of the County aforsd in the Sum of Thirty pounds Sterling
to the which payment well and truly to be made to the Ad Justices

Page 31 (says 39)
At a court held for York County March 20, 1720

The Last Will and Testament of Margaret Kendall decd was presented in Court together with . . (*missing*) Robert Clark & Mary Macarte Witnesses thereto declared that they . . (*missing*) decd as her will which is at Mr Graves Parks motion admitted to record. Test Phi Lightfoot ClCur

Know all men by these presents that We Edward Tabb Benja. Moss & Jno. Chisman of the County of York are held and firmly bound unto our Sovereign Lord George by the Grace of God Great Britain France & Ireland King defender of the Faith &c in the Sum of ten thousand pounds of Tobacco convenient in the

Ad County of York to the which payment well & Truly to be made to our Sovereign Lord the King his heirs & successors We bind ourselves and every of us Our & every of our heirs Execrs & Admins Joyntly & Severally firmly by these presents Sealed with our Seals & Dated this 20 day of March 1720

The condition of this Obligation is such that the above bounden Edward Tabb hath an order this day Granted him for a Lycence to keep an ordinary at his now dwelling house in this County for the year next ensuing If therefore the sd Edward Tabb doth constantly find and provide in his ordinary good wholesome & cleanly lodging & Diet for Travellors and Stableage & provender or pasturage & provender -as the season shall require- for their horses from the date of these presents for & During the space of one year & Shall not suffer any unlawful gaming in his sd house, nor on the Sabbath day Suffer any person to Tipple or drink nor than is necessary than this Obligation to be void & of none effect otherwise to remain in full force & virtue. Wit. Ed Tabb, Jno Chisman, Benja Moss

At a Court held for York County March 20 1720
This bond was presented & Acknowledged in Court by the partys thereto & Admitted to record. Test Phi Lightfoot ClCur

Know all men by these presents that we Mary Luke & Thomas Jones of the County of York are held & firmly bound to our Sovereign Lord George by the Grace of God of Great Britain France & Ireland King defender of the faith in the Sum of ten Thousand pounds of Tobacco convenient in the Ad County of York to Which payment well & truly to be made to our Sovereign Lord the King his heirs & Successors We bind ourselves & every of us our & every of our heirs Execrs & admins Joyntly & Severally firmly by these presents Sealed with our Seals and dated this 20th day of March 1720.

The Condition of this Obligation is such that whereas the above bounden Mary Luke hath an order this day granted her for a Lycense to keep an Ordinary at her now dwelling house in Williamsburgh in this County for the year next Ensuing if therefore the sd Mary Luke doth constantly find & provide in her ordinary good wholesome & cleanly lodging & diet for Travellors & Stableage & provender or pasturage & provender - as the season shall require- for their horses from the date of these presents nor Shall suffer any unlawful gaming in her sd house nor on the Sabbath day Suffer any person to Tipple or drink more than is necessary Then this Obligation shall be void or of none effect otherwise to continue in full force & Virtue. Mary Luke. Thos Jones

At a Court held for York County March 20 1720
This Bond was presented in Court by the partys . (*missing*) admitted to record.

Phi Lightfoot ClCur

Page 34
Know all men by these presents that We Robert Loughton Robert Ballard & Thomas Cripps of the County of York are held and firmly bound to our Sovereign Lord George by the Grace of God of Great Britain France & Ireland Kind and Defender of the faith &c in the Sum of ten thousand pounds of Tobacco convenient in the sd County of York to the which payment well & Truly be made to our Sovereign Lord the King his heirs & successors We bind ourselves and every of us our & every of our heirs Execrs & admins Joyntly & Severally & Sealed with our Seals and dated this 20th day of MArch 1720/21

The Condition of this Obligation is Such that whereas the above bounden Robt Laughton hath an order this day Granted him for a Lycence to keep an ordinary at his now dwelling house in Williamsburgh for the year next ensuing If therefore the sd Robt Laughton doth constantly find & provide in his ordinary good wholesome & Cleanly lodging & Diet for travellors & Stableage & provender or pasturage & provendner - as the season shall require- for their horses from the date of these presents for & Dduring the term of one year & Shall not Suffer any unlawful gaming in his sd house not on the Sabbath day Suffer any person to Tiple or drink more than is necessary Ten this Obligation to be void & of none effect Otherwise to remain in full force & virtue

At a Court held for York County March 20 th 1720.
Robert Laughton, Robert Ballard, Thos Cripps. This bond was presented & Acknowledged in Court by the partys & Admitted to Record. Test Phi Lightfoot ClCur

The estate of James Goodwin Dr.
To cash paid to the estate of Rachel Wise - £56. 9. 10
To Sundry disbursements allowed the Exectr - 68. 7. 10 ½
To Capt Lawr. Smith & Mildred his wife for her 1/3 pt of the Negroes valued @ £117
To the Exctr Jno Goodwin for the remaining 2/3 of £117 78.
To Capt Lawr Smith & Mildred his wife for her ½ of person estate 67. 12. 4 ¼
To the ball. Remg. to the Exctrs Jno Goodwin 67. 12. 4 ¼
=======
£377. 2. 5

Pr. Contra.
By the Inventory of James Goodwins estate including his part of his mothers estate £377. 2. 5

In Obedience to the order of the Worshipfull the Justices of York County Court to Audit State & Settle the Amts in difference between Capt Lawr Smith & Mildred his wife late Mildred Goodwin Complts & Jno Goodwin Exctr &c of James Goodwin decd respondr the above is the Settlement

At a court held for York County March 20 1720 Thos Nelson, J Walker, Richd Ambler

This settlement of the accts in difference between Capt Lawr Smith & Mildred his wife complr & Jno Goodwin Execrs &c of James Goodwin decd respondr is admitted to record. Test Phi Lightfoot ClCur

Page 35
An Inventory of the estate of Jane Allen late of Williamsburgh in York County decd Vizt. including: 2 gold rings, 1 pr ear Rings,2 bibles,1 gold girdle & silver buckle, 15 new plates 1 nes pewter Tankard etc
sold to D. Blair 1 Calf £--. 10--
sold of above goods =====
£ 12. 1. 10 ½ James Shield Excr
This invry of the estate of Jane Allen decd was presented in Court & Admitted to Record. Test Phi Lightfoot ClCur

In obedience to an order of this Court dated the 20th day of February 1720. We the subscribers have appraised the estate of Jno. Laton decd as followeth Vizt including: 3 Cows, 3 two year olds, 2 yearlings ,1 Sow 6 shoats , 2 horses and 1 pair old pistols & Sword, 1 Old Negroe man given as a Legacy to the widow £15.

===

£41.
. . . (*missing*) Page Mel Pierce & Rob Cobb

Page 36
(Continuing pages 36/37)

At a Court held for York County March __?__ 1720 This inventory of the estate of Jno. Laton __?Court & Admitted to Record. Test Phi Lightfoot Cl Cur

An Inventory & Appraisement of the estate of Susa. Allen decd. £184. __.__
In obedience to an order of the Court of York County the Eighteenth day of July 1720. We the subscribers being first sworn have appraised such estate of Susanna Allen as was produced to us amounting as above to One Hundred Eighty Four pounds& one penny which We report under our hands this 8th day of February 1720. Thos Jones, Lewis Delony, Joseph Davenport, Jean Pasture

At a Court held for York County March _? 1720
This inventory of the estate of Susa Allen dec'd was presented in Court & admitted to Record. Test Phi Lightfoot Cl Cur

At a Court held for York County May the 15th 1720
Present: Jno. Holloway, Thos Nelson, Lawr. Smith & Wm Sheldon Genl.

The Rates of Liquors are further continued for this present year

Edw. Tabb came into Court & made Oath that Jno. White departed this life without making any will as far as he knows or believes & he having together with Antho . Robinson & Saml. Tompkins his Security entered & Acknowledged their bond to the Court for his Just & Faithful Mon. on the ad. Estate (which bond is admitted to record) On his mon. Certificate is granted him for obtaining a Comission of Admn on the estate in due form.

The Last will & testament of Wm Jackson Decd. was presented in Court by Mary Parkson the Execr therein named who made Oath to it & being proved by the Oaths of all the Witnesses thereto is admitted to record & She having together with Robt Cobbs junr. & Jno. Harris her Security entered into & Acknowledged their bond to the Court for her just & Faithful admin. On the sd estate on her motion the Certificate is granted her for obtaining a probate thereof in due form.

Wm Wise, Bennet Tomkins, Thos Kerby & Robert Kerby or any three of them being sworn before a Justice of the County are appointed to Appraise the estate of Jno. White dec't & Make Report thereof to the next Court. On the petition of Dianah Hayward praying that Robert Shields may deliver unto her, her share of the estate of Wm Hayward dec'd in his hands, It is thereupon ordered that the Sheriff summon the sd Robert Shields to the next Court & Answer the Ad petition.

On the petition of Mary Clifton praying that Robt Shields may deliver unto her, her share of the estate of Wm Hayward dec'd in his hands, It is thereupon ordered that the Sherif summon the sd Robert Shields to the next Court & Answer the ad petition.

The last will & testament of_?_ Cully dec'd was presented in Court by Thos. Chisman the Execr thereupon made oath thereto & being proved by the Oath of all Witnes__?___ & he having together with Antho. Robinson Into & al__?_ their Bond _?_admin & to Record __?_ due fro_.

Page 38

Thomas Sandifer & Eliza his wife presented & acknowledged their Deed of Lease & Release & Bond for the performance of Covenants for land lying in this County To Eliz. Hayward. the sd Eliza Sandifer _?_relinquishing her Right of Dower to the sd Eliz. Hayward the sd Haywards mon. to Deeds bond & relinquishment are admitted to Record.

A Power of Atty from Jno. Wise & Margaret Wise to Cole Diggs & Richd Ambler was proved in Court by the Oaths of Mary Thorrowgood & Jno. Cannon & Admitted to Record.

On the petition of Jno. Walsh & Jno. Patrick setting forth that they being Securitys for Eliza. Burtons true & faithful admin of the estate of Lewis Burton decd. & the sd Eliza, having intermarried with Saml. Styles & The petitrs. conceiving themselves in danger pray to be released or that the said estate be delivered up to them. It is thereupon ordered that the Sherif Sumon the sd Saml. Styles & Eliza. his wife the late Eliza Burton to appear & Answer the sd petition at the next Court.

The petition of Margaret Wooldon agst Law. Smith upon hearing the partys is dismist.

The last will & Testament of Jno. Thebo decd. was further proved in Court by the Oath of Chas. Hansford & ordered to be Certyfied.

_?_os. Thebaut presented & Acknowledged her Deeds of Lease & Release of Lands lying this County to Saml. Hyde, On whose motion they are admitted to Record.

Robert Kerby Foreman, Peter Goodwin &c were this day Sworn a Grand Jury for this County & They having made several presentments were discharged.

In the action of Trespass in the case between Ann Wakefield plt & Francis Sharp deft for Twenty pounds damages issue being Joyned a Jury to witt Js Mountfort &c were Sworn & they having heard the evidence retired to Consult their verdt. & being agreed returned the same in these words {to witt} We find for the deft which Verdt. at the deft mon. is admitted to record. & the Suit is dismist with Costs als Ex. It is ordered that the Sherif Sumon Ann Combs of Chas. Parish presented by the Grand Jury for having a Bastard child & Thomas Wooten Senr for Suffering Seconds to grow at his Plantation. To answer the sd presentments at the next Court.

On the petiton of Lewis Deloney agt his Servant maid Marg. Flora for having a Bastard Child & the Charges of her lying in, It is ordered that the sd Margaret serve her Master one year for the trouble of his house at the time of her lying in after her time by Indenture Custom or former Order is Expired.

Peter Brewer being Sumd. On evidence for Ann Wakefield agt Francis Sharp & Having attended one day . It is ordered that the sd Ann pay him fourty pounds of Tobo. For the same according to law with Cost als Ex.

Chas. Cornwall the Same.

Andr. Laprade on Evidence for Francis Sharp in the suit brought by Ann Wakefield having attended one day. It is ordered that the sd. Francis pay him fourty pounds of Tobo. For the Same according to Law with Cost et Als.

Theb. Hardman the Same.

Mary Peale before the court for a Valuable consideration agreed voluntarily to Serve Wm Livingston her Master Two years after her time by Indenture Custome or former order is expired.

Wm Livingston in his petition hath an Order granted him for an ordinary Lycense in WmsBurgh in the County he having together with Wm. Gordon & Wm Blakely his Securitys entered into Bond for that purpose which bond is admitted to record.

The difference between Jno. Welsh plt & Thos Robins deft is dismist.
The difference between Francis Sharp plt & James Netter deft is dismist.

The action _?_between Jno. Abbott plt & Jno. Ness deft for Ten Pounds__?__& ten pence current money issue being Joyned the Cause__?__ next Court.

The act. __?_& Lawr. Smith_ deft _?__ is cont.

Page 39
__?____ on the 30th of May if fair if not the next fair day.

In the petition of James Bates& Jno. Bates for Admin in the estate of Mary Brewer decd. On hearing the the Arguments of both partys the Right of the sd admin is adjudged by the Court to Jno. Bates.

Jn Bates came into Court & on his solemn affirmation declared that Mary Brewer departed this life without making any will than the nuncupative will annext& he having together with Jno. Tyler & Rich Stewart his securitys entered into & acknowledged their bond to the court for his Just & faithful Admin is the sd Mary Brewers estate which bond is admitted to Record, On his mon. certificate is granted him for Obtaining a Comission of Admin on the sd estate with the will annext in due form.

Ralph Holdes Servant to Thomas Jones having been Run Away It is ordered that he Serve his Master three hundred & Fourty eight days for absent time & the tow hundred pounds of Tobacco for taking him up after his time by Indenture custom or former Order is Expired according to law & that his sd Master have liberty to inflict on his bare back punishment when he sees fit not exceeding thirty nine lashes & That the sd Thos Jones have leave to bring in a further acct agt him at the next Court.

The difference between Lawr. Smith plt & James Wall deft is dismist.

To the action of Dentinue between Jno. Wall plt & & Lawr. Smith deft for thirty Shillings Current money an Imparlance is granted the deft until the next Court.

In the Action of debt between Saml Sweny plt & Ls. Delony deft for £91. 5__ (91 pounds 5 shillings) Current money due by debt the deft failing to appear Judgement is granted the plt for the sd Sum & Costs agt the sd deft & Thos Jones his security unless the deft appears at the next Court & Answers the plts action.

The difference between Jno. Harris plt & Geo. Lilburn deft is dismist.

In the action of debt between Kathn. Craig Execr. &c of Wm Craig Decd. plt & Lewis Delony deft for thirty pounds Current money due by bond. Oyer is granted def until the next Court.

The difference between Francis Hayward &c plt & Eliza. Hayward deft is dismist

In the action upon the Case between Anna Maria Timson Excr &c of Wm Timson decd plt agt Dav. Flournoy & Mary his wife Admint. &c of Orlando Jones decd. Deft for Twenty pounds damage . On the deft motion an Imparlance is granted them until the next Court.

The difference between Philip Lightfoot Plt & Jno. Brush deft is dismist.

In the action of trespass between Jno. Page plt & Jno. Brooke def for Twenty pounds damage on the deft motion an Imparlance is granted until the next Court.

On the action upon the Case between Philip Lightfoot plt & Eliza. Hansford surviving Execr of Thos Hansford decd deft for one pound eighteen shillings &

Three pence half penny Current money due by acctg the def failing to appear Judgement is granted the plt for the sd Sum & Costs agt the sd deft. Unless she appear at the next Court & Answer the plt mon.

In the action of debt between Jos. Walker Genl. Plt & Eliza. Hansford surviving Execr &c of Ths. Hansford decd deft for One Hundred & fourteen pounds & eleven Shillings Current money due by bond, by consent of both partys Thos Nelson gen. & Philip Lightfoot & Jno. Hansford or Any two of them are appointed to Audit State & Settle the bond & auts in difference between the plt & Deft & make report thereof to the next Court.

A power of Attorney from Geo. Winter, Thos. Nelson & Jos Walker was proved in Court by Thos Danrie & Jno. Jones & admitted to record.

The action upon the Case between Chas Marshall plt & Chas Rowan deft for Five pounds Current money due by acctg _?__ until the next Court.

On the petition __? Thos Cripps Security for Saml Millington __? & Faithful admin. __?_ Norris decd praying to be reli__?__ to Ser__?__ that the sd Mill__?__ (illegible but in the margin is indicated that this is a Judgement between Hudson &c Millington)

Page 40
In the action of trespass between John Page plt & Danl Thomson deft (for__S) on the plt mon. an Atta. is granted him agt the defts estate for the sd Sum & Costs & returnable to the next Court for Judgement.

In the action upon the Case between Archib. Blair plt & J? Mundell deft for eleven pounds nineteen shillings & five pence farthing Current money due on ball. of Auct. the deft failing to appear Judgement is granted to the Plaintiff for the sd Sum & costs against the sd def & Jos Walker genl Sherif unless the sd deft appears at the next Court & Answers plts. Action. Judgement being this day passed unto Archibd. Blair agt Jos Walker Genl. Sherif for £11. 19 . 51/2 Current money & Costs by means of the non appearance of Jno. Mundell &c at the sd Blair suit on the Ad. Sherifs motion an att. is granted him for the sd Sum & Costs agt the sd Mundells estate returnable to the next Court for Judgement.

The difference between Donl. Taylor plt & Plany Ward deft is dismist.

The difference between Archib. Blair plt & Jos Freeman deft is dismist.

The difference between Jos Chapman plt & Rob Innes deft is dismist.

The difference between Benj, Weldon plt & Wm Blaikeley is dismist.

In the action upon the case between Philip Lightfoot plt & Dane. Thomson deft for twenty pounds one Shilling & three pence Current money due by acct. the deft failing to appear Judgement is granted the plt for the sd Sum & Costs agt the sd deft & Francis Tyler his Security unless the sd deft appears at the next Court & Answer the plt action.

Judgement being this day granted unto Philip Lightfoot agt Francis Tyler for twenty pounds one shilling & three pence Current money & costs by means of the nonappearance of Danl Thomson at the sd Lightfoot's Suit on the sd Francis his mon. on att, is granted him for the sd Sum & Costs agt the sd Daniels estate returnable at the next Court For Judgement.

The action of Benj Moss & Thos Chisman agt Elia. Tabb is dismist.

On the Action upon the case of Elizabeth Moody Execr &c of Philip Moody decd plt & Thos Barber deft for Two pounds two Shillings & Six pence Current money due by Ball. of acct. & the deft failing to appear the Judgement of the last Court is confirmed agt the deft & Frans. Tyler his Security & it is ordered that they pay the same to the plt with a lawyers fee according to law with Costs als Exo.

In the action upon the Case between Eliza. Moody Execr &c of Philip Moody decd plt & Thos Barbar Admin &c of Wm Barbar decd def for three pounds Six Shillings current money proved by the Plts. Oath. Judgement is granted the plt for the sd Sum & its ordered that the deft pay the same to the plt out of the decd estate with Costs als Exo.

The difference between Benja. Weldon plt & Jer. Hill deft for four pounds eight shillings & Eight pence Current money due by Acct the Atta. is further continued until the next Court.

In the Suit in Chancery between Jno. Hay & Mary his wife Complts and Thos. Tomer Surviving Exer &c of Jno. Tomer decd. Respondt. The respond. hath further time allowed him to answer until the next Court.

In the action on the Case between Jos. Stacy plt & Robt Ross def for five pounds damage time is allowed to Argue the Spec Verd. until the next Court.

In the action upon the Case between Wm Fleming plt & Lawr. Smith deft for Seven Hundred pounds of tobacco & costs The Cause is continued until the next Court.

The action _? between David Morse plt & Jos Frith deft for Ten pounds two shillings _? Pence is continued to argue the Specl. vert. at the next court.

In the action __? between Jno. Eyre plt & Jos Freeman deft for £3. 14. 8 ½ due by acct. __?_the Cause is refd. for tryall until the next Court.

In the Action __?Thos. Tomer plt & & Saml. Tompkins deft. For one hundred pounds __?_issue being Joyned the Cause is refd. for Tryall next Court. (Bottom line unreadable except: “plt & Geo. Butler deft for Two”)

Page 41
The action upon the Case between Thos Jones plt & Eliz. Powers Exectr of the estate of the Last Will & testament of Edward Powers decd for (blank space) Current money is continued until the next Court.

In the action upon the case between James Terry plt & Jas Maskinds deft , the plt failing to prosecute on the deft mon. has nonsuited And its ordered that the plt pay the deft damages according to Law with Costs als Exo.

In the action upon the Case between Mary Read plt & Geo. Butler deft for fifteen pounds fifteen shillings & four pence Current money due by Acct the deft failing to appear Judgement is granted the plt for the sd Sum& Costs agt the sd deft & Mary Butler his Security unless the sd defendant appears at next Court & Answers the plt action.

In the Action of debt between Coles Digges Esqr. plt & Lewis Delony deft for twenty Seven pounds Twelve shillings Current money due by note the deft failing to appear Judgement is granted the plt for the sd Sum & Costs agt the deft & Joseph Walker genl Sherif unless the def appears at the next Court & Answer the plt action.

The difference between Edward West plt & Jno. Longford deft is dismist.

In the petition between John Brookes plt & Jno Jackson deft for Two pounds eight shillings & Six pence Current money due by act. It is ordered that Mrs Eliza Jones be Summoned by the Sherif to render an Act of the sd Jacksons estate in her hands at the next Court.

In the petition of Samuel Cobbs &c Execr of David Cuningham decd agt John Jackson deft for Seven pounds Curnt money . It is ordered that James Bates be Summoned by the Sherif to render an Act of the sd Jacksons estate in his hands at the next Court.

Thos Wooten, Thos Wooten Jr Addiston Rogers & Peter Goodwin or any three of them being sworn before a Justice of the County are appointed to approve the estate of Dianah Blaxton decd & make report thereof to the next Court.

Ordered that the Court be Adjourned until the Court in Course. Jno. Holloway Truly Entred by Phi. Lightfoot ClCur

Know all men by these presents that we John Bates, Jno. Tyler and Richd Stewart of the County of York are held & firmly bound unto the Worshipful the Justices of the County Aforesaid in the Sum of Two Hundred pounds Sterling to the which payment well & Truly to be made to the sd Justices their heirs or Sucessors or Some of them. We bind ourselves & every of us our & every of our heirs , Execrs or Admins. Joyntlyor Severally firmly by these presents Sealed with our Seals & Dated this 15th day of may 1721

The conditions of this obligation is Such that if the Above Bounden John Bates Admin with the will annext of the Goods Chattels credits of Mary Brewer decd do make or cause to be made a true & perfect inventory of all & Singular of the Goods Chattels & Credits of the sd Mary Brewer Decd. which have or Shall come to the hands possessions or knowledge of him the sd John Bates or into the hands possessions or knowledge of any Other person or persons for him & The Same to make or exhibite or cause to be exhibited into the County Court of York at such time as he shall be thereunto required by the sd Court the Same Goods Chattels Credits & All other the Goods Chattels & Credits of the sd Mary Brewer decd at the time of her death which any time after shall come to the hands or _? him the sd John Bates or into the_? Or possessions of any other persons_?_ do well & Truly administer according to law & Furthur do make at__?_his actings & Doings therein when thereto required by the sd Court _?_ all the Legacys contained & Specifyed _?_ the sd testament _?__Goods Chattels & Credits will thereunto entered __? To the value Sh?__arge him Then this Obligation to be void ? to re__?__ Jno. C_?

Page 42

Know All men by these presents that We Edw. Tabb Anthony Robinson and Saml. Tompkins of the County of York are held firmly bound to the Worshipfull the Justices of the County aforesaid in the Sum of Fourty pounds Sterling to the which payment well & truly to be made to the Ad. Justices their heirs & Successors & Some of them We bind ourselves & every of us, ours & Every of our Heirs Execr. & Admin Joyntly & Severally firmly by these presents Sealed with our Seals & dated this 15th day of May 1721.

The Condition of this obligation is such that the Above bounden Edward Tabb Admin of a;; the Goods Chattels & Credits of John White decd to make or cause to be made a true & perfect Inventory of all & Singular the Goods Chattels & Credits of the sd John White decd. Which have or Shall come to the hands & possession of knowledge of him the sd Edward Tabb or into the hands & Possessions of any other person or persons for him & the Same to make do exhibite or cause to be exhibited into the County Court at York st such Time as he shall be thereunto required by the sd Court & The& The Same Goods Chattels & Credits & all other the Goods Chattels & Credits of the sd John White decd at the time of his death which at any time after Shall come to the hands or posessions of the Sd Edw Tabb or into the hands or possessions of any other person or persons for him to well & Truly administer according to law & Furthur do make a true & Just accounting of his actings & Doings therein when thereto required by the sd Court & all the rest & residue of the sd Goods Chattles & Credits which Shall be found remaining upon the Admin Acct/ the Same being first examined by the Justices of the sd Court for the time being Shall deliver & pay Unto Such person or persons as the Justices by their order & Judgement Shall direct pursuant to the law in that case made & provided & if it Shall hereafter appear that any last will or testament was made by the sd decd. & The Execr or Execrs. Therein named do exhibite the same into the ad Court making request to have it approved & allowed accordingly. If therefore the sd Edwd. Tabb being thereunto required to deliver up his letters of Admin approbation of Such Testament being first had & made in the Ad. Court Then this Obligation to be void otherwise remain in full force & Vertue. Edward Tabb

At a Court held for York County May 15th 1721. Anthony Robinson

This Bond was presented & Acknowledged. Saml. Tomkins.
In Court by the partys thereto & Admitted to record. Test Phi Lightfoot ClCur

Know all men by these presents that We Wm Livingston Wm Gordon and Wm Blaikley of the County of York are held firmly bound to our Sovereign Lord George by the Grace of God of Great Britain France & Ireland King Defender of the Faith &c in the Sum of Ten Thousand pounds of Tobacco convenient is the sd County of York to which payment well & truly to be made to Our Sovereign Lord the King & successors we bind ourselves & Every of us our & Every of our heirs Execrs & admin Joyntly & Severally firmly by these presents Sealed with our Seals $ Dated this 15th Day of May 1721.

The Condition of this obligation is Such that whereas the above bounden Wm Livingston hath an order this day granted him for a Lycense to keep an ordinary in his now dwelling house in Williamsburgh for the year next ensuing If therefore the sd Livingston doth continually find & provide in his ordinary good wholesome & Cleanly lodging & Diet for Travellors & Stableage & provender or pasturage& provender (as the Season shall require) for their horses from the date of these presents for & during the term of one year & prohibit Any unlawful gaming is his sd house nor on the Sabbath day Suffer __? Tipple or drink more than enough Than this Obligation shall be __? Otherwise remain in full force & virtue.

At a Court for York County May 15 1721. Wm Blaikley. Wm Gordon __?__Test Phi Lightfoot Cl Cur

Page 43
Know all me by these presents that We Mary Jackson Robt Cobbs Junior & John Harris of the County of York are held firmly bound into the Worshipfull the Justices of the the County aforesaid to the sum of Six Hundred pounds Sterling payable to the sd Justices their heirs__? Or Some of them to the which payment shall be well & Truly made We bind ourselves__? Every of us our heirs Exectr & Adminrs. Joyntly & Severally firmly __?Presents Sealed with our Seals & Dated this 15th Day of May 1721
The Condition of the Above Obligation is Such that if the above Bounden Mary Jackson Exectrx of the last will & Testament of the sd William Jackson decd do make made or cause to be made a _? & perfect Inventory of all & singular Goods Chattels & Credits of the sd Wm Jackson decd. Which have or shall come to the hands, Possession or knowledge of the sd Mary Jackson or into the hands & Possession of any other person or Persons for her The Same To make exhibite or cause to be exhibited into the County Court. At which time She shall be hereto required by the sd Court of the Goods Chattels & Credits & All other Goods Chattels & Credits of the sd Wm Jackson decd at the time of his death which at anytime after Shall come to the hands & Possessions of her the sd Mary Jackson or into the hands & Possession of any other person or persons for her to Well & Truly Administer according to law & & further do make a true & Just Admin of her Makings & Doings therein when thereto required by the sd Court & Also pay & Deliver all the Legacys contained & Specyfyed in the sd testament as far as the Goods Chattels & Credits will thereunto extend according to the value therof & The law Shall charge her. Then this Obligation to be Void & of none effect to otherwise to be in full force & vertue.

At a Court held for York County May 15 1721. Mary Jackson. Robt Cobbs jun .
This bond was presented & Acknowledged in Court. John Harris.
By the partys thereto & Admitted to Record. Test Phi Lightfoot ClCur

Know All men by these presents that we Thos Chisman Saml Tompkins and Anth. Robinson of the County of York are held & Truly bound unto the Worshipfull the Justices of the County aforesaid in the Sum of Fourty pounds Sterling payable to the Justices their heirs & Successors or Some of them to the Which payment well & Truly to be made We bind our Selves & every of us our

& every of our heirs Exectrs & Adminst.
Joyntly & Severally firmly by these presents Sealed with our Seals and dated this 15th day of May 1721.
The condition of this Obligation is such that the above bounden Thos Chisman Exectr of the last will & testament of of Jane Cully decd do make & Cause to be made a true & perfect Inventory of all & Singular the Goods Chattels & Credits of the sd Jane Cully decd. which have or Shall come to the hands possession of him the sd Thos Chisman or into the hands & possession of any other person or persons for him & The Same to make do exhibite or cause to be exhibited into the County court of York at such time as he shall be thereunto required by the Sd Court the Same Goods Chattels & Credits & all other the Goods Chattels & Credits of the sd Jane Cully decd at the time of her death which at any time after shall come to the hands & possessions of him the sd Thos Chisman nor into the hands possessions for him to well & Truly administer according to the Law further do make a true ? auct of his actings & Doings therein when thereto required by the Court & Also pay & Deliver all the Legacys contained & Specyfied in the sd Testament as far as the Ad Goods Chattels & Credits will thereunto extend according to the value thereof & The law shall charge him or this obligation shall be void & of none effect otherwise to Remain in full force & virtue.

At a Court held for York County May 15 1721. Thos. Chisman. Anth Robinson. Saml Tompkins.

This bond was presented & Acknowledge in Court By the partys thereto & Admitted into Record. Test Phi Lighfoot ClCur

Page 44
Know all men by these presents that I John Wise of Coulton in the County of the City of York within the Kingdom of Great Britain &c also Margaret my now wife formerly called by the name of Margaret Bikardike only sister & heir to Bikardike late of YorkTown in Virginia M_? decd for divers good Causes & Considerations is thereunto Severally moving have _?ordained Constituted and appointed & in our Heads & places Putt & by these presents do make Ordain Constitute & appoint & in our heads & Places put Cole Diggs Esq of York Town in Virginia aforesaid & Rich Ambler of York Town aforesaid represent our true & lawful attorney for us & in our names & to our own proper uses to enter into & upon & to the professions of all & every the houses La?Tenem into & here ditaments with their & every of their Rights members & oppurtances Situate lying &c being in Virginia aforesaid or any part thereof here of & Whereto he the Sd Arthr. Bikardike died Siezed or had any right Tale or Interest therein & the same or any part or parcel thereof to dispose & make an absolute Sale of for the best prices or prices they can get for the Same & we do also authorize &

impower our sd Attorneys for us & our names & to our own proper uses to Sell & dispose of all & every the Negroes whether men or women Boys or Girls & also all the stock of horses Cattle & hoggs & all other the Goods Chattels personal estate & effects of what nature or kind __? The Same be whereof he the Sd Arthr Bikardike did possess or anyway entitled to within the Continent of Virginia aforesaid & we do furthur nominate & appoint our sd attorneys for us in our names & to our own uses to ask Demand aquire receive all and every the Rents & arrears of Rents for the Lands & tenements abovementioned or any part thereof & also all the debts Sum & Sums of money in any kind due or owing to the sd Arthr Bickardike at the time of this decease upon bond bill or any other Specialty or otherwise howsoever & from any person or persons whomsoever & for nonpayment thereof to take & use Such Legal ways & means to recover the Same as to our sd Attorneys Shall Seem meet and Convenient & upon receipt & payment thereof to make Seal & deliver acquit or acquitance or other Sufficient discharge or Release to & for the Same & We do hereby Ratify confirm allow of & establish whatsoever our sd Attorneys Shall lawfully do or cause to be done in & about the sd premises or any of them as fully & effectually & to all intents constructions & purposes as if we ourselves were Actually by & present in our own proper persons. In Witness whereof we have hereunto Sett our Hands & Seals at the City of York aforesaid this Thirtieth day of August in the Seventh year of our Sovereign Lord George by the Grace of God over Great Britain France & Ireland King Defender of the Faith & Anno Domine one thousand Seven Hundred & Twenty. Wit. John Wise, Margaret Wise. With a Trible Six penny Stamp according To the act of Parliament.

Mary Thorrowgood of Gloucester County wife of Timo. Thorrowgood. Her mark. John Cainin

At a court held for York County May the 15th 1721
On the Power of Attorney from John Wise & Margaret Wise to Cole Diggs & Richard Ambler was proved in Court by the Oaths of Mary Thorrowgood & John Cainin witnesses therto & Admitted to record. . Test Phi Lightfoot ClCur

Page 45
On the Twenty Fourth Day of January 1720 & on the _? (Seventh?) year of the Reign of Our Sovereign Lord George by the Grace of God of Great Britain, France & Ireland King Defender of the Faith &c by __? John Exton At_? Publick dwelling in London duly admitted & Sworn into __?_ of the Witnesses hereafter named personally appeared Capt George Winter, London, Mariner who declared to have made ordained & Constitutes & By these presents doth make ordain & constitute Thomas Nelson & Joseph Walker of Virginia Esqrs. His true & Lawful attorneys Giving and by these presents granting unto his sd Attorneys & Either of them Joyntly & Severally full power & Lawful Authority for him the

sd constituent in his name & to his uses to ask, demand Levy Sue for & by all lawfull ways & means Recover & receive of & from all & every person & persons of what Degree or quality Soever whom it shall or may contain all & every Such Sum & Sums of money Goods wares merchandises effects estate & things whatsoever to him the sd Constituent due owing belonging or in any wise appertaining whether by __? Bill book debt Account consignment or for or by what other reason or means Soever nothing excepted or reserved & to that end with all & every person & Persons whom it shall or may concern to amount & to view Settle & Adjust all Accts & the balance therof to receive & upon Recoveries & Recis. To give one or more acquittances or other or Sufficent discharges in due form of law but in case of refusal or delay by any person or persons whom it Shall or may concern to make & render just & true anot. And payment & Satisfaction in the premises him her or them. thereunto to compel by all Lawfull ways & means whatsoever Also if need be to Appear before all Lords Judges & Justices in any Court or courts therto to answer defend & reply in all Matters & Causes touching or concerning the premises to do say pursue Impound Seize Sequester attach imprison & to condemn & out of prison again to deliver. Also to Compound Conclude & agree by arbitration or otherwise as his sd Attorneys or either of them Joyntly or Severally Shall think feel and Generally in & concerning the premises to do perform & execute all & whatsoever Shall be requisite & Necessary as fully amply & effectually to all intents constructions & purposes as he the Sd Constituent might or Could do if personally present & That altho the cause Should require more ample or especial power than is herein before particularly esprest with Power to Substitute one or more Attorneys under them or either of them with like or limited power & the Same again to revoke. He the Sd Constituent hereby promising to ratify confirm & hold for good & valid all & whatsoever his sd Attorneys or either of them Joyntly or Severally their or either of their Substitutes Shall do or cause to be done in or about the premises by virtue of these presents Thus done & passed in London aforesaid in the presence of the underwritten. Wit. George Winter.
First Duly Stampt in the presence of- In Querum fidem Johes Exton
1720 Nois pul
T. Danzie
Jno Jones

At a Court held for York County May the 15th 1721
This Power of Attorney from George Winter & Thomas Ne__? Was proved in Court by the Oaths of Thomas Danzie & Joh__? is admitted to record . Test Phi Lightfoot

(Torn page)

In the name of God Amen . . . In York County being Sick & weak of body_? I do

make & ordain this my last will & __? Enulling by these presents all other__?
And first I Commend . . . My Lord & Savior. . . .
(Margin says Jackson's Will)
__? pian Bur__?
Page 46
(continues)
Land belonging to him & his heirs forever __? Item g__? To my son William Jackson Sixty pounds Current money to be payed Him at the age of Twenty one years. Item I do give & bequeath to my daughter Elizabeth Jackson the Sum of Sixty pounds Current money to be payed her at the age of Eighteen years or married Item I Do give & Bequeath to my Sons Phips Jackson the sum of Sixty pounds of Current money to be payed to him at the age of twenty One years Item I do give & Bequeath to my son Ambrose Jackson the Sum of Sixty pounds Current money to be payed him at the age of Twenty One years Item I do give to my loving wife all my Negroes Cattle Household Stuff horses & Mares And I do appoint my loving wife Mary Jackson my whole Execrx to this my last Will and Testament whereunto I Sett my hand & Seal this ninth day of in the year of our Lord God 1721. William Jackson.
Test Wm Stone, John Harris

At a Court held for York County May 15th 1721. John Harris, Sarah Bee

This Last Will & testament of Wm Jackson decd was presented in Court by Mary Jackson the Excrx therein named who made oath to it & being proved by the Oaths of all the witnesses thereto is admitted to record. Test Phi Lightfoot Cl Cur

In the name of God Amen I Jane Culley of of Charles Parish in York County being sick in body but of perfect Sense & memory do make constitute ordain & appoint this to be my last will & Testament in manner & form following Vizt. Imprs. I bequeath my Soul into the hands of Almighty God my Creator &c Item after all my debts & funeral Charges are complied with I do give & Bequeath all & every particular part & Parcell of my estate as goods Chattels moneys Debts that & All things whatsoever unto John Davis Junr. The son of John Davis of Charles parish in York County & if the Sd John Davis junr. should die before he comes to the age of Twenty One years then it is my will that my sd estate shall be distributed among the poor of the Ad. Charles Parish according to the discretion of my Execrs hereafter mentioned Item I do constitute my loving friend Thomas Chisman my whole and Sole Excer of this my last Will & testament revoking & Making vow all other will or wills formerly by me made As Witness my hand & Seal this first of February 1720/1721. Jane Cully. Wit. Thos Pet_? Mary Sta_? Sarah Burnham her mark, Mary {M}Lewellen, her mark
This last Will and Testament of Jane Cully decd was presented in Court by Thos

Chisman the Execr therin named who made Oath to it & being approved by the Oaths of all the Witnesses therto is admitted to record. Test Phi Lightfoot ClCur

? The last Will & Testament of Mary Brewer widow decd in York ? Mrs Brewer being asked by Mr John Bates whether she had a mind
_________?ll in presence of me Peter Brewer & Mrs Hannah Bates and
__________?a Second time the same words & further asked whether she had
___________? These words vizt. (No I have no will nor will make no will
_____________?ates my grand Son all do you hear me I answered I Do
_______________?Trob _? Declared by Mrs Brewer dec'd
_________________?about nine aclock. - Anderson her mark

Page 47
At a Court held for York County May 15th 1721
This Depon of Sarah Anderson was presented in Court & Admitted to Record. . Test Phi Lightfoot Cl Cur

Hannah Bates in her affirmation being asked declared that Mary Brewer being asked by Jno. Bates whether She had made any will made answer that she had no will & would make none And being further asked whether she would give anything to her sons Sackfield or Peter Brewer & She answered No and that Sarah Anderson was not present at the time when she heard Mary Brewer Declare as above & that she was present at the drawing up of the above writing. .

At a Court held for York County May 15th 1721
This depon. of Hannah Bates was presented in Court admitted to Record. Test Phi. Lightfoot ClCur

Peter Brewer on Oath declared that he went to visit his mother Mrs Mary Brewer before her sickness he asked whether She had made any will answered that she was designed to give it Ed. Brewer & after his death to his brother John Bates but they being both dead it might be the better for you meaning this "depon", and in her sickness the 2nd of may 1720 This depon was to visit her again & he bid John Bates ask her if she had settled her affairs & accordingly he did ask her Sevll. Questions to which she made no answer & The reason he supposed was because he this Depon was in the Room. He thereupon went out & he farther Says that Mrs Brewer was in perfect Sense. That he left Sarah Anderson when he left it & That she dyed on Saturday 8 Aclock in the morning and that the written paper was drawn up on Monday.

At a Court for York County May 19th 1721
This depon. of Peter Brewer was presented in Court & Admitted to record. Test Phi. Lightfoot ClCur

John Hope committed to the Gaol of this County on Suspicion of Felony & Burglary in breaking in & Robbing the Store of Dr Archibald Blair in Williamsburgh & he being before the Court on Examination of the Witnesses they are of Opinion that the sd John Hope ought to be tried for the sd fact at the Genl Court Therefore it is ordered that he be remanded to the prison of the County under the Custody of the Sheriff & from thence to be Conveyed to the publick Gaol at WmBurgh in order for a Tryal at the genl Court as the Law in such cases direct.
Jonathon Drewet Wm Keith, Wm Prentis Jos. Freeman Patrick Ferguson Richd Brand & Frans. Elinor Severally before the Court acknowledged themselves indebted to our Sovereign Lord the King in the Sum of Seventy pounds to be levied on their Goods & Chattels on Condition that if they Shall appear before the Genl. Court on the fourth day theres_? & Attend from time to time then & There to give evidence for our Sovereign Lord the King agt John Hope who stands committed for felony & Burglary &c then the above Recognizance to be void or else to remain in full force.

Patrick Ogilvie the same for Jane his wife (Margin says Ogilvie's Recognicance)

________? Henry Tyler & Greves Pack Genl.
____________? County as Accessory to a Robery lately
____________? of Dr Blair in WmBurgh. (Margin seems to indicate Sharp to be conveyed to publick Gaol.)

Page 48
Cont. Nightime & he being before the Court for examination of Witnesses they are of opinion that the sd. Frans. Sharp be remanded to the prison of the County under the custody of the Sheriff & there to remain 20 days in which time he is to give Security in the Sum of One Thousand pounds Sterling with 3 Securitys in the Sum of five hundred pounds each for his appearance on the fourth day of the Genl. Court otherwise that he be conveyed to the publick jail.

Archibald Blair Genl. In Open Court acknowledged himself indebted to our Sovereign Lord the King in the Sum of one Thousand pounds Sterling to be levyed on his Goods Chattels &c on Condition that he Shall appear at the next Genl. Court on the fourth day thereof & from time to time attend & prosecute John Hope & Frans. Sharp this day examined committed on Suspicion of felony and Burglary then the above recognizance be void or else remain in full force.

At a Court held for York County June the 19th 1721. Present Jno. Holloway, Lawr. Smith, Hen. Tyler & Wm Sheldon. Gent. Justices

It being represented that Mary West hath made use of the estate of her decd husband without giving an Inory. (inventory) or taking Admin. It is ordered that She be Sumoned by the Sherif to appear at next Gen, to show Cause why she does exhibit an Inv. ny. of her Sd husbands estate & take Admon. Thereof according to law.

Kate a Negroe Girle belonging to Wm Lee is adjudged to be 12 years old.

Robert Cobbs presented & acknowledged his Deeds of Lease & release of Lands lying in this County to Matt Pierce which on his mon. are admitted to record.

The last Will & Testament of Henry Gill decd was presented in Court by Margt. Gill the Execrx therein named who made Oath to it being proved by the Oaths of all the Witnesses therto is admitted to record & She having together with Archib Blair ,Lewis Holland & Saml Cobbs her Securitys entered into & Acknowledged their bond to the Court for her just & faithfull admon on the sd estate on her mon Certificate is granted her for Obtaining a probate thereof in due form.

Henry Boucock hath an Order Granted him for a Lycence to keep an Ordinary in Wmburgh in this County he having together with Jno. Randolph & Matthew Pierce his Securitys entered into & Acknowledged their bond to the Court for that purpose which bond is admitted to Record

John Cooke on his petition hath an Order Granted him for a Lycence to keep an ordry. At his now dwelling house in York Town he having together with Wm Gordon & Nathel. Hook his Securitys entered into & acknowledged their bond to the Court for that purpose which bond is admitted to Record.

Thomas Cobbs Robt Crawley Jos. Forth & Robt Cobbs or any three of them Sworn before a Justice of the County are appointed to appraise the estate of George Browne decd unadministered by Eliza. his Relict & Make report thereby to the next Court.

On the petition of Robt Kerby Setting forth that his Negroe woman being afflicted with fitts & Having burne her self & So rendered incapable of working It is ordered that the sd Robert Kerby pay no County Levy for the sd Negroe woman until She is capable of working.

Benja. Buck is appointed Constable in the Upper prets. of Yorkhampton parish in the Room of Wm Lark he giving Notice thereof to the sd. Benja. it is ordered that he immediately repair to Some Justice of the Peace of the County & Take the Usual Oath.

On the petition of Lane Jones, Jon J__? Flournoy is appointed his guardian he having together with __? & Jen__? His Securitys entered into & acknowledged ___? That he take care of the sd_____?

Page 49

On the petition of Thos Cripps & Saml. Millington praying to be released from the Securityship of Mary Brethwaite Adm on the estate of Jno. Brethwaite decd or to have an order the sd. Brethwaited estate, the Sd Brethwaite having intermarried with Wm Bigges. It is ordered that the Ad. Bigges be Sumoned to answer the sd petition at the next Court.
An Inventory of the estate of Wm Jackson was exhibited in Court by Mary Jackson & admitted to Record.

The Last Will & testament of Philip Dedman decd was presented in Court by Mary Dedman the Exctrx therein named who made Oath to it & being proved by the Oaths of Lawr. Smith genl & Ann Allen Witnesses thereto is admitted to record & She having together with Jno. Tinkam & John Wrighther Securitys entered into & Acknowledged their bond to the Court for her just & Faithful admon on the sd estate which bond is admitted to record. On her mon. Certificate is granted her for herObtaining a probate thereof in due form.

Henry Tyler genl complaining that Lewis Davis refused to Serve being legally Sumoned on an Request. It is thereupon odred that he be Sumoned to answer the sd Complt at the next Court.

An inventory &c of the estate of Dianah Blaxton decd was presented to Court & Admitted to record.

Jane Given Servant to Mary Dun having been Run away days & The sd Mary Dun having expended fourty shillings & Six pence half penny . It is ordered that She Serve her sd Mistres Twenty One Weeks after her time by Indenture custom or former order is required.

An Invry &c of the estate of Jno. White decd was presented in Court by Edw. Tabb which is admitted to Record.

An Inventry of the sate of Dennis White decd was presented in Court by Mary White which is admitted into record.

The petition of Dianah Hayward agt Robt Shield for her shared of the estate of Wm Hayward her decd father is continued until the next Court

In the action upon the Case between Wm Fleming plt & Lawr. Smith deft for

Seven Hundred pounds of Tobo. & Cash due by Note the deft confessed Judgement to the plt for Six Hundred pounds of Tobo. convenient in King Wm County. And it is ordered That the deft pay the same with a Lawyer fee according to Law & costs als Ex.

The petition of Mary Clifton agt Robert Shields for her Share of the estate of the Wm Hayward her decd father is continued til the next Court.

It appearing to the Court that Margt. Croney Servt to Mary Gill did resist & Assault the sd Mistriss. It is therefore ordered that she serve her sd Mistriss one whole year after her time by Indenture Custom or former order is expired.

Ann Combs failing to appear & answer the Grand Jurys presentment is ordered to be taken into Custody.

Thos. Wooten presented by the Grand Jury on his mon. the sd presentment is continued until next Court.

In the action upon the case between John Abbott plt & John Ness deft for ten pounds Ten Shillings & ten pence Current money due Accot. The Cause is continued at the deft mon. & Costs & it is ordered that the deft pay the plt a Lawyers fee & if the same is not paid at the determination of the suit that Exo. Go in like manner for the same.

The action of trespass on the Case between Wm Gordon plt & Lawr. Smith deft for one Hundred pounds damage is continued to perform the Survey on the first Thursday in July if fair if not the next fair day .

In the action of detinue between James Wall plt & Lawr. Smith de for __?ngs Current money issue being Joyned the Cause is cont. __?xt Court.

(Margin indicates Craig vs Delony) ________?between H_?Craig Execr &c of Wm Craig decd plt plt for _? Thirty poundsCurrent money due by bond the deft having-

Page 50

Had time to plead & being now called & failing to do the same on the plt mon. Judgement is granted him for the sd Sum & costs by Nihil Duit confirmable at the next Court on the like default.

The difference between Anna Maria Timson Exectx &c of Wm Timson decd plt & Jno. Jas. Flourney & Mary his wife Execr &c of Orlando Jones decd deft. is dismist.

In the action of trespass between Jno. Page plt & John Brook deft for Twenty pounds damage issue being Joyned the cause is refd for tryall until the next Court.

On the petition of Achillis Saunders praying to be exempted from paying levies he being very old & infirm It is thereupon ordered that he be exempted therefrom.

In the action of Detinue between Thos Tomer plt & Saml Tompkins deft for One hundred pounds damage issue being Joyned a Jury (to witt} Matt. Pierce &c were Sworn & they having heard the evidence and recd a Special verdt. Drawn up by both partys retired & After some time returned into Court & Delivered their verdt. In these words (to witt) We find the will of Jno. Tomer hereunto annexed We find that Ann Tomer daughter of the sd John in the sd will mentioned departed this life under Coverture & With out other issue then one son named Saml. Born before her espousal with the deft. We find that Thos. Tomer the plt is the only brother of the whole blood of the sd Anne . We find the negroes in the plts despn. Mentioned are in the possession of the deft who intermarried with aforesaid Anne & are of the price following Vizt- Nemo of the price of £20. __ __ Jimmy of the price of £18. __ __ & Judy of the price of £12. __ __. We find a Deed bearing the date the 28th day of February in the fourth year of King George & in the year of of our Lord 1717 from Saml. Tompkins & Anne his wife unto Saml. Tompkins the sone of the Ad. Saml. & Anne hereunto annexed. We find the Negroes Nemo & Judith in the sd Deed mentioned. Are the Negroes in the Declon. We find that the sd Anne is the daughter of the sd John Tomer in the will mentioned. We find that at the time of making the sd Deed the sd Anne was under Coverture. If upon the whole law before the plt we find for him the Negroes of the value above & the damage of one Shilling for detaining otherwise We find for for the deft. Matt. Pierce fforeman by consent of the partys the matter of Law arising from the sd Verdict are ref. to be argued at the next Court.

The action upon the Case between Philip Lightfoot plt & Eliza Hansford Surviving Execr. &c of Thos. Hansford decd. Deeft for £1-18-9/a Current money dued by Audt is cont until the next court.

In the action of debt between Jos Walker genl . plt & Eliza Hansford surviving Execx. &c of Thos Hansford decd deft for one hundred & fourteen pounds & Elven Shillings Current money due bt bond the Audrs Report is admitted to record-& it appearing that fifty four pounds & Fourteen shillings is due to the plt it is ordered that the deft pay the Ad. Sum out of the decd estate with costs als Exo.

On the action of Trespass between Jno. Page plt & Dane. Thompson deft for Twent pounds damage the deft confessed Judgement to the plt for fifteen shillings & its ordered that he pay the Same to the plt with costs Als Exo.

In the Actions of debt between Same. Sweny plt & Lewis Delony deft for Ninety one pounds five shillings Currt money due by note Thos Jones became Special bail for the deft & Issue being Joyned the Cause is ref. for Tryal until next Court.

The action upon the Case between Arcgibd. Blair plt & Jno. Mandell deft for £11-19-51/4 Current mony due on balla. Austs. is cont. until the next Court.

A power of Att from John How & Isaac Clayton to Thos. Strangbe was acknowledged by the Ad. Isaac Clayton & proved by the Oath of Wm Gwine to be the Act & Deed of Jno. How is admitted to record.

The difference between Jos Walk Sherif plt & Jno. Mundell deft is dismist.

In the action upon the Case between Phi Lightfoot plt & Dane. Thomson deft for £20-1-3 Currt money th ?? The Suit is continued until the next Court.

Page 52

In the action upon the Case between Edwd Sparks Mariner plt & Jos. Barry deft for £500 damage Wm. Robertson became Security for the plt for Costs & Issue being Joyned the Cause is referred for tryal on the mon. of the defts att. liberty is given to either party to take the depons. of any Witnesses as they may have occasion to make use of in the Coun. Before Thomas Nelson Gent giving Notice thereof which Depon. Shall be admitted as evidence on the Tryall at the next Court

In the action upon the Case between Chas Marshall plt & Chas Rowan def Judgement is granted the plt for Costs of Suit & a Lawyer for the aforesaid Sum of Five pounds being paid & its ordered that the deft. Pay the Costs aforesaid & A Lawyers fee to the plt Als Exo.

In the petition of Benj Weldon plt & Jere Hill def for Four pounds Eight Shillings & Eight pence Current money on Attr. being returned executed by the Sherif for the sd Sum in the hands of Ja. Rowan Esqr. & It appearing by Acct that the Sum of four pounds Eleven Eleven Shillings & Three pence is in the hands of Jas Roscow aforesaid Judgement is granted the plt for his debt & costs & its ordered that the Ad Roscow pay the sd Sum of four pounds eleven Shillings & Three pence to the plt.

In the suit in Chancery depending between John Hay & Mary his wife Complts

& Thos Tomer Surviving Execr. &c of Jno. Tomer decd Respond. Delivered in his answer on Oath & the Complt hath time allowed him to consider the Same until the next Court.

The action upon the Case between Jos. Stcy plt & Robt Ross deft for five pounds damage is continued until the next Court .

The action upon the Case between Jno. Eyre plt & Jos Freeman deft is cont. at the deft mon & Charge until the next Court.

In the action upon the Case between Jno Hope plt & Geo Butler deft for two pounds Current money due by Act
Judgement is confirmed agt the deft & & Mary Butler his Security for one pound Sixteen Shillings & its ordered that they pay the Same to the plt with Costs als Exo.

The action upon the Case between Thos Jones plt & Eliza Powers Execr &c of Edwd. Powers decd is cont. until the next Court.

The action upon the Case between Mary Read plt & Geo Butler deft is continued until the next Court.

The action of Debt between Cole Digges Esq. plt & Lewis Delony deft for Twenty Seven pounds Twelve shillings Current money due by Note is ordered to be dismist & that the deft pay Costs als. Exo.

In the petition of Jno. Brooke agt Jno. Jackson for fourty eight Shillings an Atta. being returned Executed by the Sherif for the Sd Sum in the hands of Eliza Ives it is ordered that She deliver the Goods & She acknowledges to be in her Custody belonging to the sd Jackson to the sd Jno. Brooks & That the sd atta. Be dismist.

In the petition of Wm Robertson & Saml Cobbs Execrs of David Cuningham decd agt Jackson for Seven pounds Crrt money by bill proved James Bates being examined the Atta. is discontinued.

The difference between Jos. Stacy plt & Ja Dixon deft is dismist.

The difference between Jno. Bratt plt & Jere Turner deft is dismist

The difference between Richd Howell plt & Edw Sparks deft is dismist.

The difference between Thos. Holliday plt & Joseph Freeman deft is dismist

In the action of trespass on the Case between Benj. Clifton plt & Wm Bigges deft for Ten pounds damage the deft failing to appear on the plts mon. an Atta is granted him agt the deft estate for the aforesaid Sum & Costs confirmable at the next Court on the like default.

In the Suit in Chancery brought by Armiger Parsons & Eliza. His wife Complt __? To answer until the next Court. _??minr &c of Robt Hay decd respondts on the responds mon. until the next Court.
(Margin indicates Bell & Power) ? Power deft is dismist

Page 52
The difference between Wm Rogers plt & Augt. Moore &c Excr. of John Baylor decd is dismist.

In the action upon the Case between Philip Lightfoot plt & Thos. Bell deft for £9. 4. 2 ¼ due on balla. of Auts on the defts mon. an Imparlance is granted him until next Court.

The difference between James Mackindo plt & Wm Elliot deft is dismist.

In the action upon the Case between Edwd Sparks Mariner plt & Philip Lightfoot Genl Deft. the plt failing to prosecute on the defts mon. he is nonsuited and its ordered that the plt pay the deft damage according to law & Costs Als Exo.

In the action of debt between Thos. Posford plt & Jos Davenport deft for fifteen pounds damage Jno. Randolph became Security for what Costs Shall accrue on this suit on the Aust of the plt on the plts mon. judgement is granted him agt the deft & Security for the aforsd Sum & costs unless the deft appears at the next court & answer the plts mon.

On the action upon the Case between Jno Hay plt & Armiger Parsons & Eliz his wife deft for £8. 7. 8 ¼ Curt money due by Acct. on the defts mon an imparlance is granted him until the next court.

In the action of Trespass on the case between Edward Sparks plt & Saml Weldon deft for £500 damage Wm Robertson became Security of the Plts paying Costs on the plts motion he hath time allowed him to consider the defts plea until the next Court.

The action of Debt between David Morce plt & Jos. Frith deft for Ten pounds Two shillings & eleven pence due by note is continued until the next Court.

A power of Att from Rebc. Tyler to Phi Lightfoot was proved in Court by the

Oath of Saml Weldon & admitted to record.

Philip Lightfoot by virtue of a power of Att from Reba. Tyler relinquished her right of Dower in Certain Lotts of Land Lying In Wm Burgh conveyed to Gavin Corbin by Francis Tyler by certain Deeds which relinquishment is admitted to Record. Barnard Cowdert on Evidence for Thos Tomer agt Saml Tomkins having attended one day ordered the sd Thomas pay him fourty pounds of Tobo for the same with Costs als Exo

John Stewart in open Court made an Oath that George Browne dec departed this life without making any will So far as he knows or believes & he having together with Matt. Pierce his Security entered into & acknowledged their bond to the court for his Just & faithful Admon on the sd Browns estate unadministered by Eliza his Relict & Excetx. (which bond is admitted to record on the sd Stewarts mon. Certificate is granted him for a Comission of Admon on the Sd estate in due form.

The petiton of Jno. Welch & Jno. Patrick agt Saml Styles is dismist the petrs not appearing.

Ordered that the Court be adjourned until the Court in Course. Lawr. Smith Truly Entred by Phi Lightfoot ClCur

Be it Known unto all men by these presents that I Rebecca Tyler wife of Francis Tyler of James City County have constituted & appointed by these presents to constitute & appoint Mr Philip Lightfoot to be my true & Lawfull attorney for me & in my name to Relinquish my right of Dower in & To four Lotts lying and being in the City of Williamsburg Sold by my husband to Coll. Gaven Corbin to do execute & perform all & every matter & thing which which in or about the promises Shall be requistite & necessary to fully& effectually as I myself might or could if I was personally present. __??Ratified allowed & confirmed Witnesses my hand__? 1721. Rebecca Tyler

Page 53
At a Court held for York County June 19th 1721.
This Power of attorney from Reba. Tyler to Phi Lightfoot was proved in Court by the Oath of Saml Weldon & admitted to Record. Test Phi Lightfoot Cl Cur

In the Name of God Amen I Henry Gill of the City of WmBurgh & County of York being sick & weak of body but of Sound & perfect memory praised be God therefore do make this my last Will & Testament in manner of form following Imprs after my Just debts are paid I give & Bequeath unto my Son John Gill & The heirs of his body lawfully begotten for ever the Two Lotts whereon I now

dwell with all the edifices buildings & improvements thereupon to be kept in good repair until he comes to the age of Twenty one years & if my Son John Gill die without issue then I give & bequeath the Two Lotts aforesaid with all the Improvements aforesaid to my Daughter Eliza Gill & The heirs of her body lawfully begotten forever. And if my daughter Eliza Gill happen to died without issue than I give the Two Lotts with the housing aforsd To my loving wife Margaret Gill her heirs & Assigns forever. Item I give my Tan yard with the Lotts thereunto belonging & my Negro man named Will equally between my Son Jno Gill and my loving wife Margt Gill during her natural life & after her decease to be & remain wholly to my son Jno Gill & The heirs of his body lawfully begotten forever. & if my Son John should happen to died without issue as aforesaid than I give the sd Lotts & Tanyard to my daughter Eliza Should she happen to died without lawfull issue Then I give the Lotts & Tannyard to my loving wife Margt Gill her heirs & Assigns forever. Item I give & bequeath to my son John Gill my Sirvntore press bed with the furniture thereunto belonging. Item I give & bequeath the three Lotts with the housing & Improvements thereupon (being where Mr. Lewis Holland now keeps store) to my loving wife Margt Gill during her natural life & after her decease I give and bequeath the three Lotts with housing to my daughter Eliza when She doth come of age or marry fifty pounds Current money. Item my Will is that my Son John Shall live with his mother till come of age to possess his estate Item I give & bequeath unto my brother Mark Gill in England one Guinea value Twenty Six Shillings here in Vira. Item I give all the rest & residue Reversion & remainder of my whole estate both real & personal unto my Loving wife Margt & her heirs forever & doth hereby appoint my loving wife whole & Sole Execrx of this my last Will & testament revoking all former wills by me at any time heretofore made in testimony whereof I have hereunto Sett my hand & Seal this Sixteenth day of December 1720. Henry Gill
Wit. John Abbott, Lewis Holland, Morgan Conner, C. Evans
This last will and Testament of Henry Gill decd was presented in Court by Margt Gill the Exectx therein named who made Oath to it & being proved by the Oaths of all the Witnesses thereto is admitted to record.
Test Phi Lightfoot Cl Cur.

Page 54
Know all men by these presents that We John How & Isaac Clayton mariners In St Christophers do hereby assign ordain Authorize constitute and appoint & in our Stead & Place put & Depute Thomas Strangle Mariner of London to be our true & lawfull Deputy & Attorney & for us & in our name & to our use benefit & behoof to ask demand & Require Sue for & Recover and to our use benefit receive all Such debts dues Sum & Sums of money or other demands whatsoever as now or hereafter Shall be due payable belonging or to be delivered to us from Capt Chalender Williams Commander of the Ship Gascoyn the Sd Thos Strangle

to use all lawfull ways & means for recovery thereof by action Suit arrest bill plain Atta. Address reentry or other ways as fully & employ in every respect as I my Self might or Could if I were personally present Granting unto my Sd Attorney full whole & Lawfull authority in the Execution of all & Singular the premises & to Substitute & appoint one or more Att. Or attorneys & The same again at pleasure to revoke to make or to give any acquittance release or discharge upon the recovery & rect. four Debt Sum & Sums of money & generally to Say execute compound conclude agree determine & Finish all & everything & things whatsoever my sd Attorney & His Substitute Shall lawfully do touching the premises by virtue of these presents In Witness wherefor we have hereunto Set our hands & Seals

This 10th Day of May 1721. Jno. J (mark) How.

Wit. Wm Gwinner, Isaac X Clayton, Jno Jones, Geo. Gosmold

At a Court held for York County June 19th 1721. This power of attorney from Jno How & Isaac Clayton to Thos Strangle was acknowledged by the sd Isaac Clayton & Proved by the Oath of Wm Gwine to be the Act & Deed of Jno. How & admitted to record. Test Phi Lightfoot Cl Cur

In the Name of God Amen I Philip Dedman of Yorkhampton parish in the county of York being Sick & weak but in Perfect sense & memory (Blessed be God) do make my last will & Testament in manner & Form in manner & Form following Imprs I do resign my Soul in to the hands of God that gave it to me & my body to the earth from whence it came to be decently buried at the discretion of my Excr. -hereafter named item I give & Bequeath to my loving Son Philip Dedman all my dividend or tract of Land I now liveupon, being in Yorkhampton parish in York County to him & the male heirs of his body lawfully begotten forever & For want of Such heirs to my grandson Francis Luck & the male heirs of heirs of his body lawfully begotten for ever & for want of such heirs to my daughter Martha & the male heirs of her body lawfully begotten forever & for want of such heirs to my Daughter Susanna & The male heirs of her body lawfully begotten forever & for want of such heirs to my daughter Mary & The male heirs of her body lawfully begotten forever & For want of such heirs to my daughter Ann & The male heirs of her body lawfully begotten for ever. Item I give & bequeath to daughter Elizabeth Pollin twenty Shillings Current money Item I give I give & bequeath to my daughter Martha Dedman the best feather bed of furniture belonging to me Three Rushia Cather high chairs three matted chairs one Square Table one hackaback Tablecloth & Six Napkins, Six new plates, four new dishes to weigh about four pounds each one iron pott about Twenty Four pounds, one new frying pan and new Pewter Quart Tankard Six new pewter spoons Four Breeding Ewes & One young Cow & Cow year__?? To daughter Martha when she arrives to the age __?? Marriage by my Execr h__? Loving wife have &

Page 55
enjoy all the remaining part of my estate during her widowhood but if my said wife should marry then it is my will & Desire that my Ad remaining part of my estates be equally divided between my sd wife & her children (Vizt) Philip Dedman Susaa. Dedman Mary Dedman & Ann Dedman Lastly I do make constitute & appoint my loving wife Mary Dedman my whole & sole Exectx of this my last will & Testament revoking all other Wills heretofore by me made in Witness whereof I have hereunto Sett my hand & Seal this 7thday of February 1718. Phill Dedman. Wit. Lawr. Smith, Ann Allin, Basill W (Mark) Wagstaff

At a Court held for York County June 19th 1721
This Last Will & Testament of Philip Dedman decd was presented in Court by Mary Dedman the Execrx therein named who made Oath to it & being proved by the Oaths of Lawr Smith & Ann Allin Witnesses thereto is admitted to Record. Test Phi Lightfoot Cl Cur

June 17th 1721
An Inventory of the estate of Wm Jackson decd as followeth (includes 3488 pounds tobacco & 1 young negroe man - no totals)

At a Court held for York County June 19th 1721
This inventory of the estate of Wm Jackson decd was presented in Court by the Exectx & admitted to record. . Test Phi Lightfoot Cl Cur

In Obedience to an order of the Court bearing date March 20 1720 We the - subscribers being first Sworn have appraised all the estate of Dennis White decd that was offered to us as followeth : June 19 1721 £4-17-6
At a Court for York County June 19 1721 __?estate Dennis White decd was admitted to record. Robert Kerby, Bennet Tompkin, Thos Kerby

Page 56
In Obedience to an Order of York County Court bearing date May the 15th 1721. We the Subscribers being first Sworn have appraised all the estate of John White decd . June 19 1721. £3-13-6 Robt Kerby, Wm Wise, Thos Kerby

At a Court held for York County June 19th 1721
The Invry &c of the estate held for Jno. White decd was presented in Court & admitted to Record. Test Phi Lightfoot ClCur. £51-12-11

£3-1-1 2 years interest =========

£54-14-

Contra Credit 1725 Tobo. 1724@ 2of

£ 17-5-

Cash --9

51=12=11 ½

=========

69-6-11

Errors excepted P. Walker

June 6 1721

We the subscribers having met & examined the above pursuant to an order of York County dated May 15th 1721. do find the ball. Due the plt fifty four pounds fourteen shillings Current money now under our hands. Thos Nelson, Jno Hansford, Phi Lightfoot

At a Court held for York County June 19th 1721 This Amt & settlement of the estate of Thos Hansford decd was presented into Court & admitted to record. . Test Phi Lightfoot Cl Cur

Page 57

Know All men by these presents that We Mary Dedman Jno Tenham & John Wright of the County of York are held & firmly bound unto the Worshipfull the Justices of the county aforesaid in the Sum of One hundred & Fifty pounds Sterling payable to the Sd Justices their heirs & sucessors or Some of them to the which payment well & Truly to be made We bind ourselves & every of us our & every of our heirs Execr & admin Joyntly or Severally firmly by these presents Sealed with our Seals & Dated this 19th day of June 1721

The condition of this Obligation is Such that if the above Bounden Mary Dedman Execr of the Last Will & testament of Philip Dedman decd do make or cause to be made a true & perfect Inventory of all& Singular the Goods Chattles & Credits of the Sd Philip Dedman decd which have or Shall come to the hands or Posession or knowledge of her the Sd Mary Dedman or into the hands or possession of any person or persons for her & the Same to be made do exhibite or cause to be exhibited in the County Court of York at Such Time as She Shall be thereunto required by the sd Court & The Same Goods Chattles & Credits & all other the Goods Chattles & Credits of the sd Phi. Dedman decd at the time of his death which at any time after Shall come to the hands profession of her the sd Mary Dedman or into the hands or possession of any person or persons for her to well & truly administer according to law & further do make a true & just Acct of her actings & Doings therein when thereto required by the Sd Court & also pay & deliver all the Legacys contained & Specyfied in the Sd testament as far as the Ad Goods Chattels & Credits will thereunto extend according to the value thereof & the Law Shall discharge her , Than this obligation to be void & of none effect otherwise remaining in full force & Vertue. Mary (mark) M Dedman

At a Court held for York County June 19th 1721

John Tenham.

This Bond was presented & acknowledged in Court John Wright

By the partys thereto & admitted to Record. Test Phi Lightfoot ClCur

Know all men by these presents that We Margt Gill Archibald Blair , Lewis Holland & Sam Cobbs of the County of York are held & firmly boundunto the Worshipful the Justices of the County of York in the Sum of four hundred pounds which payment well & truly to be made we bind our Selves & every of us our & Every of our heirs Execrs & admin jointly & Severally firmly by these presents. Sealed with our Seals & dated this19th day of June 1721
The Condition of this Obligation is Such that if the above bounden Margt Gill Execrx of the last Will & Testament of Henry Gill decd do make or cause to be made a true & perfect Inventory of all & singular the Goods Chattels & Credits of the sd Henry Gill decd which have or Shall come to the hands possessions or knowledge of her the sd Margt Gill or into hands or possessions of any other person or persons for her & The Same to make do exhibite or cause to be exhibited into the County Court of York at Such time as She Shall be thereunto required by the sd court & The Same Goods Chattles & credits & all other the Goods Chattels & Credits of the sd Henry Gill dec at the time of his death which at anytime after Shall come to the hands & Possessions of her the sd Margt Gill or into the hands or possessions of any other person or persons for her to Well & Truly Administer according to law & further do make a true and Just Acct. of her actings & doings she__? Thereunto required by the Court & also pay & deliver all the Legacys contained & Specyfied in the sd Testaments far as the sd Goods Chattels & Credits will thereunto entered according to the value__?Then this Obligation to be void & of none effect or __?vertue. Lewis Holland Margt Gill. Saml Cobbs. Arch. Blair

Page 58
At a court held for York County June 19th 1721
This bond was presented & Acknowledged in Court by the partys thereto & Admitted to record. Test Phi Lightfoot Cl Cur

Know all men by these presents that we Jno. Cooke Wm Gordon & Nathaniel Hook of the County of York are held & Firmly bound by the grace of God of Great Britain France & Ireland King Defender of the faith &c in the Sum of ten thousand pounds of tobacco convenient in in the sd County of York to the which payment well & Truly be made to our Sovereign Lord the King his heirs & Successors we bind our Selves & every of us our & Every of our heirs Execrs & Adminrs Joyntly & Severally firmly by these presents Sealed with our Seals & dated this 19th day of June 1721
The Condition of this Obligation is Such that Whereas the above bounden Jno. Cooke hath an order this day granted him for a Lycence to keep an Ordinary at his now dwelling place in York Town for the Year next ensuing. If therefore the Ad Jno. Cooke doth constantly find & provide in his sd ordinary good

wholesome & Cleanly lodging & diet for Travellers & Stabling &c and provender or pasturage & provender (as the season Shall require) for their horses from the date of these presents for & during the term of one - year & Shall not Suffer any Unlawful gaming in his sd house nor on the Sabbath day suffer any person to Tipple or drink more than is necessary. Then this Obligation to be void & of none effect Otherwise to remain in full force & virtue.

At a Court held for York County June 19th 1721. Jno. Cooke.
This Bond was presented & Acknowledged in Court . Wm Gordon
By the partys thereto & Admitted to Record. Nath. Hook Test Phi Lightfoot Cl Cur

Know all men by these presents that we Henry Bowcock Jno. Randolph and Matt Pierce of the County of York are held firmly bound to our Sovereign Lord George by the Grace of God of Great Britain France & Ireland King Defender of the faith &C in the Sum of Ten Thousand pounds of Tobo. convenient to the sd County of York to the which payment well & truly to be made to our Sovereign Lord the King his heirs & successors We bind our Selves & every of us our & every of our heirs Execrs & Admins Joyntly & Severally firmly by these presents Sealed with our Seals & Dated this 19th day of June 1721.
The condition of this obligation is Such that where as the above Bounden Henry Bowcock hath an Order this day Granted him for a Lycence to keep an ordinary at the now dwelling house in WmBurgh for the year next ensuing if therefore the sd Henry Bowcock doth constantly find & provide in his ordinary good wholesome & Cleanly lodging for Travellors& Stableage & Provender or pasturage & Provender (as the Season Shall require) for their horses from the date of these presents for & During the term of one year he Shall not Suffer any illegal gaming in his sd house nor on the Sabbath day Shall Suffer any person to Tipple & drink more than is necessary. Then this obligation to be void & of none effect otherwise to Remain in Full Force & Vertue.

At a Court held for York County June 19th 1721 Henry Bowcock.
This __? Acknowledged in Court by the partys__? Jno Randolph, Pierce

Page 59
Know all men by these presents that We Jno. James Flournoy Saml Cobbs & Jno. Pasture of the county of York are held & Firmly bound unto the Worshipfull the Justices of the County aforesaid in the Sum of five hundred pounds Sterling payable to the Justices their heirs & successors or Some of them to the which payment well & truly to be made we bind ourselves & every of us our & Every of our heirs Execrs and Adminst. Joyntly & Severally firmly by these presents Sealed with our Seals & Dated this 19th day of June 1721.
The conditions of this Obligation is Such that if the Above Bounden Jno. James

Flournoy Shall well & Truly pay or cause to be paid unto Lane Jones Orphan of Orlando Jones decd all Such estate or estates belonging to th sd. Orphan as is or hereafter Shall come to the hands & Professions of him the Sd Jno. James Flournoy or into the hands or professions of any person or Persons for him when or upon as the sd orphan Shall attain to lawfull age when thereunto required by the sd court & Shall also Save & Keep harmless the Ad Court from all trouble or damage that Shall or may accrue to them about or concerning the sd estate Then this Obligation to be void or else to remain in full force & virtue. John James Flournoy
At a Court held for York County June 19th 1721
This Bond was presented acknowledged in Court by the partys thereto & admitted to record. Saml Cobbs, Jean Pasteur. Test Phi Lightfoot Cl Cur

1 bed & bedstead & rug & 1 sheet & blanket & pillow 1 Table & 1 Box & bloster & 4 chairs. £3-9-6. Addiston Rogers, Thos Wooten, Thos Wooten Jr

At a Court for York County June 19 1721.
This Invenry &c of the estate of Dianah Braxton decd was Presented in Court & admitted to Record. Test Phi Lightfoot ClCur

At a Court held for York County July 17th 1721. Present Lawr Smith Graves Park, Thos. Nelson, Wm Sheldon - Genl Justices

JnC_?ry a Negroe boy belonging to Wm Rogers is adjudged to be Twelve years old.
Rumford a negroe boy belonging to WmRogers is adjudged to be Ten years of age.
Phillis a Negroe Girle belonging to Do. is adjudged to be eight years old.
_? Negroe boy belonging to Jno. Robinson is adjudged to be nine yrs old.
Will a Negroe boy belonging to Do. is adjudged to be Eight years old.
Hannah a negroe Girle belonging to Benja Buck is adjudged to be fourteen.

In the petition of Christo. Jackson agt John Ness for fourteen pounds Six shillings & one farthing an Att__? Executed by the Sherif in the hands of Dr Jno. Br, __? Jones it is thereupon ordered at __?sd Ness's estate in their hands

__? Jno. Ness for fifteen pounds eleven shillings & nine __? Executed in the hands of Thos Danrie. It is __? of the sd Ness's estate. (Margin says Jones @ Ness)

Page 60
In the petition of David Prior agt John Ness forty three pounds four Shillings proved to be due on ball. of Aust an Atta. Being returned executed on Corn &

wheat, It is ordered that Jno. Harris Thomas Cripps Richd Easter & Wm Davis or any three of them being sworn are appointed to appraise the sd Corn& Wheat & deliver So much thereof to the petr. As will be sufficient to pay the aforesaid . Debt & Costs & make return thereof to the next Court
Eliza Powers on her petition hath an Order granted her for a Licence to keep an ordinary in YorkTown. She having together with Wm Gordon & Saml Cobbs her Securitys entered into & Acknowledged their bond to the Court for that purpose which bond is admitted to record.
John Dowsing presented & acknowledge his Deed for Land lying in York Town to his son Robt Dowsing on whose motion it is admitted to record.

On the petition of John Abbott prisoner in the gaol of this County Setting forth that he having been in the aforesaid Gaol above the Space of Three months & having likewise made Oath that he hath no estate real nor personal of the value of fifty Shillings. It is thereupon ordered to be certified to the Sherif.

Ezekial Gilbert on his petition hath an order granted him for a Lycence to keep an ordinary in York Town he having together with Butler & Wm Gordon his Securitys entered into & Acknowledged their bond for that purpose which bond is admitted to Record.

In the petiton of Jno. Jones agt John Ness for Sixteen pounds due by Acct proved an Atta. being returned executed in the hands of Capt Rich Pitts The sd Pitts appeared & Made Oath that he is indebted to the sd Ness no more than Seven pounds five Shillings& Eleven pence Current money And its ordered that he pay the same to the plt.

In the petiton of Dr. John Browne agt John Ness for the Sum of three hundred pounds Current money the plt proved his Acct. for Sixty pounds fourteen Shillings & Seven pence Currt Money on atta. Being returned executed on one Silk Mantua & Petticoat &c in the hands of Capt Clark, Mr Blackwell Lawr. Smith Wm Biggs & Capt Keeling-
It is ordered that the sd Clark & Keeling appear before Some Justice of the County & render an Acct. of the sd Neffs effects in their hands & pay Same to the Sherif & That the sd Blackwell Smith & Biggs appear and render an Acct at the next Court & further that the Jos. Davenport John Brooks Henry Bowcocke & JohnBr_? Any three of them being Sworn before a Justice of the County _? The sd Goods& Make a report therof to the next Court

In the petition of Samuel Cobbs agt John Ness for twenty two pounds Seven Shillings Seven pence due by Acct proved by the petrs Oaths an atta. being returned executed on _? & furniture in the hands of Wm Robertson & Dr John Browne It is ordered that Henry Bowcocke Jno. Pasture Jos Davenport & Lewis

Holla_? of them being Sworn before a Justice of the County appraise the Sd _?the same to the petr & Furthur that Sherif Sumon the sd Robertson & Browne to appear & render an Acct of the Sd Ness's estate in their hands at the _? ___? (poss Geo) Gilbert agt Jno Ness for three pounds five shillings Current __?proved by the plt Oath on Att. Being returned executed __?Allen Andr. Laprade it is ordered that the sd Allen& Lapr_?Ness effects__?

Page 60 A
(Left side and Top part of page gone) Test Phi Lightfoot Cl

?By these presents that We Mary Laton Thos Wade & James
___?York are held & firmly bound unto the Worshipfull theJustices
___?D in the Sum of One Hundred pounds Sterling payable to
___?heirs & Successors or Some of them to the which payment
___?de We bind ourselves & every of us our & every of our
___?minors Joyntly & Severally firmly by these presents
___?& dated this 17th day of November 1720.
___?n of this obligation is Such that if the above bounden Mary
___?the Last Will & testament of Jno. Laton decd do make or
___? A true & perfect Inventory of all & Singular the Goods Chattles
___?John Laton decd which have or Shalle come into the hands
__
___? dge of her the sd Mary Laton or into the hands or possessions
___?Or persons for her & the Same to make do exhibite or cause to be exhibited
___?County Court of York at Such time as She Shall there
___?the Ad Court & the same Goods Chattles& Credits & All other
___?& Credits of the sd John Laton decd at the time of his death
___?after Shall come to the hands & possessions of her the sd Mary
___?& Possessions of any other person or persons for her
___?according to Law & Furthur do Make a true & Just Acct
___? Therein when thereto required by the SdCourt & also
___?the Legacys contained & specified in the sd Testament as
___?Chattles or credits will thereunto entered according to the value
___?& charge her Then this Obligation to be void & of none
___?charge her Then this Obligation to be void & of none
___?full force & virtue. Mary X Laton (her mark) . Thos Wade, James Taylor,
__? For York
___? 20th 1720
___? Acknowledged by the partysthereto & admitted. Test Phi Lightfoot ClCur

_? All men by these presents that We JohnHollway Maj Nathaniel ? Blair of the County of York are held & firmly bound unto___?his heirs Admins. One Hundred Fifty pounds Sterling to the which

_________?be made We bind ourselves & every of us Our & Every
__________?joyntly & Severally firmly by these presents
_____________of Februart 1720

60B
(Fragment of a page)
At a court held for York Cou
This Bond was presented & ackn
The parts thereto & admitted to Recor
Test Phi Lightfoot

In Obedience to an Order
Day of December 1720 We the Subscr (Margin says Pollings Invry & C)
Chattles of John Polling late of the pa
This Eleven day of January 1720
One of his Majesties Justices of the sd
William W Lilborn Edw_?

At A Court held for . . . .

Page 61
The atta. of Edwd Sparks agt Jos Barry Wm Robertson having entered himself Security for costs & damages on the mon of Phi Lightfoot & Saml Weldon the sd Atta is further continued until the next Court.

Thomas Robins on his petition hath an order granted him for an ordry Lycence he having together with Richd Baker & John Matlocke his Securitys entered into & Acknowledged their bond to the Court for that purpose which bond is admitted to Record.

An Invry. of the estate of Phi Dedman decd was presented in Court & Admitted to Record.
The last Will & testament of Nathl. Sebrell decd was presented in Court by Jno Mundell & Susa Sebrell the execrs therein named who made Oath to it & being proved by the Oaths of James Robinson Dennis Reynolds and Wm Bayley Witnesses thereunto is admitted to record & the Exectrs having together with Wm Bayley & Andr Laprade their securitys entered into and acknowledged their bond to the Court for their just & faithfull admon. In the sd estate Certificate is granted them for obtaining a probate therof in due form.

On the petition of Alexander Atkinson & His making Oath that a Silk Gown & Petticoat attached by Dr Browne as the estate of John Ness is his. It is thereupon ordered that the Sherif deliver the sd Gown & Petticoat to the petr.

Comrey a negroe boy belonging to Danl Thompson is adjudged to be Nine years old.

Miles Wills & Eml Wills presented & acknowledged their Deeds of lease & release of Lands lying in York County & bond for performance of Covenants to William Stark on whose mon they are admitted to Record

On the petition of Wm Livingston agt Essex Weller the court having given the deft a reprimand the Same is dismist.

Robert Clarke Jno Hubbard,Richd Stewart & Wm Spencer or any three of them being sworn before a Justice of the County are appointed to appraise the estate of Nathl Sebrell decd & make Report therof unto the next Court.

Ordered that the Court be adjourned until the Court in Course. Lawr. Smith Truly recorded Phi Lightfoot ClCur

At a private Court held Augt, the 8th 1721Present Lawr Smith Thos Chisman, Graves Park & Wm Sheldon

Elinor Conner committed to the Gaol on suspicion of Felony & Burglary in breaking & Robbing the house of Collo. Philip Ludwell__?robbing of Christo. Degraffenreid of Sundry Goods & being before the Court on Examination confessed the fact wherefore it is the Courts opinion that the Sd Conner ought to be tried for the sd fact at the Genl Court—Therefore it is ordered that She be remanded to the prison of the County under the Custody of the Sherif & from there conveyed to the publick Gaol at WmBurgh in order for a Tryal at the next Court as the Law in Such cases Directs.

(Cary & Broaddribbs Recognizance)
__________???before the Court acknowledged themselves
_______?the King to the Sum of twenty pounds to be levied
_____?Shall appear before the Genl Court on the
_____? There to give evidence for our Sovereign
?to be void

Page 62
Know all men by these presents that We John Mundell Susa. Sebrell Wm Bayley & Andr Laprade of the County of York are held & Firmly bound unto the Worshipful the Justices of the County aforesaid in the Sum of fifty pounds Sterling payable to the Sd Justices their heirs & Successors or Some of them to the which payment well & truly to be made We bind ourselves and every of us

our & every of our heirs Execrs & adminrs Joyntly & Severally firmly by these presents Sealed with our Seals & dated this 17th day of July 1721
The condition of this Obligation is Such that if the above bounden John Mundell & Susa Sebrell Execrs &c of the Last Will & Testament of Nathl Sebrell decd do make or cause to be made a true & perfect Inventory of all & Singular the Goods Chattels & Credits of the sd Nathl. Sebrell dec which have or Shall come to the hands or possession or knowledge of the sd John Mundell & Susa. Sebrell or into the hands or possessions of any Other person or persons for them & the same to make exhibite or cause to be exhibited into the county Court of York at Such time as theyShall be thereunto required by the sd Court & the Same Goods Chattels& Credits & all other the Goods Chattels & credits of the sd Nathl Sebrell decd at the time of his death which at anytime after Shall come come to the hands & possessionsof any other person or persons for them do well & truly adminr. According to law & further do make a true & Just Acct of their actings & Doings therin when thereto required by the sd Court also pay & deliver all the Legacys contained & Specyfied in the sd Testament as far as the sd Goods Chattels & Credits will thereunto extend acccccording to the value thereof & The law Shall charge them Then this Obligation to be void or else to Remain in full force & Vertue.
At a court held for York County July 17 1721. John Mundell, Wm Bayley, Andr Laprade
This Bond was presented & Acknowledged in Court by the partys thereto & admitted to Record. Test Phi. Lightfoot ClCur

Know all men by these presents that we Thomas Robins Rich Baker & John Mattlock of the County of York are held & firmly bound unto our Sovereign Lord George by the Grace of God of Great Britain France & Ireland King Defender of the faith &c in theSum of Ten Thousand pounds of Tobo. Convenient in the sd County of york to the which payment well & truly to be made to our Sovereign Lord the King his heirs & Successors we bind our Selves __? Our & every of our heirs Execrs & adminrs Joyntly & Severally firmly by these presents Sealed with our Seals & dated this 17th day of July 1721.

The Condition of the obligation is Such that whereas the above bounden Thos Robins hath an order this day granted him to keep an Ordinary at his now dwelling house in the __?year next ensuing. If therefore the sd Thos Robins doth constantly obtain & provide in his said Ordinary good wholesome & cleanly lodging & dyet for travelors and Stableage & provender or pasturage & provender (as the Season Shall require) for their horses from the date of these presents for & during the term of one year Shall not Suffer any unlawful gaming in his sd. house nor on the Sabbath day Suffer any person To tipple & Drink more than is necessary. Then this Obligation Shall be of none effect otherwise remain in full force & virtue. Thos X Robins. Rich Baker, John Mattlock

At a Court held for York County
This Bond was __?
Sworn__?

Page 63
Know all men by these presents that We Eliza Powers Wm Gordon & Saml Cobbs of the County of York are held & firmly bound to our Soverign Lord George by the Grace of God of Great Britain France & Ireland King Defender of the faith in the Sumof Ten Thousand pounds of Tobo convenient in the sd County of York to the which payment well & truly to be made to our Soverign Lord the King his heirs & successors we bind ourselves & every of us our heirs Execrs & adminrs Joyntly & Severally firmly by these presents Sealed with our Seals & dated this 17th day of July 1721.

The Condition of this obligation is Such whereas the above bounden Eliza Powers hath an order this day granted her to keep an Ordinary at her now dwelling house in York Town for the year next ensuing & if therefore the sd Eliza Powers doth constantly find & provide in her sd ordinary good wholesome & Cleanly lodging & dyet for travelers & Stableage & Fodder or pasturage & provender (as the season shall require) for their horses from the date of these presents for & During the Term of one year. & Shall not suffer any unlawful gaming in her sd house nor on the Sabbath day to Suffer any person to tipple or drink more than is necessary . Then this obligation to be void & of none effect otherwise to Remain in full force & Vertue. Eliza Powers. At a Court held for York County July 17th 1721. Wm Gordon, Saml Cobbs. This Bond was presented & acknowledged in Court & admitted to Record. Test Phi Lightfoot ClCur

Know All men by these presents that We Ezekial Gilbert, Walter Butler & Wm Gordon of the County of York are held & firmly pound to our Sovereign Lord George by the Grace of God of Great Britain France & Ireland King defender of the Faith &c in the Sum of Ten thousand pounds of tobo. Convenient in the sd county of York to the which payment well & Truly to be made to our Sovereign Lord the King his heirs & Successors we bind our Selves & every of us our & every of our heirs Execrs & Admins Joyntly & Severally firmly be these presents Sealed with our Seals & dated this 17th day of July 1721.
The Condition of this Obligation is Such that where as the above Bounden Ezekial Gilbert hath an order this day granted him for a Lycence to keep an ordinary at his now dwelling house in York Town for the year next ensuing therefore the sd Ezekial Gilbert doth constantly find & provide for his Ordinary Good wholesome & cleanly lodging & dyet for Travelers & Stableage & provender or pasturage & Provender (as the season shall require) for their horses for the date of these presents for & During the term of one year & that not Suffer

any unlawful gaming at his sd house nor on the Sabbath day Suffer any person to Tipple or drink more than is necessary, Then this Obligation to be void & of none effect Otherwise to remain in full force & Vertue. Ezekial Gilbert. Walter Butler, Wm Gordon. At a Court held for York County July 17th 1721. This Bond was presented & acknowledged in Court and admitted to record. Test Phi Lightfoot ClCur

Page 64
In the Name of God Amen I Nathl. Sebrell being Sick & weak of body but of Sound & perfect mind & memory Thanks Be to God for the Same, Do make this my last Will & Testament in manner & Form following. Impris I give & Bequeath Soul into the hands of Almighty God that gave it & my body to the Earth to be buried at the discretion of my Exectr hereafter
Named & as to my Worldly estate which it has pleased God to bestow upon me I dispose of as follows. I give & bequeath all my land to my brother David Sebrell & to his heirs forever. Item I give & bequeath my Negroe Girle Moll unto my sister Susa Sebrell & to her heirs forever. Item I give & bequeath my Negroe Girle Judith to my sister Sarah Sebrell & to her heirs forever. Item I give & bequeath unto my sister Susanna Sebrell my black horse branded with RH. Item I give & bequeath unto my brother David Sebrell my Saddle & Bridle Item I will that all the rest of my estate of what nature or kind Soever be Sold by my Execrs hereafter named named or if any remain after my just Debts & funeral charges are paid to be divided between my brohter David my Sister Susa. & my sister Sarah equally, Lastly I make ordain & appoint Jno. Mundell & my sister Susa. Sebrell Execrs of this my last Will & testament hereby Revoking all other wills by me heretofore made in Witness thereof I have hereunto Sett my hand & Seal the 20th day of February 1720. Nathl Sebrell (His mark) . Wit. Ralph Gough, James Robinson, Dennis Raymond, Wm Bayley (all their marks) At a Court held for York County July 17th 1721----This Last Will & testament of Nathl. Sebrell decd was presented in Court by John Mundell & Susanna Sebrell the Execr therein named who made Oath. To it & being proved by the Oaths of James Robinson Dennis Reynolds & Wm Bayley witnesses thereto is admitted to record. Test Phi Lightfoot ClCur

An Inventory of the estate of Philip Dedman decd
To a Negroe man named Frank. To a Negroe boy named Dick. 33 feather beds. & furniture 11 chairs 1 Round Table 15 chests. . . Mary Dedman
At a Court held for York County July 17th 1721 This invory. of the estate of Philip Dedman decd was presented in Court by Mary Dedman the Execr & Admitted to Record. Test Phi Lightfoot ClCur

In the Name of God Amen this twenty fourth day of Aug in theyear of our Lord One Thousand Seven Hundred and Twenty One. William Tabb of the County of

York being sick & Weak of body but of sound & perfect memory Praise be to God.

Page 65
This my present last will and testament in manner and form following (that is to say) first and principally I commend my soul into the hands of Almighty God hoping through the merits death Passion of my Savior Jesus Christ to have free pardon & Forgiveness of all my Sins and to inherit everlasting life and my body I commit to the earth to be decently buried at the discretion of my executor hereafter named and as touching the disposition of all Such temporal estate as it hath pledged almighty God to bestow upon me. I give and dispose therof as followeth First I will that my debts and funeral charges Shall be paid and discharged Imprimis I give and bequeath unto my two loving Sons William and Thomas Tabb and their heirs for ever these three Negroes to wit. Beckah Ned and George together with the increase if any may to be equally divided between them when they come of age And as for my other Negroes I have together with my Cattle Hogs Horses and all other my household goods to be carefully be Sold and the value thereof together with my mony to be equally divided between my two said sons when they come of age or the Survivor And as for my Gold rings I have My will and desire is that they may be equally divided between William Tabb and Thos Tabb my two said sons said Sons shall not choose a guardian nor have any part of their Estate before they come of age without the consent of my three brothers Edwd. Tabb John Silater and Morris Sweney And if it should pleased God to take William and Thomas Tabb my two sons to his mercy before they come of age then I give unto Edward and Martha Tabb Children of my brother Thomas Tabb twenty five pounds apiece and in the provisor aforesaid I then give to Martha and Mary Selator twenty five pounds apiece and five and twenty pounds likewise to Martha Sweney my brother Edmund Sweneys Child and Twenty five pounds to Charles son of my brother Samuel Sweney and for the remainder of my Said estate upon the above said proviser I give and bequeath unto my brother Edward Tabb and his heirs and I do appoint and constitute and ordain my beloved brother Merit Sweney Sole and Lawful executor of this my last will and testament revoking and disannulling all other wills heretofore made by me or given as witness my hand and Seal the year and day first __? William Tabb. Wit. Bernard Cond_t, Plany Hard___, Richd Gallawa__ At a Court held for York County Sept 15th 1721. This will and Testament of Wm Tabb deceased was presented in Court by Merrit Sweney The Executor who made Oath thereto and being proved by all the witnesses is admitted to Record and Probate granted the said Executor. Test Phi Lightfoot ClCur

Know all men by these presents that we Merrit Sweney Edmund Sweney and John Gibbons of the County of York __and firmly bound unto theWorshipfull the Justices of the County aforesaid in the Sum of five hundred ____? To the sd Justices their heirs and Sucessors __?payment well and truly to be made we bind ___? Every of our heirs Executors.

Page 66
Administrators Joyntly and Severally firmly by these presents sealed with our Seals and dated this 18th day of Sept 1721

The condition of this Obligation is such that if the above bounden Merit Sweney Execr of the last will and testament of Wm Tabb decd do make or cause to be made a true and perfect Inventory of all and Singular the goods Chattels and Credits of the sd Wm Tabb decd which have or Shall come to the hands possessions or knowledge of him the said Merrit Sweney or into the hands and possession of any other person or persons for him and the same so made to exhibite or cause to be exhibited into the County Court of York at such time as he shall be thereunto required by the said Court and the same goods Chattles and Credits and all other the Goods Chattels and Credits of the said Wm Tabb decd at the time of his death which at any time after shall come to the hands and possessions of of him the said Merrit Sweny or into the hands and possessions of any other person or persons for him to well & Truly administer according to Law and further do make a true and Just account of his actings and doings therin when thereto required by the sd Court and also pay & Deliver all the Legacys contained and Specyfied in the said testament as far as the said Goods Chattles and Credits will thereunto extend according to the value thereof and the Law shall charge him Then this obligation to be void or else to remain in full force and virtue. Merrit Sweney. Edmund Sweny, John Gibbons.
Sept 18 1721
This bond being acknowledged in Court by the partys thereto is admitted to record. Test Phi Lightfoot Cl Cur

Know all men by these presents that we Mary Archer and Robt Holland of the County of York are held and firmly bound to the worshipfull the Jsutices of the County aforesaid in the Sum of two hundred pounds Sterling to the Which payment well & truly to be made to the said Justices their heirs and Successors or Some of them we bind our Selves and every of us and our and every of our heirs Executor and administrators Joyntly and Severally firmly by these presents Sealed with our Seals and dated this 18th day of Sept 1721.

The Condition of this Obligation is such that if the above bounden Mary West Administrix of all the Goods Chattles & Credits of John West decd do make or cause to be made a true & perfect Inventory of all and Singular the Goods Chattels & Credits of the sd John West decd which have or shall come to the hands or possession of any other person or knowledge ofher the sd Mary West or into the hands or possessions of any person or persons for her and the same so made to exhibit or cause to be exhibited into the County Court of York at such time as she shall be thereunto required by the said Court and the same goods Chattels and Credits and all other the goods Chattels and Credits of the said John West Decd at the time of his death which at any time after shall come to the hands or possessions of her the said Mary West or into the hands and possessions for her do well and truly administer according to Law & __? Do make a true and Just account of her actings and doings therein when when therefore required by the sd Court and all the rest and residue of the sd __?which shall be found remaining upon the administration__?examined by the said Justices __?Shall deliver and pay.

Page 67
Unto such pson. or psons as the said Justices by their order of Judgement shall direct pursuant to the Law in that Case made and provided if it shall hereafter appear that any Costs Will and testament was made by the sd. decd. and the Executor or Executors therein named to exhibit the same into the said Court making request to have it allowed and approved accordingly if therefore the said Mary West being there to required do render and deliver up letters of Administration approbation of such testament being first had in the said Court then this obligation to be void and of none effect or else remain in full force & virtue. Mary West her mark.
At a Court held for York County Sept 18th 1721 Robert Gallard
Eliz Archer
This bond being presented in Court and acknowledged
By the partys thereto is admitted to record. Test. Phil Lightfoot ClCu

Know all men by these presents that we Mary Dun and Wm Robertson of the County of York are held and firmly bound to our Sovereign Lord George by the grace of God of Great Britain France Ireland King defender of the Faith &c in the Sum of ten thousand pounds of tobacco convenient in the sd County of York to the which payment well and truly to be made to our Sovereign Lord King and his heirs and Successors we bind ourselves and every of us our and every of our heirs Exects & administrators jointly and Severall firmly by these presents Sealed with our Seals & dated this 18th day of Sept 1721
The Condition of this Obligation is such that whereas the above bounden Mary Dunn hath an order this day granted to her to keep an ordinary at her now dwelling in Wm Burgh in this county for the year next ensuing and if therefore the said Mary Dunn doth constantly find and provide in her sd ordinary Good Wholesome and Cleanly Lodging and dyet for travellors and Stableage and provender or pasturage and provender (as the Season shall require) for their horses from the date of these presents for and during the term of one year and Shall not Suffer any unlawful gaming in her sd house nor on the Sabath day

Suffer any person to tipple or drink more than is Necessary then this Obligation to be void & of none effect otherwise remain in full force and virtue. Will Robertson
At a Court for York County Sept 18 1721
This bond was presented & acknowledged by the said Witness and admitted to Record. Test Phi Lightfoot ClCr
Know all men by these presents that we Robert Ballard Benj. Moss and John Goodwin of the County of York are held and firmly bound unto the Worshipful the Justices of the County Aforsaid in the Sum of One Hundred pounds Sterling payable to the said Justices their heirs and Successors or Some of them to which payment well and truly to be made We bind ourselves and every of us our and every of our heirs Exectrs and Adminstrators Joyntly & Severally firmly by these presents Sealed with our Seal and dated this 18th day of Sept 1721

(Margin says Ballard Bond for Monnis)
(left side of page missing) . . . tion is such that if the above bounden
. . . be paid or Casue to be paid unto John Monnis
. . . estate or estates belonging
Page 68
to the sd Orphan as is or hereafter Shall come to the hands or possession of him the sd Robt. Ballard or into the hands or possession of any other person or persons for him when or as soon as the said Orphan Shall attain to lawfull age or when thereunto required by the said Court he shall also save and keep harmless the said court from all trouble and damage that shall or may accrue to them about or concerning the said estate then this obligation to be void or else to remain in full force & Virtue. Sept 18 1721. Robt Ballard, Benj Moss, John Goodwin. This was presented in Court & acknowledged by the parts thereto & Admitted to Record. Test Phi Lightfoot ClCor

In Obedience to an order of York County Court bearing date June 19th 1721 Wherein it was ordered that a Jury in Company with ye County Surveyer should go upon the Land in Difference between Wm Gordon plt & Lawr Smith deft we the Subscribers being first Sworn before Mr Thomas Melson oneof his Mjties. Justices of the peace for the sd County did meet upon the land in Controversie having regard to all patents and evidence that were laid before us did begin as followeth (vizt,) At Allens hundred acres Corner tree in a beaver trench thence South East one hundred Sixty two Chains to a Corner Gum in a Run that runs to Pocoson River thence North North East half a point Easterly to Morses Road ye leads to back Creak adjoining Esq. Wormley's line we find the deft no Trespassor In witness whereof we hereunto set our hands & Seals this Sixth day of July 1721. John Chisman, Peter Goodwin, Charles Collier, Edwd. Tabb, Robt Kerby Jun, Thos Powel, John Gibbins, Nath Hook, Jno. Mattlocke, Benj Moss, Jno. Potter, Robt. Ballard. Jno. Selator Survr.

At a Court held for York County Sept 18th 1721
This report was presented in Court and at the motion of Lawr Smith Genl. is admitted to Record. Test Phil Lightfoot ClCr

An Inventory of the estate of Henry Gill Decd as follows:
Page 69
Page 70
Includes: 300 hides and Skins Just put into the Second Lig. of bark when my husband dyed, 1 Turnbrel Cart 3 old harnesses for horses 3 horses 1 Mare 1 Cow A Negroe man named Will about Thirty years old. Daniel A white Servt. 3 years to serve at the time of my husbands death. Wm Sherman a Boy Six years and a half. Morgan Conner 5 months. Margaret Croney a year and a half
This is the whole account of the estate of Henry Gill deceased my late husband that hath as yet come to my hands this 18th day of August 1721. Margaret Gill her mark At a Court held for York County Sept 18th 1721. This inventory of the estate of Henry Gill decd was presented in Court by the Executrix and admitted to record. Test Phil Lightfoot ClCr

The estate of Ann Morland decd to due upon acc
2/5 paid to Mary Wagstaff
to Wm Lee 4/4
to Wm Stark 3/15/
to Wm Gording 2/2
to Joseph Cral_? 3/15

Page 71
To John Hansford 20/ to Don Phillips 1/11/6
To Phi Lightfoot 1/5/2
To Henery Gibbs 2/
To Eliz Jones for Wheat 0/4
To Edw. Morland 2:7
To Jno. Watkins /15
To Charles Hansford /10
Contra Credit £257-6
By the hire of a Negroe man one year 8-
Excrs excepted by Franc. Morland Exr Aug 20 1720 £257-6
This acct and Settlement of the estate of Ann Morland decd
Was presented in Court and admitted to record Test Phil Lightfoot Cl Cr
The estate of Ann Morland decd is Dr. - to Sundry persons
Vizt. To Tho: Morland his part in the said estate- 18. 29 -
To Edwd Morland - 18. 29 -
to Matthew Morland - 18. 29 -
to Edwd. Slate- 18. 29-

to John Gibs - 18. 29-
to John Morlands Orphans - 18. 29 -
to Fra: Morland Execr. - 18. 29-
to Do. Acct. against the Said estate - 1776
1447
by the Inventory and appraisement amounting to 1447 1 August 29 1720 Essrs . exsptd Fra: Morland Execr
___? ion of the estate of Ann Morland dec
___? ted in Court by Fra Morland & admitted to Record. test Phil Lightfoot Cl Cor
York County Aug 17 1721

In Obedience to an order of this Court dated June 10 1721 we the Subscribers have inventory'd and appraised the estate of Geo. Brown decd as followeth vizt.
Cows, Steers Bulls Calves horses & Mares
Robt Cobbs at 1. 15-

Page 72
1 Old negro woman and Beding - 13-
1 Mullato Boy named Jack given to___?
Of the said decd Geo. Brown to his grandson (name illeg) - 12-15
1 ornamented & two stone rings given __ gift by Elizabth Brown
to her grandson Geo. White 1-17
========
1 1 5 14
At a Court held for York County Sept 18 1721. Thos Cobbs, Joseph Smith, Robt Cobbs, Robt. Crawley
This inventory and appraisement__?estate of Geo. Brown decd was Presented in Court & admitted to Record. Test Phi. Lightfoot ClCur

Page 73
At a private court held for York County Sept 21 1721
Present : Henry Tyler, Thos. Nelson, Lawrence Smith Wm Sheldon, Thos Chisman - Gentl. Justices

Matthew Read committed to the Gaol of this County on suspicion of felony in Robing of Joseph Dowding of the Sum of one hundred and ninety pounds Current mony and the said Mathew Read was brought before th said Justices and being examined confessed tha he did open a Chest and trunk of the sd Joseph and took out of the same a Considerable Sum of mony but how much he could not tell that the said chest and trunk was in a boat belonging to the said Joseph at YorkTown Landing and were left under the care of the sd examl and some part of the sd mony being found upon him vizt. DdLoons [doubloons?] & moiders 1 piece Gold millo mony 13/6 Spanish and other silver 48/ 1 pair large silver buckles. In a Large Purse 1ddLoon. 5 moiders 7 Luidores 13 pistols 2 half pistols and 4 chickeens wherefore it's the opinion of the Court that the said Mathew Read ought to be tried for the sd fact at the Genl court therefore its ordered that he be remanded to the prison of the County under Custody of the Sheriff and from thence to be conveyed to the public Gaol at WmBurgh in order for a tryal at the Genl. Court on the fourth day thereof according to Law. Joseph Dowding being before the Court acknowledged himself indebted to our Sovereign Lord the King in the Sum of fifty pounds Sterling to be levied on his Goods & Chattels lands __ on Condition of the said Joseph Dowding shall__? Before the Genl. Court on the fourth day and from time to time as the said Court shall direct __? Mathew Read who stands committed for felony then the above recognizance to be void or else remain in full force power and virtue.

At a Court held for York County Sept 18 1721
Present: Jno. Holloway, Graves Pack, _? Tylerm _?Smith, Wm Sheldon Genl.

Page 74
In the action upon the Case between John Welch plt and Joseph Stacy deft for 3-16-1 current mony dued upon acct. the deft being called and failing to appear and no Security being returned for him at the Plts motion Judgement is granted him for the sd Sum and costs against thesaid deft and Jos. Walker gentl. Sherriff of this County unless the sd deft appears at the next Court and answers the plt accn.

Judgement being this day passed unto John Walsh agt Jos Walker Gent Sheriff for the sum of 3-16-1 and Costs by means of the non appearance of Jos. Stacy at the suit of thesd John Welch therefore at the said Walkers motion an attachment is granted him agt thesaid Stacys estate for thesaid Sum and Costs returnable to the next Court for Judgement.

In the action upon the Case between Benj. Moss plt and Jos. Stacy deft for 3-10-0 Current mony due upon acct the dft. being called and failing to appear and no Security being returned for him at the plt. Motion Judgement is granted him for the sd Sum and costs agt the sd deft and Jos Walker Gent Sheriff of this County unless the said deft appears at the next Court and answers the plt action.

Judgement being this day passed unto Benj Moss agt Jos Walker Gent Sherriff for the sum of3-10-0 and Costs by means of the non appearance of Jos Stacy at the suit of the said Benj Moss therefore at the sd Walker's Motion an attachment is granted him against the sd Stacy's estate for the sd Sum and Costs returnable to the next Court for Judgemnt.

In the action of Trespass upon the Case between Benj Clifton plt. and Wm Biggs deft for ten pounds damage by means of the deft concealing to his own use a Certain Mare belonging to the plaintiff . The deft being served with a copyof the writ and failing to aaaappear an attachment is granted to the Plantf. For the sd Sum and costs agt deft estate returnable to the next Court.

In the action of Essix Weller agt Wm Livingston for abuse upon hearing the Evidences & Suggestions of both partys the Court were of opinion that the petition be dismist.

Mary Dunn on her petiton & giving Security hath an ordr, granted her for a Lycense to keep an ordinary at her dwelling house in WmBurgh in this County. Wm Robertson entered into bond for that purpose & acknowledged the bond in open Court wi bond is admitted to record.

_?rs Ripping on his mtion hath an order granted him for a Lycence to keep an ordinary at his dwelling house in WmBurgh . . . ing this county giving Security,

The petition of Katherine Craig for a Lycense to keep an Ordny . is rejected.

The last Will & testament of Wm Tabb decd was presented in Court by Merritt Sweny Proved by the Oaths . . .

Page 75
of Bernard Caubert Plerny Ward & Richd Gallaway witnesses thereto is admitted to Record and he having together with Wm Sweny & Jno. Gibbons his Securitys entered into & Acknowledged their Bond to the Court for his Just & faithfull administration of the decd Estate wo. bond is admitted to Record & on the motion of the sd Merritt Certificate is granted him for obtaining a probate thereof in due form

In the accn. of Debt between Wm Livingston assignee of Eliza Ives plt & Essex Weller deft the deft on his motion hath a Specl. Imparlance granted him until the next Court.

Ann Sullivant on her petition hath an Order granted her for a Lycence to keep an ordinary at her dwelling house in WmBurgh giving Security

The accon upon the Case between Justinian Love plt & John Gossett & Eliza his wife his wife deft is dismist.

Katherine Cary Servant to Katherine Craig before the Court confessed that she had a bastard child. On the sd Craig's motion that the ad Cary serve her for health of her house in the time of lying in one whole year after her time by indenture custom or former order is expired

Katherine Cary Serv. To Katherine Craig having had a bastard child & The sd Craig having assessed the payment of? Tobo. Being her fine to the Parish of Bruton in consideration thereof the sd Cary does agree & it is hereby ord. That she serve her sd Mistress the Space of one whole year for the same after her time of Indenture custom or former order is expired.

Katherine Craig proved her accn. Agt Authe. Iverton Jno. Bolton Giles Sidenach Genl. w. and ordered to be Certified.

In the petition of Joseph Stacy & John Bond agt Richd Homes & Jane his wife ordered that unless the defts do give the plts good Security indemnify them before the next Court from the Childrens parts of the Estate of James Bennit decd or that they Surrender the Same to the plts appraisd by the former apprs. of als. Exo.

On the petiton of John Morris orphan of James Morris decd Robert Ballard is appointed his Guardian & the sd Ballard have together wth Benj. Moss & John Goodwin _? Securitys entered into & Acknowledged their Bond for that purpose wch. Bond is admitted to record, Ordered that the sd orphan & His estate be committed to the care & Custody of his Guradian.

__? (probably a Mrs West) came into Court making Oath that John West departed this life __?any will _?Knows or believes & She having together _?Ballard _?Securitys enterd into Bond for her just__?Estate to Bond being acknowledged __? On the sd Estate in due form-
Thos Cripps Richd. Easter John _? Uriah Hudson or any three of them being Sworn are _?Appraise the estate of John West decd & Make report thereof-

In the __?n & Dianah his wife agst Robt Shields for a Child part __?ard decd. _?of both partys Col Lawrence Smith_?estate _?the sd Haywards Estate __?next Court.

(margin says Hansford & Moss) ___? For his portion oof the estate of his father Wm __?Moss be served with a copy of this order that __?mit to Seek further order herein as shall be

Page 76
Francis Morland Exhibited accts & & Settlem: of the estate of Ann Morland decd wl. are admitted to record.

The petition of Dianah Hayward agt Robt Shield is dismist.

In the petiton of Thomas Crippes & Saml Millington Securitys wth. Mary the wife of Wm Riggs for the children parts of the estate of John Brathwait decd agt Wm Biggs Ordered that the sd Biggs give them good Security to indemnify them, to that he Surrender so much of Mr Brathwaits estate as is the childrens parts to the petts. Appraised by the former appraisers wi. Costs als Exo.

The presentment of the grand jury agt. Ann Combs is dismist.

The presentment of the grand jury agt Thos, Wolten is dismist.

In the accon. Upon the case between Joseph Stacy plt & Robt Ross deft for five pounds damage by means of the deft refusing to deliver a Saddle & furniture &c the matters of law arising from the Spl. Verd. being this day fully argued & heard the Court were of Judgement for the plt whereupon it is considered that the plt recover agt the deft & Wm Gordon his Security the Sum of Fifty Shillings being his damages by the Jurors aforesaid with Costs als Exo.

The accon upon the Case between Jno. Abbott plt & Jno. Ness deft is dismist.

The petition of Mary Clifton agt Robt Shield is cont for a Settlement of Wm Haywards estate.

In the accon. of trespass on the Case between Wm Gordon plt & Lawrence Smith deft the Jurys verdict in this cause at the defts. mon is admitted to record & the Suit dismist ordered that the plt pay Costs als Exo.

The accon of Detinue between James Wall plt & Lawrence Smith deft is continued by consent until the next Court.
In the accon of _? Between Katherine Craig Extx. of the Last Will & testament of Wm Craig decd plt & Lewis Delony deft for 30l due by bond dated the 17th day of June 1718 Judgement is granted the plt for the sum of fifteen pounds Current mony too her with Interest thereon amounting to two pounds nine Shillings __?hereupon ordered that the deft pay the sum of Seventeen pounds Nine Shillings and Six pence with Costs als Exo.

The accon of detinue between Thos Toomer plt & Saml Tomkins deft by consent of the partys is continued until the next Court.

The action between Eliza. Hansford plt & Joseph Walker deft is dismist

.

The accon _? (Margin says Lightfoot) plt & Eliza Hansford deft a__?

The accon _ (margin says Sweny/Delony) __? wis Delony deft is contined until the next Court by Consent.

The accon on the Case between Archibald Blair plt & __?Mundell deft is dismist,

The accon upon the Case between Phi Lightfoot plt & Daniell Thomson deft is by consent continued until the next Court

In the accon __?Jn Cage plt & Jo_?Brookes deft __?confessed whereupon ordered __?deft __?with a lawyers fee Costs als Exo.

In the accon upon_?Sparks plt & Joseph Berry deft the plt failing to _?is nonsuited & ordered that he pay deft __?costs als Exo

The Suit __? (Hay & Toomer) . __?
Page 77
In the action of the case between__? (Eyre & Freeman) is dismist neither appearing.

In the accon between Thomas Jones plt & ?Powers deft case is continued by consent.

Wm Robertson is appointed to prosecute Lewis Davis for his contempt for failing to obey the Coroners summons.

In the accon upon the case between Mary Read plt & George Butler deft issue being Joyned the Cause is referred until the next Court for tryall

In the suit in Chancery depending between Armiger Parsons & Eliza his wife Complts. And John Hay Admins &c Robert Hay decd respondts. The Respondt on his mon has further time until next Court to answer.

The accon upon the case between Phi Lightfoot & Thos Bell is cont. until the next Court.

In the accon of debt between Thos. Cosford plt & Jos Davenport deft is dismist & ordered that the deft pay Costs als Exo.

In the accon upon the case between John Hay plt & Armiger Parson & Elizabeth his wife for 8-7-8 ¼ due by acct the defts having had time given to them at last Court to plead & being called failed to appear to answer anything in barr or exclusion of the plts accon One plts mon Judgement is granted him by Nihil dicit for the sd sum & costs returnable at next Court on the like default.

Upont the accon of trespass between Edward Sparks plt & Dan Weldon deft is nonsuited & Voided & it is ordered that the plt pay a Lawyers fee & Costs according to Law als Exo.

In the accon of Debt between _? Morce plt & Joseph Frith deft the case is continued until next Court.

In the accon upon the Cause between George Allen plt & Francis Sharpe deft for the Sum of 1-15-2 Deft failed to appear & No Security was returned Judgement is granted for the Sum & Costs agt the deft & Joseph Walker Genl Sheriff unless deft appear at the next Court & answer Plts accon.

The accon upon the case between Jno Jones plt & Thos Hubbard deft is dismist.

The accon of Dentinue between John Brown plt & John Ness deft is dismist.

The accon of Debt between Henry Bowcock plt & Morris Walker deft is dismist

In the accon upon the Case between Henry Bowcock plt & David Watson deft is dismist.

In the accon of Debt between ?Weller plt & Eliza Ives deft Deft has a Special Imparlance granted on her mon. until the next Court.

(Butler& Collier) __? (Walker or Walter) Butler plt & Charles Collier & Mary his wife & Natht. __?decd praying that that he may be_?ake. ordered that the Sheriff at the next Court.

__?the lower precincts of YorkHampton __? Ordered that (on notice here of) he repair
__? Take the usual Oath.

__?Levingston plt & Thos Wyatt deft __?nt an attached issue agt the __able to the next Court for Judgement.

___? By Richad Haughton her _?ounds be acct the deft failing __?her agt the defts estate __next Court fo Judgement.

__? uina Maria Timson Exr. If the last --?John Jacob Flornoy & Mary his wife _?or the defts on an Imparlance.

Page 78
Lightfoot & Timson__?between Phi Lightfoot plt & Anna Maria Timson__?

In the accon upon the case between Wm Rogers plt & Augistine Moor Robert Baylor Wm Tabb& James Garnett Execrs &c of John Baylor decd deft the defts on their motion have an Imparlance granted them until next Court.

In the petition of Chrs Jackson agt the estate of John Ness in the hands of Mr Hugh Jones at the plt moton the Same is continued until next Court.

The petition of David Prior agt the Estate of John Ness on the plts motion the former ordere is furthur continued until the next Court.

In the petiotn of John Brown agt the estate of John Ness for Sixty pounds fourteen Shillings & Seven due on ball of _agt proved by the plt ?Judgement is granted him for the Said Synca_?v. Ness & on the plt mon. the attachment is further continued agt Lawr. Smith & M Blackwell who are to appear & render an acctof the ?effects in their hands at the next Court _?appraisement Entered into Record.

The petiton of__? Cobbs agt the estate _?Ness is discontinued.

The petiton of Geo Gilbert agt the Estate of John Ness is continued. & ordered the Aud. Lapade & geo Allen appear & under anaced. of the sd Ness's Effects_?their lands at the next Court.

In the petition _?Edward Sparks agt Joseph Barry for 199-6-6 by acct : are attached having been returned Executed in the hands of Phi Lightfoot & Saml. Weldon _? Phi Lightfoot having rendered an acct : if what Effects properly belonged ? sd Barry in his custody as by accd. & he having also before the court _? In behalf of the sd Barry to Hand hand by the awardof Court in case he_? In thisaccon. So far _? The sd Effects will answer & pay the sd attachment _? & the plt ordered to declare by the sd Barry at the next Court.

John Mundall abt_? Susanna Sebrell Exr of Nich Sebrell have further time given them to ? &c of _?Sebrells estate at next Court

In the accon _? The Case between D? Shield plt & Saml Sweny Excr of Aml. Har_? For3-6-0 by acct & the deft failing to appear & No Security ret _? Him on the plt mon. Judgement is granted him for the sd Sum & Costs__? The sd deft appear at the next Court.

In __?John Batesdeft for 55-2-10Sterl_?gent. is granted him for the appears

_?Security unless the deft. (Tucker & Bates)

In the ___? For 5-2-6 __?ep. mon. pls act. (Tucker & Bates)

(Wooden & Chapman) _? is dismst.

(Dalton & Moor &c) _? is dismst.

(Palmer & Stedds) _?Stedd deft_?

(Laughton & Barbar) _accon__?Thos Barbar dismst.

(Good & Cobbs &c) Accon__? & Saml Cobbs &c Excr of David Livinston_?granted them untill next Court.

(Waters Chapman) ___? Deft is dismst.

(Blair & D__tt) In the__?& Martha his wife __?referred for tryal_?

Page 79
In the accon of debt between Ed. _Lattemore plt & Law Smith deft the deft appeared & on his motn hath an Imparlance granted him until the next Court.

The accon upon the Case between Phi Lightfoot plt & Wm Perkins deft is dismist.

In the accon of debt between Thos Charles plt. Edward Jacquelin Excr &c of Harwood Cary decd deft on the defts mon. an Imparlance is granted him till next Court.

The accon of Frover(?) between John Graves plt & John Phripp deft is dismist.

On the accon of debt between Susanna Townsend plt & James Haison deft for £1-2-9
By bill the deft failing to appear & no Securrity returned for him Judgement is granted the plt for the sd Sum & Costs sgt the sd deft & Joseph Walker Genl Sheriff unless the sd deft appears at the next Court & answers the plts accon.

The acoon of debt between James Shields plt & Wm Robertson deft is dismist

In the accond upon the Case between John Goodwin plt & Lawrence Smith & Mildred his wife late Mildred Goodwin deft issue being Joyned the cause is referred for tryal at next Court

In the accon of debt between John James plt & Thos Nash deft issue being joined the case is refered until next Court for Tryall.

The accon upon the Case between Saml Cobbs plt & Ann Magriggar deft is dismist

The accon upon the Case between Isaac Phinness plt & Edw. Whitaker deft is dismist

The accon upon the case between Edw. Whitaker plt & Isaac Phumiss deft is dismist.

The accon upon the Case between Edward Carter plt & Thos Dilks deft is dismist.

In the accon between the Case between Saml Cobbs plt & Joseph Sutton deft for £6. 7. 8by acct the deft failing to _? On the plts mon. Judgement is granted him for the sd Sum & Costs agt the sd deft & Joseph Walker his Security unless the sd deft appears at the next Court & answers the plt accon.

The accon between the case between Robt Laughton plt & Thos Barbar deft is dismist.

The accon upon the Case between John Borland plt & Wm Morgan deft is dismist.

In the accon of debt between _?Shields plt & Wm Robertson deft the deft on his moton hath an_?is granted him untill the next Court.
In the accon of trespass between Richd Bellamie & Sarah his wife plts & Charles Rowan__? The deft failing to appear on the plt mon. an attachment : is granted _? Defts estate for the sd Sum & Costs returnable to the next Court for __?

The accon upon the Case _?Edward Tabb plt & James Haisan deft is cont. (?)

The accon upon the Case _?Lilly D & Shisack Marr. Deft is dismist.

In the accon upon the Case _?Joseph Walker plt & Elizabeth Hansford Excx. &c of Sarah Hansforddecd deft on her moton hath an Imparlance granted her until the next Court.

In the acccon upon the Case between Joseph Walker Gent plt & Eliza Huller__?

Huller decd deft for Thirty Five pounds Six Shillings _? The plts_?appeared personally & confesses Judgement_? The Sum of Thirty Five _? Decds estate with Costs als Exo.

___? Joseph Walker Gntl plt & Eliza Moody ___? rty Six pounds Eleven Shill & Seven__? Wm Robertson attorney of the deft __?whereupon it is ordered that the deft __?Twelve Shillings & five pence being the balance __? Als Exo.

__? Goodwin Execr &c of Maes __?respond. appeared & on her__?

(Weldon & Sharpe) __?don plt & Francis Sharpe deft __?& no Security being returned ffor him __? The sd Sum & Costs agt the sd deft. __?appears at the next Court.

After Page 80
The petition of Andrew Leprade agt John Mundell is cont until next Court.

Ordered that the Sheriff Summons twenty four freeholders of the County to appear at the next Court to be the grand jury.

John Sadler Servant to Joseph Mountfort having been runaway four days & The sd Mountfort having expended two hundred pounds of Tobo, in taking him ordered that he serve his sd Master three months & eight days for the Same after his time by Indenture Custom or former order is Expired.

It appearing to the Court that John Sadler Servt to Joseph Mountfort resisted & Struck his Sd Master wherefore it is ordered that he serve his sd master one whole year after his time by Indenture Custom or former order is expired for the sd offence as the law directs,

Ordered that the Court be adjourned until the next Court in Course. Signed Hen. Tyler. Truly entered by Phi Lightfoot ClCur

At a Court for York County November the 20th 1721. Present John Hollowell Lawrence Smith. Henry Tyler & Graves Pack Gent Sheriff

In the accon between Peter Beverly of Gloucester County gen. plt & Robert ... (*missing*)
Tobo. Augustin Moor & James Garnett Exctrs of the last will & testament of John Baylor late of the county of King & Queen gent decd defts . . (*missing*) Currt mony due by bond dated the 26th day of November 1721 plt having proved his debt by his Oath John Holloway Gent appeared in behalf of the defts &

confesses Judgement to the plt for the Sum of One thousand one hundred & twenty pounds Currt mony the sd plt. (*missing*) thereout what should (*unclear*) to have been received & him from . . (*missing*) in his life, Ordered that the deft pay the same to. . (*missing*) of the decd. . (*missing*) with Costs als Exo.

On... *(missing)* Hansford . . (*missing*) rec, for his part and prof... (*missing*) of his . . (*missing*) Hansford decd by consent of both parties . . (*missing*) and Jno Hubberd or any two of them according to his Will ... (*missing*) appears thereby (*missing*) at Court.
(Hansford & Morce Judgement)

In. y (*missing*) Tomkins defend. (rest is missing except for margin which reads Tomer & Tomkins Ex isue bona Nov 24th 1721) and- damaged or defaming.

Page 81
On ye pet. John Welch & John Rogers praying to be discharged from being Securitys with (Jonas?) Bell for ye estate of Jno. Fergusan orphan. it is ordered that ye said Bell be summoned to answer sd pet. at the next Court.

On ye petition Edw. Stringer and Francis his wife praying that Richd Palmer an orphan may be removed from the Guardianship of William Palmer by reason of Severall abuses in ye sd petition set forth It is ordered that ye Sheriff Summon said William to appear at the next Court to answer same pet.

The Power of Att by (*missing*) Lutwidge to Thos Nelson was proven by oath of Thomas Craghill & admitted to record.

Mary West exhibited an Invy. &c of Jno. West decd which was admitted to record.

A further Invry of the estate of Henry Hayward decd was admitted to record.

In ye petition of James Cathern & Dinah his wife against Robt Shields agt ye petitioners motion is continued until next Court.

The petition of Wm Hansford agt David Morse is dismist.

In ye petition of Mary Clifton agt Robt Shields at ye pets. Motion the former Order is continued until the next Court.

In the action of Detinue between James Walls plt & Lawr. Smith deft neither partys appearing the action is dismist.

The action of debt between Saml Sweny plt & Lewis Delony deft is Continued until the next Court.

Ye petition of Richd Burt praying that he be appt Guardian to Martha Eliza. & Judith daughters of Rich Burt decd upon ye death of their former Guardian . he having given Security. it is ordered accordingly that he be Guardian and that they and their estate be Committed to his care.

Will a Negro boy belonging to John Potter was this day adjudged to be six years of age.

Ned a negro boy belonging to John Monnis was this day adjudged to be twelve years of age.

Ye action upon (*missing*) Phi Lightfoot plt & Danl. Thomsin deft is dismist.

The suit in Chancery (*missing*) Hay & Mary his wife complt and (*missing*) next Court and examine witnesses. (Hay & Toomer)

z) & Eliza Powers is cont till next court (Jones & Powers)

(*missing*) (Davis dismist) Contempt in refusing to obey ye court (*missing*) paying costs als Exo

(*missing*) (Smith &) that Alex Atkinson &c (*missing*) fair or believes (*missing*) & Robt Laughton his Security (*missing*) admon on the decd estate w. Gen. (*missing*) & on the mon. of the sd Lawrence Smith (*missing*) for obtaining letters.

(*missing*) Wm Cross his Securitys proved (*missing*) Burt Guardianship (*missing*) record.

(*missing*) Benja. Clifton plt & Wm Biggs deft (*missing*) estate is Continued until the next Court

Page 82

The Last Will & testament of Wm Lindsay decd was presented in Court by ... (*missing*) . Keith & Eliza. Powers Excrs who made Oath to it and it being proved by the Oaths of Robt Wills and James Taylor witnesses thereto is admitted to record and they together with Will Gordon and James Shields their Securitys entered into and acknowledged their bond to ye court for their just and faithfull administration of the decd estate which bond is admitted to Record and on ye motion of the sd excrs Certificate is granted them for Obtaining a probate thereof in due form.

The action upon the Case between Phil Lightfoot plt and Thos Bell deft is continued until the next Court.

John Butterworth on his motion and giving Security hath an order granted him to Obtain a Lycence to keep an ordinary at his dwelling house in York Town.

Giles Moody on his Motion and giving Security hath an order granted him to Obtain a Lycence to keep an ordinary at his dwelling house in Bruton Parish in Ye County.

The petition of John Abbott for a Lycence to keep an Ordinary is rejected.

Jn Hansford on his Motion and giving Security hath an order granted him to Obtain a lycence to keep an ordinary in Yorkhampton Parish in ye County.

The petition of James Minzie's for a Lycence to keep an ordinary is rejected.

In the suit in *Chancery* depending between... (*missing*) ayer Parsons & Eliza his wife Complts & Jno. Hay Adm. &c of Robert Hay decd respond. has until next Court to Consider the respondts answer.

In the Case between Mary Read plt & Geo Butler deft for £ 15-15-4 by acct issue being joyned *(missing)* Court) Robt. Cobbs Sam. Cobbs &c were Sworn to try the issue joined they having heard the evidence retired to Consult their verdict & being returned into Court & Delivered the same in these words we find for the plt £5-9-7 Currt mony which verdict is at the Plt mon recorded & its ordered that the plt recover ags the deft the sum of Five pounds nine shillings and seven pence by the jurors aforesaid w costs als Exo.

Wm Cross foreman Joseph Mountfort &c were Sworn a grand jury for the body of . . *(missing)* they having finished their present. Were discharged & . . *(missing*) ordered to be Summoned at the next Court.

In the accon. Between Archbd Blair & Jonathon Drewitt & Martha. . (*missing*) Wm Kaine decd deft both partys having . . (*missing*) of law arising therof.

In . . (*missing*) Joseph Frith deft the Court . . (*missing*) the Special verdict given. IN . . (*missing*) ordered that the Suit be dismissed. (Morce & Frith written in margin)

Mary. . *(missing*) ordered to Serve her... (*missing*) in the . . (*missing*) her time

(Gill & Crony in margin)

(Cronby from Jackson deed acct. in margin)

(Minzie's pet. Rejected in margin)

Page 83

YORK COUNTY DSo.
LEVY Tobo.
To the Secretary for fees - 90
To Hen. Tyler Sheriff for def *(missing)* - 132
To Col Lawrence Smith for Coroner fees - 243
To Wm Bradribb for - 130
To Mr Henry Tyler for fees - 785
To Robt Clerk for services - 50
To Wm Gordon - 585
To Eliza. Powers for . . . . . this Courthouse - 100
To the Sheriff for. . . . . - 1080
To Wm Frickner for . . . wn bridge - 1080
To Jno. Juncock for m. . . . . windows - 112
To Phil Lightfoot Extra Services & Sp. Courts - 1880
To Wm Gordon deling - 60
To Jno. Randolph for Benj. Reads tryall - 216
To Wm Robertson ...Dr Butterly - 216
To Arthur Dickenson. . . . . Beaver dam ridge - 500
To . . . . . to lye in the Sheriff hands towards purchasing - 1325
=====
8634

Ordered that the name of . . . . . every person mentioned in the List of Tithables . . . Roll for paying the Contingent charges of County & . . . . . pay ins to Levy

The same by Distress & its ordered . . . . . Same to Such persons as is appointed in the County . . . . .

Ordered that the Court be adjourned Untill the next Court in Course
Signed Jno. Hollowell. Phi Lightfort Cl Cur

. . . . . Garret Joyce late belonging to ye town . . . . . assigned and made in
(Joyce power Att to Abbott)
Page 84
(continuation of Garret Joyce Power att to Jno. Abbott)

as witness my hand this 4th day of November 1721. Signed Sealed and Dated Garrett Joyce (mark) . Wit. Jno. M ... ocke, Ann M .... cke

At a court held for York County November 18 1721
The power of Att of Garrett Joyce to Jno. Abbot was presented in Court and proved by the Witnesses named within and entered into record. Test Phi Lightfoot ClCur

Know All men by these presents that I P Lutwidge of white haven in County of Cumberland Norch. have made nominated constituted and appointed and do hereby make nominate constitute and appoint Mr Thos Nelson Merch. of Virginia my true and lawfull attorney for me and in my name to ask demand recover and receive of and from Capn. George Eskridge in Virginia or any other person or persons whatsoever all or any Sum or Sums of money Accounts debts dues or any Effects whatsoever to me now belonging or after shall or may be inhibited unto and upon receipts of such . . . of mony accounts Debts dues or Effects aforesaid ac . . . actual discharge in my name to make . . . for me and in my name to accept of all. . . . . of mony Accompt debts dues or effects whatsoever . . . I do hereby Ratifie confirm and allow all and wha . . . attorney shall do or Cause to be done. . . . . by virtue of these presents In witness whereof. . . . . my hand and Seal this 26th day of February . Signed . . . Lutwidge, . . . 1721. . . . Lightfoot ClCur

Page 85
Know all men by these presents that we Wm Kieth Eliza Powers and Wm Gordon and Jno. Shields of ye County of York are held and firmly bound unto ye Worshipfull ye Justices of ye County aforesaid in ye Sum of One Hundred pounds Sterling payable to . . . their heirs and Sucessors or some of them to the which payment shall well & Truly be made We bind ourselves and every of us our and every of us our heirs Exectrs Admin Joyntly and Severally firmly by these presents and Sealed with our seals this 20th day of November 1721.

The Case of. (. *missing)* above bounden Wm Kieth Eliza Powers Exectrs . . . of Wm Lindsey decd do make or Cause to be made a true and perfect Inventory of all and Singular ye Goods Chattels and Credits of the aforesaid Lindsey decd which has or shall come to ye hands and possessions or knowledge of them ye sd Excrs or into ye hands or possession of any other person or persons for them the same so made shall exhibite or cause to be exhibited into ye County court of York at such time as they shall thereunto be required by ye said Court and ye same goods Chattels and Credits and any other Goods Chattels and Credits of ye sd Lindsey decd by ye time of his death which at any time after shall come to ye hands or possessions of them ye sd Execrs. Or into ye hands or possessions of any other person or persons for that . . . . . Well and Truly administer according to Law and further do make a true acct of their actings and doings therein when thereto required. . . . . Court and also pay and Deliver all ye Legacys contained and Specyfied in ye Last will and Testament as far as ye Goods Chattles and Credits will. . . . . according to ye values thereto and ye Law. Shall discharge according . . . . . bligation to be void otherwise shall continue in full force and virtue.

Nov 20 th 1721 This matter was presented in Court
By . . . . . Wm Kieth, Eliza. Powers, Wm Gordon, James Shields. Admitted to Record. Phi Lightfoot ClCur

Know all men by these presents that we John Hansford Francis Sharp & Arth Dickerson of ye County of York are held and firmly bound to our Sovereign Lord ye King in ye Sum of ten. . . . . . convenient in ye County of York to which payment well & Truly be made to our Sovereign Lord ye King his heirs Successors we bind . . . . . and every of our heirs Execrs and Adminrs Joyntly and Severally and Sealed with our Seals and dated this . . . . . such that whereas ye above bounden Jno. Hansford . . . . . Lycence to keep an Ordinary at his now residence . . . for ye year next ensuing and fully if there . . . . . and provide in his ordinary good wholesome and cleanly . . . . . amd Stableage and provender or pasturage and provender (as the season shall require) for their horses from ye date . . . . . year and shall not suffer any person to
. . . . . Sabath day & suffer any person to . . . . . then this Obligation to be void and of none. . . . . and virtue. Jno. Hansford. Fra Sharp, Arth Dickerson ……. . . acknowledged by ye partys therto and Phi Lightfoort ClCur

Page 86
Know all men by these presents that we Lawr. Smith Wm Gordon & Robt Laughton of ye County . . . . . held and firmly bound to ye Worshipfull ye Justices of ye said County . . . . . of twenty pounds Sterling which payement well & Truly to be made to ye said Justices their heirs and successors or some of them we bind our Selves and every of us our and every of us our heirs Execrs and Adminrs Joyntly and Severally firmly by these presents Sealed with our Seals and dated this 20 day of Nov. 1721

The condition of this Obligation is such that the above bounden Lawr. Smith and Lucinda his wife admn of ye Goods Chattels and Credits of Alex Atkinson decd . . . . . Cause to be made a true & perfect Invy. of all and Singular . . . . . Credits of ye sd Atkinson decd which have or shall come to the hands possessions knowledge of them ye sd Lawr, and Lucinda Smith or into ye hands possessions of any other person or persons for them the same so made to whit or cause to be exhibited into ye County Court of York at such time as they shall be thereto required by ye sd Court and ye same goods chattels and Credits and all of ye

goods Chattles and Credits of ye sd Atkinson decd at ye time of his death which at any time after shall come to ye hands and possessions of them ye sd Adminsrs or into ye hands or possessions of any other persons or persons for them to well and truly admintr according to Law and further do make a true & just account of their actings & Doings thereupon when therto required by ye sd Court and all ye rest and . . . . . goods Chattells and Credits which shall be found remaining . . . . . account ye Some being first examined by the Justices of ye sd . . . . . being Shall deliver and pay unto such person or persons as ye . . . . . their order or Judgement shall direct pursuant to ye Law in that . . . . . provided and if it shall hereafter appear
That any last will and Testament was made by ye said decd and ye Exr or Excrs therein named . . . . . in ye sd Court making request to have it allowed and appraised . . . . . therefore ye sd Adm being thereto required do render and. . . . . letters of Admin Approbation of such testament being first had. . . . . then this obligation to be void and of none effect or else remain in full force and virtue.
Lucinda Smith, Wm Gordon, Robert Laughton,
This bond was presented by the partys . . . . . .

Know all men. . . . . Butterworth Wm Gordon and Richd Baker . . . . . firmly bound unto Our Sovereign Lord the King . (. *missing*) pounds of Tobacco convenient in ye County of York which payment well and truly to be made to our Sovereign . . . . . successors we bind ourselves and every ... adms jointly and Severally . . . . . Seals and dated this20 day of Nov 1721 ... Obligation is such that where. . . . . this day granted him to keep. ... dwelling house in York . . . . . Butterworth ... pasturage ... (*missing*) not suffer Butterworth. Wm Gordon

Page 87
Know all men by these presents that _______________ 26-4. 8
Of the County of York are held and ________________ 2. 0. 10-
. . . . . resaid in ye Sum of... . . . 29. 1. 1 -
. . . . . Heirs and Successors or Some. . *(missing*) well & Truly to be made we bind ourselves. . . . . our heirs Execrs and Adms Joyntly . . . . .
. . . . . to yet accounted for. Phi. Jones, Wm Wharton, Dr Philipson

(*The margin states Burks Bond for Guardianship . . . . but there are figures written down and partially missing that indicate it could be something else, Below is a Guardianship bond that also has much missing. Page is in poor shape*)
... . . . Thos Bell Jno. Power Jno Hay of the
... . . . bound unto ye Worshipfull ye Justices of ye County
... . . . Sterling payable to ye sd Justices their heirs
... . . . which payment well & Trult to be made
... . . . our and every of our heirs Execrs and Adminrs.

… . . . these presents sealed with our Seals and dated
… . . . That whereas above bounden Thos Bell at a
… . . . Guardian of Jno. Fergason Orphan of
… . . . Care and Custody ye whole estate of ye said Orphan
… . . . Thomas Bell do well and truly perform ye trust he hath
… . . . and his estate and pay or cause to be paid his
… . . . some when he shall attain to lawfull age or Sooner
… . . . from time to time and at all times hereafter shall
… (*missing* (ye said Justices their heirs &c from all damages
… . . . then concerning ye said estate and perform all other
… . . . of this Court Than this Obligation to be void or
. . . . . acknowledged. Thos. Bell (mark) , Jno. Powers, Jno Hay . Phi Lightfoot ClCur

York County this 18 1721
. . . . . lloway Thos Nelson
Graves Park Gent
. . . . . ye Estate of Philip Moody decd is continued
. . . . . . enof Williams Hansford decd William
… . . . Guardian to ye F Thomas And it
of ye sd William Hansford
in ye Lowr precints of York County
ordered that he keep ye Roads and bridges
… . . . Mackinds & Jno. Mattock or any three
… . . . appraise the Estate of Alexr. Atkins
Court

Page 88
In ye petiton of ye Appraisal of Hen. Haywards estate July 26 1721

=========

42. 16. ½
Eliza Hayward
Edw. Tabb

(Note: this page has much of it missing. Figures are entered on right margin And left margin has the usual margin notes. Entire center missing. Any names will be entered along with legible margin notes.)

(Bacchus & Bates Atta. *Legible is said Bates s estate*)
(Bacchus & Bates Atta.)
(Bocock to be summoned . . Mary his wife be summoned)
(Gordon -Cobbs Judgement)
(Gordon & Sharp Judgt. Issue Costs 15 Jun 1721)

(Sebrels Est to be appr. . legible also... *in ye pet. . Susa. Sebrell Ex. . Estate by consent. . acct of ye sd Nat. .*)
(Hubards Est to be appr. Legible also. . G*raves Pack... of Thos Hubard dec)*
(Hawkins & Melonys Est Judgement)
(Holland & Biggs & Davis Judgement)
(npr & Frith Judgement issue Costs feb 5 1721 In Satisfaction)
(at bottom of page is beginning of a will visible is. . *my Sins*)

Page 89
and to inherit eternal Life my body . . . . . Richd Burt Joseph Moundford & W Cross
. . . . . of my Excrs, heretofor found unto ye worshipfull ye Justices of . . . . .
funeral expenses being . . . . . pounds Sterling payable to ye said Justices
Imprimis I give and bequeath . . (missing) them to which payment well ... . . .
Powers of York Town . . and every of us Our and every of. . . . . . Severally by these presents
22nd day of Nov 1721

... . . . that if ye above bounden Richd Burt shall
... . . . unto Martha Eliza. And Judith orphans
estates belonging to ye sd Orphans as is
hands or possessions of him ye said R. Burt
. . . . any other person or persons for him when or as
. . . . attain to Lawfull age or when thereunto re
also save and keep harmless ye said Court
that shall or may accrew to them about or Con
this Obligation to be void or else to remain
Richd Burt, Joseph Mountford, Wm Cross. Phi Lightfoot Cl Cur

... . . . that we Giles Moody Jno. Pasture & Jno. James
... . . . held and firmly bound to our Sovereign Lord
pounds of tobacco convenient in ye said
well and truly to be made to our Sd Lord ye King
our and every of our heirs Execrs and adminrs
presents sealed with our Seals and dated
. . . . . . such that whereas ye above bounden Giles
. . . . . . him for a Lycence to keep an ordinary
Bruton parish for ye year next ensuing
Moody doth constantly find and provide
Cleanly Lodging and diet for travelors
Forage and provender as ye Season shall
of these presents for and during the
Suffer any unlawful gaming in his house

Person to Tipple or drink more than is
Void and of none effect otherwise

Giles Moody, John Pasteur, Jame. Flourney. Test Phil Lightfoot Cl Cur

Page 90
Haywards further Invry. (in margin)
An acct of ye Estate of Jno. Miller deed in Lotts (top of page)
Appears to be two Inventories. One has a total of £47-16. 6 (probably Miller's) The date is 17 July 1721.
Bottom inventory is illegible but may be that of Henry Hayward (That name is legible)

Page 91
. . . Know all men by these presents that I commit to ye Earth to be decently interred at . . . . . my Wordly estate . . . . . Sum of three hundred pounds . . . . . paid/I give and dispose of us . . . . . unto ye sd Justices their heirs and every of us . . . . . Keith of ye county of York . . . . . of us our and every of our heirs . in ye sd County all my estate that is due . . . . . persons whatsoever in ye aforesaid colony of Virginia as also what goods and chattels . . . . . be shipped by Mr William Hay in return . . . . . by Coll. Cole Diggs on Mr Arthur . . . . . year. . . . . . equally divided between them y said Jas. Keith . . . . . hereby nominateand appoint ye sd. Jas. Keith . . . . . this my last will and testament revoking & Dis . . . . . and legacys by me heretofore made in Witness . . . . . my hand and Seal dated at York Town this . . . . . 1721 Wm Lindsay.

At a Court held for York County Nov 20 1721
. . (*missing*) and testament of Wm Lindsay decd was presented in Court
. . . . . and Eliza Powers ye Execrs who made Oath thereto
by ye Witnesses is admitted to Record. Test Phi Lightfot ClCur

. . . . . Est of Jno. West of York County is as follows

=======
£55. 18. 6

... . . . above estate witness our hand
... . . . Nov 1721 Thos Crips, Jno. West decd, Uriah Hudson, Mary West Adm.
(Margin states Hansfords Bond Guardianship Hansford))

Page 92
An Account of ye estate of Giles Tavernor decd

=========
£45 . 11. 8

(visible on page is. . *Susa. Tavernor. . Wm Walke. . Security*)

next is (Sebrells Inveny)
In obedience to an order . . . . .
Subscribers have . . . . .
Of Nath Sebrel decd...
A Negro wench named W. . .
A Negro wench named Juo. . .
This invry was. . .
Admitted to Rec. . . .

Page 93
In Al-------------------Jn Jones Wm Gordon and Edw. Tabb of the
Balance due to me from ... . . . Worshipfull Justices of ye said Court Excepted . .
. . . or Some of them we bind our ... . . . and dated this19 day of cber 1721

. . . . . . above bounden Jno. Jones adm of all ye
. . . . . . do make or cause to be made a true and
. . . and credits of ye said decd which have
. . . ye sd Jones or into ye hands possessions
. . . so made do exhibit or cause to be
...he shall be thereunto rev
...Chattels and all other Goods
...death which at any time after shall
...or into ye hands or possessions of
...truly administer according to law
...of his acting & doings therein when
...due if ye sd Goods chattels & Credits
...ye adm account ye same being first
...being shall deliver & Pay unto
. . . or Judgement shall Direct
...provided and if it sshall hereafter appear
...ye sd Decd and ye Excr or Excrs therin
...request to have it allowed & approved
...therto required do render and deliver
. . ,testamentCausing first in ye sd Court
...Jones, ...Gordon, Edw. Tabb. ...Lightfoot ClCur

This ... . . . that we Wm Hansford Richd Stewart & Geo Gilbert
By ye... . . . worshipfull ye Justices of ye County
... . . . hundred pounds Sterling payable to ye sd Justices their heirs
... . . . them to ye which payment well and truly to be made

...our and every of our heirs Execrs and admrs. Joyntly
...presents seals with our Seals and dated this 18 day

...... tion is such that whereasye above bounden Wm Hansford at
...... York County became Guardian of Thos. Hansford Orphan of
... Care and Custody of ye whole Estate of ye sd orphan
.... do well and truly perform ye trust that he hath undedr
...pay or Cause to be paid his full dues acc
...Lawfull age or sooner if ye Courts shall
...es hereafter shall save harmless and
...damages that shall or may arise
...other things enjoyned by Law

...... or else to remain in full force
...... Wm Hansford, ..., Rd Steward, ... Geo Gilbert
acknowledged. .... Lightfoot Cl Cur

Page 94
An *Action* ..... Brown agt Jno. Ness's Estate the atta. is further continued

To a ..... lor ye appearance of Law. .... and ordered that ye Sheriff ..... Blackwell into Cus (probably custody) ..... security for him ..... Sufficient Security for ..... next Court & rendering ..... Ness's Est in his hands further ordered that return be made hereof.

..... being this day confirmed ... . ambs. . (missing) £54. 2. 8 Sterl of non appearance ..... Jno. Bates at ye court Robr. Tucker ..... for ye aforesaid Sum agt ye... .... for Judgement ... . Bacchus for 55. 2. 10 Sterling ..... at ye suit of Robt Tucker on... .... ye Sum & costs agt ye sd Sheriff

... . ter & Mistress Henry Bocock ... . Cloathing the Court do. .... until next Court that he ... (*missing*) ye sd Henry Bowcock & ..... at ye next Court.
... . & Saml Cobbs Surviving
... . Tobacco due by acct proved by
... . is granted ye plt. For ye sd Tobacco
..... twelve pounds fourteen
...... with Costs Als Exo.
...... plt & Thos Wyat deft for
..... yds of Camlet & 9 yds of Sattonett
..... protesting his debt before some
..... James Mackinds & Nath Hook
..... reqt thereof to ye next Court
..... plt & Fra Sharpe deft for

. . . . . plt oath ye deft making no Object
. . . . . Sum and ordered that the deft
. . . . . . one fathing to ye plt together

... . . . David Sebrel agt Jno. Mundal and
. . . . . . Davids Share of ye Testators
. . . . to audit state & settle the
... ... to ye sd Davd. To ye next Court
. . . . . er Sisland & Evan Morgan
. . . . . . to appraise ye estate
... . . . Meloy for 700 of Tobacco
. . . . five pounds
... ... Davis deft.

Page 95
Rachel a negro Girl belonging to Wm Houghton is adjudged to be 9 years old.
... (*missing*) boy belonging to ... Calthrope is adjudged to be nine years old.
... . . . Surveyor of . . . . . upper precincts of Charles
. . . . for not keeping the roads
... ... he had put the sd roads
. . . . . discharged paying fees als exo. (margin says Tuckam discharged from Roads)
. . . . . . Hay & Armiger Parsons & Eliza his wife deft is dismist.
... ... between George Allen plt & Francis Sharpe deft issue. . . . . referred until the next
. . . . Court for Tryall. ... Court presented his deeds of lease & release
... ... County together with his bond for performance of Covenants
. . . on his motion are admitted to record. (Walker from Stock. . deed &c)
... (*missing*) (between Jno. Welch plt & Joseph Stacy deft is dismist
. . . . by Joseph Walker Gent Sheriff agt the Estate of Joseph Stacy
... ... nonappearance at the suit of John Welch is discontinued.
... . . . debt between Essex Weller plt & Eliza Ives deft for 100£
. . . . . . to plead Judgement is granted the plt by Nihil Dicit
. . . . . . next Court on the like default.
. . . . . . between Wm Levinston assignee of Eliza Ives plt & Essex Weller . . . Sterling damage the deft failing to plead , Judgement
. . . by Nihil Dicit Confirmable at the next Court

In the Action between Anna Maria Timson Execrs &c of Wm Timson decd . . (*miss*)
Flournoy & Mary his wife Exers &c of Orlando Jones deft . . . . . having had time allowed them to plead & being . . . . . judgement is therefore granted the plt by Nihil Dicit Returnable at the next Court on the like default

In the Action on the Case between Wm Rogers plt & Augustine Moor &c Exers of John. . (*missing*) deft for £3. 13. 6 by acct failing to plead Judgement. . (*missing*) the plt by Nihil Dicit confirmable at the next Court on the like default.

. . . . . er Jackson agt the estate of John Ness is dismist.

. . (*missing)*... (Pryor agt the Estate of John Ness is dismist the debt. . . .

... . . . (Nelson's negro Adjudged) belonging to Thomas Nelson was this day adjudged. . . . . .

... . . . (Abbott from Joyce power Att.) Joyce to Jno Abbott was this day proved & admitted to record

... . . . the estate of John Ness the att is
... . . . Allens appearance & recognizance
. . . . . . & ordered that Leprade pay the. . . . . . . (Gilbert & Ness)
Page 96
& ordered to pay the sd Sum of fifty four pounds & Eight Shillings to the plt with Cost als Exo.

The Action of Debt between Robt Tucker plt & John Bates deft for fifty pounds two Shillings& ten pence is a protested Bill of Exchange . . . . . called & Failing to appear to answer the motion the Judgement of . . . . . the sd James Bacchus his Security ... confirmed & its . . . . . . Sum of Fifty pounds two Shillings and ten pence & cost als Exo.

John Mundale . . . . . Nathl Sebrell decd Exhibited an Invr. of the sd Sebrells estate and it is admitted to record.

In the accon upon the Case . . . . . plt & Joseph Barry def issue being joined the Case is continued until the next Court for tryall.

In the petition of John Randolph. . . . . John Cranston setting forth that the sd John for... . . . eight pounds Sterling armum did warr. himself to be. . . . . & that he was not capable to perform either & praying... . . . paying him any wages the Court upon hearing the defence . . . . . Cranston are of opinion that he is not capable... . . . contract & thereupon to adjudge that the sd John Cranston. . . . . or his assigns the remaining part of his ... . . . that he the ptr be released & Discharged from the sd ... . . . him in lieu thereof apparel meet & fitting for Sur. . . . . .

In the accon upon the Case ... . . . Haughton by Richd Haughton her next friend plt & John... . . . mon the attached agt the deft Estate is continued until the next Court. (margin says Haughton-Rhodes)

The accon of Debt between (Lattemore) plt & Lawrence Smith deft is dismist & ordered that the deft pay. . . . .

In the accon of Debt between ... . . . plt & Edwd Jacquelin Exer &c of Harwood Cary decd deft. Deft ... . . . hath time allowed him (or her) consider the deft plea . . . . . next Court (Charles & Jacquelin)

The pet of Andrew Laprade agt. Nathl. Sebrell decd is dismist.

In the petition of John Brookes... . . . John Wright for abuse the court upon hearing the . . . . . Submission do order & adjudge that he serve . . . . . after his time by indenture custom or former order has expired.

The accon of Debt between ... (*missing* ((Townsend) & James Faison deft is continued until the next Court.

In the accon . . . . . & Josiah Stacy deft the def . . . . . to the plt for thirty Shills . . . . .

(Walker & Stacy) discontinued

(James & Nash) continued

(Shields & Robertson)

Page 97
The accon on the Case between (Edw?) Cobbs plt & Joseph Sutton deft is cont until the next Court.

The petition of David Walker agt Thos Lark & Mary his wife Execr &c Florence Mc Carty decd Ord that the Sheriff Sumon the sd Thos Lark to appear to answer at the next Court.

The accon of trespass & assault between Richd Ballamie & Sarah his wife plt & Charles Rowan is dismist.

The accon upon the Case between Edw. Tabb plt & James Faison deft is dismist.

In the Suit in Chancery depending between John Goodwin Excr &c of James

Goodwin decd ptr & Mary Read Respondt the respondt demurrer being joined by consent its referred until the next Court to be argued

John Jones came into Court & Made Oath that Thos Hubberd departed this life without making any will so far as he knows or believes together withWm Gordon & Edw. Tabb his Securitys entered into & Acknowledged their bond for his just & Faithfull admon on the sd Hubberds wi. Bond is admitted to record on his mon Order is granted him for obtaining letters of administration on the sd estate in due form

The action of Walker Butler agt Charles Collier &c Excr of Jno. Young is dismist neither part appearing.

Wm Gordon Exhibited acct of the estate of Giles Tavernor & Jno. Meloy decd Wi. and admitted to record

In the petition of Philip Lightfoot Excrs of Matthew Ballard decd agt the Estate of Jno. Meloy for thirty Shillings or 3 barrels of Corn On the partys Oath Judgement is granted for the Same & ordered that Wm Gordon pay thirty Shills. To the petr. of the decd estate & Costs als Exo.

In the action upon the Case between Joseph Walker plt & Eliza Hansford Exer &c of . . . Hansford decd deft for £7. 15. 0 by acct upon the deft coming to the bar and agreeing to deliver for the use of her Sisters two Cows the plt released his debt . . . . . that the deft pay Cost als Exo.

The accon of Case between Hugh Allen plt & Wm Gilchrist deft is dismist no appearance

The accon upon the Case between Math Jones plt & Nath Hook deft is dismist

The accon upon the Case between Mathew Jones plt & Richd Baker is dismist

In the accon of Trespass on the case between Peter Brewer plt & Henry Swinfin def . . . . . his mon hath an Imparlance granted him until ye next Court

On the accon of the case between Jno. Taylor plt & Garret Joyce deft is dismist.

On the accon of the case between Garret Joyce plt & Jno Barry deft is dismist.

On the accon of the case between (?) Hyde plt & Jno. Haythorn deft is dismist.

(Lightfoot & Lawrence Smith)

. . . . . Richd Needham plt & Saml Reed deft on the plt moton an attachment . . . . . Suit agt the deft estate returnable to the next Court.

... . . . upon the Case between Thos Toomer plt & Eliza Hayward Excr &c Henry Hayward decd deft & the defts appeared on their mon and had an imparlance granted them until the next Court

. . . . . Lawrence Smith plt & Jno. Woldom deft is dismist.

. . . . . between Jno Hay & Mary his wife Complt & Thos. . ? is continued until the next Court.

Page 98
In the petition of James Cathern & Dianah his wife late Dianah Hayward one of the daughters of Wn Hayward decd agt Robt Shield for the sd Dianah's share of the sd Wms Estate the ... this cause is admitted to record & it appearing thereby that the Sum of two pounds Six Shillings & one penny half penny is due the petr. Therefore ordered that the sd. Shields pay the sd Sum with Costs als Exo.
In the petiton of Mary Clifton agt Rob Shields for her share of the estate of her father Wm Hayward decd it appearing by the Auds report that the Sum of nine Pounds & Three half pence is her part of the sd estate therefore ordered that the deft pay her the sd Sum (discounting what she has already received) with costs als exo

The accon of debt between Saml Sweny plt & ?Delony deft is continued until the next Court.

The petition of John Welch & John. . . . . agt Thos Bell is denied. The sd Bell having given fresh. . . . .

Thos Bell John Power & John Hay presented & Acknowledged their bond to the Court for the sd Bells Guradianship of John Furgeson wi. Bond is admitted to record

Ordered that theCourt be adjourned until the next Court in Couse. Signed Jno. Holloway. Truly entered by Phi Lightfoot ClCur.

An Inventory of the estate of Eliza. Goodwin
18 Negroes (no names) 2 head cattle 59 Sheep
Tobacco Shipped home 8552 pounds 45 barrels Indian Corn

Page 99
Cash £2. 1. 0. Jno. Goodwin, Rachel wife

Jan. 15 172-1
This Invry and Accn is presented in Court by Jno. Goodwin and is Admitted to record. Test Phi Lightfoot Cl Cur

Know All men by these presents that We Eliza Manson Peter Manson & John Chapman & Fran Minnis of ye County of York are held and firmly bound unto ye Worshipfull ye Justices of ye County aforesaid for ye Sum of £ 500 Sterling to Which payment well & Truly be made to ye sd. Justices their heirs & their Successors or some of them we bind Ourselves & Every of us and every of our heirs Adms & excrs Joyntly & Severally by these presents Sealed with our Seals and dated this 15th day of Jan 1721

The condition of this Obligation is such that ye above bounden Eliza Manson & Peter Manson Excrs of ye last will and Testament of Peter Manson decd do make or Cause to be made a True & perfect Invry of all & Singular ye goods Chattles & Credits of ye sd decd which have or shall come to ye hands possessions or knowledge or into ye hands or possessions of any person or persons for them and ye same so made do exhibit or cause to be exhibited in ye County Court of York at such time as ye shall be thereunto of ye sd court and ye same Goods Chattles & Credits and all other goods Chattles & Credits of ye decd at ye time of his death which any time after shall come to ye hands & Possessions of them ye said Execrs or into the hands & Possessions of any other person or persons for their use further do make a true & Just acct. of their actings & Doings . . . . . when thereto required by ye sd Court and also pay and. . . . . Legacys specified in ye sd test. As far ... . . . charge them Then this Obligation to be . . . . . Eliza Manson, Peter Manson, John Chapman, Fran Minnis, ... acknowledged . . . . . . Lightfoot ClCur

In the name of God Amen. I Peter Manson being sick & Weak of body but of Sound & perfect memory Blessed be God for it Revoking all former Wills and revisions therein this my Last Will and testament in manner and form following I bequeath my Soul to God who gave it to me in Certain . . . . . through ye merits of my Blessed Saviour Jesus . . . . . and my body to ye ground from whence it was . . . . .

Page 100
Shall name as to my Wordly estate to which ye Lord hath been pleased to lend me I bestow as followeth my just debts legacys and funeral charges being first paid ye remainder part of my estate I give and bequeath as followeth item I give unto my Loving Son Peter Manson all that stock of Cattle which I Bought by way of out Cry out of ye estate of Giles Tavernor decd with their Increase item I lend unto my Loving wife Eliza Manson for her Support and maintenance during her widowhood these following negroes (to whit) Black Betty Jude Bill and

Bess and I also lend to her all ye remaining part of my estate during her widowhood and in case she Should marry or dies my desire is that all my estate be equally be divided among all my children to wit Peter Manson Anne Horthan Eliza Manson John Manson James Manson and Walter Manson and my will and desire is that my loving wife should keep my son Walter Manson and what belongs to him until he comes of age of 14 years and give him what learning . . . . . appoint my loving wife Eliza Manson and my loving son Peter Manson to be my Execrs of this my last will and testament And I do request loving brother-in-law John Chapman to oversee and take care that this my will be performed according to my true intent and meaning thereof as witness my hand and Seal this 20 of March in ye year of our Lord 1720. Peter Manson, Wit. Robt. Kerby, John Lowry, Thos Kerby Jan 15 1721

This last will and testament of Peter Manson decd was presented in Court by Eliza and Peter Manson therein named who made Oath to it and being proved by ye oaths of Robt Kerby & Thos Kerby witnesses the will is admitted to Record. Phi Lightfoot ClCur

Part of ye appraise mi of ye Est of . . . . . Wise which came Since to my hand to be added to ye former appraisal . . . £18. 13. 10

Jan 15 1721. Edw. Curtis, Benj Moss, John Fentam

The furthur appraisal of the Invy of. . . . . Wise was presented in Court by Jno. Goodwin and admitted to record. Test Phi Lightfoot ClCur

At a court held for York County 15th Jan 1721

Page 101

Richd Ambler . . . . . them being sworn...appointed estate of Thos Hubbard decd . . . . . and make report at ye next Court

Thos Barber Arthur Dickinson Wm Stark and Charles Hansford or any three of them being sworn are appointed tp appraise ye estate of Eliza. Moody decd and make report thereof to ye next Court.

In ye petition of John Morris agt ye estate of John Meloy decd for £2. 10. 0 for ye maintenance of ye children of ye sd decd three weeks it is ordered that Wm Gordon pay petr fourty shillings out of ye decds estate with Costs als Exo.

Mary West presented by ye grand jury for having a Mullatto Bastard being Summoned and failing to appear ordered to be taken into Custody till she gives Security for her appearance at ye next Court to answer ye presentment

Richd King being presented by ye grand jury for failing to attend Church according to Law being summoned and failing to appear ordered that ye Sheriff take him into Custody till he gives Security for his appearance to ye next Court to answer ye presentment

Wm Rogers the same

Joseph Frith the same

Wm Needham being presented for keeping a woman as his wife & Having presented a Certificate of Marriage is dismist

John Fossett having been presented for Swearing is fined five shillings and ordered to pay ye same to ye Churchwarden of Charles parish at their next Levy with cost als Exo.

Uriah Hutson having been presented for Swearing is fined five shillings and ordered to pay ye same to ye Churchwarden of Bruton Parish at their next Levy with costs als Exo

Ez Gilbert having been presented by ye Grand Jury for swearing is Summoned to ye next Court to answer ye presentment

Elize Griffin having been presented by the grand Jury for having a Bastard Child being summoned and failing to appear is ordered to be taken into Custody until she gives Security for her appearance at ye next Court to answer the presentment

J. . (missing) Pain same

The case between Thos Jones plt & Eliza Powers deft is cont until next Court

The case between Wm Hansford & David Moss is dismist

In the accon on trespass cause between Benj Clifton plt & Wm Biggs . . . . . plt agrees to receive any special . . . . . continued & ye Cause is referred for tryall

. . . . . and acknowledged their deed for
. . . . . at whose mon it is admitted to record (Gordon fm Biggs bond decd- *margin*)

. . . . . and app. of ye Rachel decd (Wise)

. . . . . estate of Eliza Goodwin

. . . . . Armiger Parsons & Eliza his wife
. . . . Hay decd respond Law Smith
. . . . audit state & Settle all accs.
. . . thereof to the next Court

. . . . . Lightfoot plt & Thos Bell deft
. . . . next Court for tryall (

. . . . . . Frances his wife agt Wm Palmer
. . . of Richd Palmer (Stringer)

Page 102
. . . . . n Goodwin plt & Lawrence Smith & Mildred his wife deft late Mildred Goodwin is cont until next Court for tryall

In the accon of debt between Wm Stone plt & Wm Biggs deft the deft being in ye Custody of ye Sheriff confessed judgement to ye plt for ye Sum of Six pounds whereupon it is Ordered that he pay ye sd Sum to ye deft with Costs

On the petition of Mary Atkinson ye wife of Wm Atkinson Certificate is granted her for Obtaining Adm of . . . . . of her decd father ... . . . with the will annext in due form giving Security. (Atkinson adm Moody)

Mary Atkinson wife of Wm Atkinson came into Court & Made Oath that Eliza Moody departed this life without making any will so farr as she knows or believes On her mon & giving Security is granted her for letters of adm for the decd estate in due form

In the accon of debt between Archibald Blair plt & Jonathon Drewett & Martha his wife adm &c of W. Kaidyce deft the spec. verdict found in this cause have been certified by the court is declared void ordered thereby a new venue of these persons wi. (by consent of both partys) were by this day struck by the Court for the jury & that the suit be continued

On hearing ye complaint of Mary Williams agt her Master & Mistress Henry Bocock & Mary his wife and their defence it is ordered by ye Court that she return to her sd Master and that he sell her as soon as possible and that she serve assigns of her sd master four months after her time by Indenture Custom or former order is expired

John Moss and Eliza his wife and Eliza his mother presented their deeds for lands and bond in open court to Jno. Trotter and ye sd Eliza ye wife being privately examined voluntarily relinquished her right of dower in ye sd land deed . . . . . Trotters mon are admitted to Record

The last will and testament of Peter Manson was presented in Court by Eliza Manson and Peter Manson Excrs so named who made Oath to it and being proved by ye Oaths of. . . . . Thomas Kerby witness is admitted to record and ye sd Excrs . . . . . Jno. Chapman & Fran Minnis their Security having entered into . . . . . acknowledged their bond to ye court for . . . . . ye sd bond is admitted to record . . . . . probate thereof in due form

. . . . . Jno. Meloy decd for fourty pounds (Meloy's estate Judgement)

. . . . . be released form being Security
………… husbands estate It is
. . . . Frances to appear at ye next (Hay -Malicote)

(Hyde - Thebo)

Page 103
At a Court held for York County Janry 29, 1721

Present John Holloway Henry Tyler
Lawr Smith Thos Nelson & Wm Sheldon gentl.

Lewis Davis committed to ye Goal of this County on Suspicion of Felony For entering ye Storehouse of Wm Gordon & Taking thence some wine &c ing before ye Court upon hearing ye evidences and his examination it is ye opinion of ye Court that ye sd Lewis Davis ought to be tried for ye sd fact before ye general Court Wherefore it is ordered that he be remanded to ye prison of ye County under ye Custody of ye Sheriff & from thence to be conveyed to ye Publick Gaol at Williamsburgh in ordere for a Tryall at ye general Court as ye law is Such cases directs

Thos Neal Jno. Wooldom & Thos Quin Severally before ye Court acknowledged themselves indebted to ye Sovereign Lord ye King in the Sum of ten pounds Sterling to be levied on their Goods & Chattles on Condition that if they should appear at ye next General Court on ye fourth day thereof and attend from time to time then & There to give evidence in behalf of our Sovereign Lord ye King against Lewis Davis who stand committed for ye felony then this recognizance be void otherwise to remain in full force

Wm Gordon ye same for his servant George Blair

Nath Hook ye same for his servant Bertrand a Mullatto

In ye name of God amen 28th of Jan 1721 I John Steward of Bruton Parish being sick & Weak of body but of perfect Sense and memory praised be Almighty God do make and ordain this to be my last Will and testament in manner and form First revoking all furthur wills and Testaments hereto fore made And after my

Just debts and funeral charges paid all such estate that it has pleased God to bless me with I bestow as follows vizt Imprs I give and bequeath to my daughter-in –law Sarah Peirce my Riding horse and after . . . . . White's estate which given by his Grandfather and grandmother is . . . . . my just debts aforesaid all ye rest of my estate what. . . . . to my Godson John Pierce and to his heirs forever But . . . . . die before he comes to ye age of twenty one years of age. . . . . Sarah Peirce and to her heirs forever . . . . . my best suit of Cloaths my best frock . . . . . Mathew Peirce ye Riding Coat . . . . . and all ye rest of my wearing cloathes and Lastly I do ordain and appoint . . . . . Execr of this my Last will and testament . . . . . whereof I have hereunto set my hand and Seal when . . . . .

John Stewart

Feb 19 1721

Wit. Geo H. . . . . Far... the last Will and testament of Jno. Stewart was... . . . who made oath to it and it being . . . to record. Phi Lightfoot ClCur

Page 104

A true and Just Inventory of ye estate of Peter Manson as followeth One negro man named Will about twenty five years old One negro woman named Betty about 60 years One Negro woman named Judy about Thirty two years old One negro girl named Bess about 2 years 9 months old. . . .

Feb . . . . . Eliza Manson. Peter Manson. Phi Lightfoot Cl Cur

In ye name of God Amen. . . . . Tavernor of Charles parish in York County being weak of memory but Sound of Sense and memory do on this 5th day of 8th . . . . . Make ordain this my last will and testament In manner and form following that is to say First I send my Soul into ye Hands of My great Maker from whom I received it at first and my body into the earth from whence it was made to be decently buried at ye discretion of. . . . .

Page 105

Item I give unto my son Wm Tavernor and to ye heirs of his body lawfully begotten 100 acres of land lying and being in ye parish and ye County above written and in case If he should die before his wife Mary Tavernor I give to he ye used of ye sd land during her natural life And in case my son Wm Tavernor should die without heirs of his body then I give it unto my grandson Giles Tavernor and ye heirs of his body and in case none such these to ye next heir item I give unto my son Wm Tavernor one Negro man named Frank to him an his disposing and ye use of one Negro Girl Judy during his life and after his decease I give her and her increase unto my granddaughter Ann Morris and unto her heirs item I give unto my son-in-law Thomas Baly the Sum of one shilling Sterling The like Sum I give unto my son-in-law John Johnson Item I give unto all my Grandchildren ye Sum of One Shilling Sterling apiece item after my debts and legacys paid ye remaining pe. of my whole estate which is to say all Goods

and Chattel I give to my son Wm Tavernor & Mary his wife item I do ordain & Appoint my loving son Wm Tavernor my whole and sole Excr of this my last will and Testament revoking all former wills by me heretofore made as Witness I have hereunto set my hand and affixed my Seal ye day and year above written Signed Sealed and declared to be ye last will and Testament of ye testator in ye presence of us . . . . . Robinson, Jno. Robinson Feb 19 1721
. . . . . testament of Wm Tavernor was presented in Court by Wm Tavernor ye Excr who made Oath It being proved by ye Oaths of ye witnesses thereto is admitted to Record. test Phi Lightfoot ClCur

Know ye all men by these presents that we Wm Tavernor John Robinson and Jno. Powers. . . . . hereby bound unto ye Worshipfull ye Justices of ye County their heirs and Sucessors or some of them to which payment well and truly be made. . . . . by these presents Sealed with our Seals and dated this 19th day of Feby 1721
The condition of this Obligation is such that ye above bounden Wm Tavernor do make or cause to be made a true and perfect Inventory of all & Singular ye goods Chattels and Credits of ye sd decd which have or shall come to ye hands possessions or knowledge of him ye sd exectr or into ye hands possessions of any other person or persons ... To exhibit or cause to be exhibited . . . . . such time as her shall be thereunto . . . . . Chattels and credits and all other goods chattels and credits. . . . . time of his death which at any time shall come to the hands or possessions of him ye sd Exectr or into ye hands. . . . . person or persons for him do well & truly administer according to Law and further do make a true & Just acc. of his actings & Doings therein when thereto required by ye sd Court and also . . . . . all legacys contained and specyfied in ye sd testament . . . . . goods chattels credits thereunto extended . . . . . thereof and ye law shall charge him then this obligation . . . . . else remain in full force and virtue. Wm Tavernor, ... in Court and ,,, Jno. Power .... thereto and . . . Jno. Robinson. Phi Lightffor Cl Cur

Page 106
In Obedience to ye order of ye Worshipfull Justices of York County Court we ye Subscribers have appraised so much of ye estate of Thos Hubbard decd as was exhibited to us and we adjudge and report ye underwritten was to ye best of our Judgement ye true value thereof Given under our hands at York Town Feb 2 1721

=============

£3. 15. 7

Jno Jones Feb 19 1721

Richd Ambler, Jno. Trotter, Wm Gordon

This Invy & appraisment of ye estate of . (*miss*) Hubbard
Decd was presented in Court byJn Power and is admitted to

Record

... . . . one of ye Genl Justices
. . . Thos Hubbard as Followeth

ye Sloop named . . . . . apparel and furniture £75. 0. 0
5. 0. 0
=========
£80. 0. 0

Given into our hands this. . day Janry 1721. Fr Martin, Graves Pack, Evan Morgan
Jn Jones Feb 9 1721
This invry & Appraisal of Thos Hubbard decd was presented in Court and admitted to record. Phi Lightfoot ClCur

In Obedince to an order of the Court ... . . . Subscribers being Summoned and have admitted ye estate of Alexander Atkinson decd as followeth vizt
£16. 8. 0
In Witness thereof. . . . .

Page 107
Know all men by these presents that we Matt. Pierce Benj. Weldon and Robt Cobbs of ye County of York are bound and firmly bound unto ye worshipfull ye Justices of ye County aforesaid in ye Sum of three hundred pounds Sterling payable to ye Justices their heirs and Successors or some of them to which payment well and truly be made We bind ourselves and every of us our and every of us our and every of our heirs Execrs Adms Joyntly and Severally firmly by these presents Sealed with our Seals this 19th day of Feb 1721

The Condition of this Obligation is such that if the above bounden Matthew Pierce Exctr of the last will and testament of John Stewart decd to make or Cause to be made a true and perfect inventory of all and singular ye Goods Chattles and credits of ye sd decd or into ye hands or possessions of any other person or persons for him and ye same to make or exhibit or cause to be exhibited unto ye County court of York at such time as he shall be thereunto by ye sd court and ye same Goods Chattles and Credits and all other ye Goods Chattles and Credits of ye said decd by time of his death which at anytime after shall come to ye hands or possessions of him ye sd Excr or into ye hands or possessions of any person or person for him to well and truly admin of according to Law and further do make a true and just account of his actings and doings therein when thereto required by ye sd Cocurt and also pay all Legacys contained and Specyfied in ye sd testament of ye Goods Chattles and Credits will

thereunto extend to ye value thereof and ye Law shall charge him then this Obligation to be void or else remain in full force and virtue
Feb 19th 1721. Matt Pierce, Benj Weldon, Robt Cobbs.
This bond was presented in Court and acknowledged by ye persons thereto and was admitted to record. Test Phi Lightfoot ClCur

Know all men by these presents that we Wm Cross Jos Mountfort and Wm Gordon of ye County of York are held and firmly bound to ye Worshipfull ye Justices of ye County aforesaid in ye Sum of Sixty pounds Sterling payable to ye sd Justices their heirs and Successors or some of them to whi. payment well and truly to be made We bind ourselves and every of us our and every of our heirs Execrs and Admns Joyntly Severally firmly by these presents Sealed with our Seals and dated this 19th day of Febry 1721

The condition of this Obligation is such that whereas ye above bounden Wm Cross at a Court held for York County this day became admin of Lucy Hill orphan of Thomas Hill decd and hath recd into his Custody ye whole estate of ye sd orphan know ye therefore that ye sd Wm Cross do well and by virtue of ye trust hath undertaken relative to ye sd orphan and her estate and pay or Cause to be paid her full due according to Law and Custom when she attains to lawfull age or sooner ye Court shall sit from time to time and at all times hereafter shall save . . . . . ye sd justices their heirs &c from all damaged that shall or may occur to any of them concerning ye sd estate and perform all other things enjoyed by Law and members of this Court Then this Obligation to be void otherwise remain in full force and virtue. Feb 19th 1721 Wm Cross, Ben Weldon, Wm Gordon. This obligation was presented in Court and submitted by these presents and admitted to record. Test Phi Lightfoot ClCur

. . . . . that he may be discharged from being
. . . . . late Sarah Goodwin for a probate of
. . . . that ye Sheriff summon ye sd John
. . . . ye sd petition (Margin says Jackson & Mundell)

. . . . . Worley decd Edw Worley is appointed
.................her estate is committed to his care (Worley appt guardian)

. . . . . Robinson adjudged to be eleven. (Margin says Robertson.)

Page 108
The attachment obtained by James Bacchus agt ye estate of Jno. Bates for ye Sum of Fifty four pounds two shillings and Eight pence Sterling & costs by means of ye sd Bates Suffering Judgement logs agt him at ye Suit of Robt Tucker for ye sd Sum being returned on three Negroes to wit Will Harry &

Cesar. Judgement is granted agt ye sd Bacchus for ye aforesaid Sum and its ordered that Sam Cobbs Robt Cobbs Ralph Graves or Matt Pierce or any three of them by Some justice of ye sd County appraise ye sd negroes and deliver them or so much thereof as is sufficent satisfy ye sd debt & Costs to ye sd Bacchus unless ye sd Bates will replevin ye same and make report thereof to ye next Court until when ye attachment is further continued

The attachement obtained by James Bacchus against ye estate of Jno. Bates for ye Sum of Fifty five pounds two shillings and ten pence Sterling and costs by means of ye sd Bates Suffering judgement to go agt him at ye suit of Jno. Tucker for ye said Sum being returned Executed on three negroes to wit Grace Sucy and Sarah judgement is granted ye sd Bacchus for ye aforesaid Sum and its ordered that Sam Cobbs Robt Cobbs Ralph Graves Matt Pierce or any three of them being sworn by some Justice of the County appraise ye sd negores and deliver them or so much as is sufficient to satisfy ye sd debt and Costs to ye sd Bacchus unless ye sd bates will replevin ye same and make report therof to ye next Court when ye attachment is further continued

The pet of Robert Roberts praying that his share of ye estate of Jno. . . . . . decd now in ye hands of Mary ye wife of Wm Atkinson may be . . . . . to him it is ordered that ye Sheriff Sumon ye said Mary to answer ye said petiton at ye next Court.

In ye petition of Jas Bates praying that John Bates exectr of ye last will and Testament of Jno. Bates decd may give an account of his administration on ye said decd estate it is ordered that ye Sheriff Summon ye sd John to appear and render an acct accordingly at ye next Court.

On ye petiton of Henry Hacker agt his sd Servant Wm Bond for running away it appearing that ye sd Hacker did . . . . . Seven hundred and eleven pounds of tobacco in retaking him and that he was absent r thirty five days. It is ordered that he serve his sd master . . . . . months for ye same after his time by Indenture custom or former custom is required

. . . . . aus a Negro girl belonging to D. . Lamb is adjudged to be nine years old

Dick a negro boy belonging to Ann Alleus is adjudged to be nine years old

Sarah a Negro girl belonging to Ann Alleus is adjudged to be twelve years old

The last will an testament of Jno. Stewart decd was presented in Court by Matt Pierce ye Exctr Oath to it and being proved . . . . . witnesses therto is admitted to record . . . . . Benj Weldon & Robt Cobb . . . . . bond to ye court for ye due

Execution of ye . . . . . to record a certificate is admitted to probate. . . . . due form . . . . . decd was presented in Court. . . . made oath to it and being proved . . . . . Robinson & Jno. Powers his Security . . . . . thereof

Page 109
James Bacchus Jonathon Drewit Thos Cobbs and Robt Crawley or any three of them being sworn are appointed to appraise ye estate of Jno. Stewart decd and make report thereof to ye next court

On ye petition of Lucy Hill orphan of Thos Hill decd Wm Cross is appointed her Guardian who having given Security according to Law It is ordered that ye said orphan and her estate be committed to ye care of ye sd Wm Cross

Anthony Robinson Robert Kerby Thos Kerby and Wm Wise or any three of them being Sworn are appointed to appraise ye estate of Wm Tavernor decd and make report to ye next Court

The petition of Wm Tavernor agt ye Execrs of Peter Manson is rejected

The action of debt between Joseph Stacy and Jno. Welch and David Holloway defents neither partys appearing is dismist

The action of detinue between Thos Toomer plt and Saml Tompkins deft upon ye Sheriffs return non est inventus is dismist

The action of case between Elizabeth Powers plt and Thos Hubert deft is dismist

In ye action of debt between James Faison plt and Danl Taylor brother deft heir of Henry Taylor late of Charles parish decd deft at ye deft mon an Imparlance is granted him until ye next Court

The accon upon ye case between Robt Innis plt and Thos Bell deft is dismist

The accon of debt between Lewis Delony plt & Jno. Mundell deft neither party appearing is dismist

The accon of debt between Lewis Delony plt & Jno. Battles deft for One pound two shillings due by note ye deft being called and not appearing nor any Security being retnd for him on ye plts mon Judgement is granted him agt Fra Tyler ye Sheriff of ye County for ye sum and Costs unless ye deft appears at ye next court and answers ye sd action

The action of debt between Lewis Delony plt & Fra Young deft is dismist

The action of case between Lewis Delony plt & Wm Ingram deft neither party appearing is dismist

The action upon ye case between Danl Stoner plt & Jno. Mundall & Sus Sebrell Excrs &c of Nath Sebrell decd at ye deft mon an Imparlance is granted until ye next Court

On ye Action of ye case between Cornelius Cormack plt & Andrew Laprade deft on ye deft mon an Imparlance is granted until ye next court

In ye action upon ye case between Jno. Randolph plt & Joseph Stcy deft for twent Shillings due for presenting an action of case in behalf of ye deft agt Robt Ross in York County Court ye deft being called and not appearing nor any Security being ret... . . . judgement is granted him agt Wm Gordon Sheriff of this County for ye. . . . . appears at ye next Court and answers ye sd action

In ye action between Jos Stacy plt & Barth Burcher deft neither party appearing is dismist

(Moodys pet dismist)

. . . . . Eliza Kane for running away
. . . . . twenty five months and that she
. . . . hundred twenty six pounds of
. . . she serve her sd Master five years
. . . days after her time by indenture custom (Margin says Thompson's servant fined)

... . . . acknowledged her deed of gift for two negroes
... . . . Pescod and George Pescod her children
. . . record (Fournham's deed for negroes)

... . . . rton genl testees (?) &c trustees for ye land appraised . . . . . ye City of Williamsburgh ... . . . presented & acknowledged . . . . . four lotts of the sd land with receipts . . . . . they are admitted to record (Drewitt trustees deed)

Page 110
Manson decd and admitted to Record (top line and margin are illeg.)

John Lewellin and Mary his wife presented & acknowledged their deed for land &c bond for performance of Covenents to John Johnson and ye sd Mary being privately examined relinquished her right of dower therin which deed bond and release are at sd Johnson's mon admitted to record

The action of case between George Allen plt & Francis Sharpe deft is cont until next Court

The accon of debt between Essex Weller plt & Eliza Ives deft is cont by consent until next Court

The action of debt between Wm Levingston plt and Essex Weller deft is continued by consent until ye next Court

Wm Haughton is appointed Head borough for ye upper precinct of Charles Parish in ye room of John Bond Ordered that he repair to Some justice of ye County to take ye usual Oath

In ye action upon ye case between Mary Fruison Excectr of ye last will and testament of William Fruison decd plt against John James Flournoy & Mary his wife Excr of the last will and testament of Olando Jones decd for thirteen pounds four shillings and seven pence halfpenny due on balance of accts proved . . . . . judgement is granted plt for ye sd Sum and ordered that . . . . . ye said Sum and costs of . . . . . estate if so much they have (*much of center of page missing*)

. . . . . Ness's Estate Lawr Smith having decl- . . (*missing*) hands ye atta is discontinued . . . . . is cont agt George Allen (Ness estate) . . . . . Shield plt & Sam Sweny . . . . hath time allowed . . . untill next Court. . . . . Hubbard decd was presented . . . admitted to record

Jn Mundell. . . . . to exhibit an Inventory (Mundell's Est to be appr)

The action . . . . . ton by Richd Haughton
Her next. . . . . party appearing is dismist (Haughton & Rhodes)

. . . . . Jacquline Excr (Charles & Jacqueline cont)

Page 111
of the sd Joseph

In ye action of debt between Susannah Townsend plt & James Faison deft the deft came personally into court confessed judgement to ye plt for one pound two shillings and nine pence ordered that ye deft pay ye same to ye plt with costs als Exo

In ye action of debt between John James plt & Thos Nash deft for two pounds one shilling and five pence both psrtys having submitted ye difference to ye Courts determination who upon hearing ye evidence were of Judgement for ye deft whereupon its ordered that ye plt pay costs als Exo

The action upon ye Case between Edw Spark plt & Joseph Berry def Issue being joined for tryall next Court

Joseph Freeman in open Court presented and Acknowledged his deeds for lands lying in Williamsburgh and recx thereon to Thomas Jones and Dorcas wife of the sd Joseph being privately examined voluntarily released her right of dower in ye sd lands which sd deeds &c release are at ye sd Jones' mon admitted to record

On ye action of debt between James Shields plt and Wm Robertson deft the plt hath time allowed him to consider ye def plea

In the petition of David Walker agt Thos Lark & Mary his wife Excr &c of Flo. McHarty decd upon hearing ye partys ordered that ye pet be dismist

The pet of Andrew Laprade agt John Mundall & Sus Sebrell Excrs of Nath Sebrell decd is dismist

The action of trespass on ye case between Petr Brewer plt & Henr Swinsin def neither party appearing is dismist

The accon on the case between Phi Lightfoot plt & Lawr. Smith deft is cont by consent

In ye accon of trespass on ye case between Richd Needham plt and Sam Read deft for £ 20 damages ye att is further cont till ye next Court

In ye accon upon ye case between Thos Toomer plt and Edw Tabb & Eliza Hayward Execrs &c of Henry Hayward decd deft for Sixteen pounds current money due on balance of acc ye deft failing to plead Judgement is granted ye plt by Nihil Dict conformable at ye next Court on ye like default

The accon of debt between . . (*miss.*) Sweny plt & Lews Delony plt is cont by consent

The suit in Chancery. . (*missing*) Jno. Hay & Mary his wife Compl & Thos Toomer surviving Excr &c of Su Toomer decd respond is continued till next Court to examine witnesses

On ye pet of Robt Clark agt his servant Thos Compris for running away It is ordered that the serve his said Master One year four months and eleven days for absent time and charges in returning him after his time by Indenture custom or further order is expired

Wm Lake gave Evidence for Thos. . . . the suit of John James having . . . . . two days on his mon is ordered that the sd Nash pay . . . . . pounds of Tobacco for the same and cost als Exo

Jane Lake . . . . . evidence for Thos . . (*missing*) of Jno James having . . (*missing*) on her mon it is ordered the sd Nash pay her . . . . .

(margin says Blair & Drewit Judgement)

(margin says Cobbs & Sutton & Walker Judgement) . . (visible is *...Joseph Sutton deft.)*

Page 112
Judgement being confirmed this day agt Joseph Walker Gent for the Sum of three pounds ten shillings and Seven pence fee & Costs by means of the non-appearance of Joseph Sutton at the suit of Saml Cobbs on the mon of the sd Walker an attachment is granted him agt the sd Suttons estate for the sd Sum & Costs returnable to the next Court for Judgement

In the accon on the case between Wm Livingston plt & Thos Wyatt deft for twent seven shillings & Six pence by accd proved Judgement is granted plt for the sd Sum and Costs & ordered that the same be paid out of the defts estate appraised in the hands of Richd Baker & The actte. discontinued

Ordered that the Court be adjourned until the Court in Course. Signed Thos Nelson. Truly Ent by Phi Lightfoot ClCur

March 14 1721
In obedience to an order of Court bearing date of 19th Febry 1721
Wee ye Subscribers have mett and appraised ye estate of Wm Tavernor decd as followeth ... Wm Tavernor Excr (X his mark) , Anthony Robinson, Robert Kerby, Wm Wise
March 19 1721

An Inventory ad... . . .

Page 113
Know all men by these presents that we Robt Cobbs Matt Peirce & Wm Stone of ye County of York are held and firmly bound unto ye Worshipfull ye Justices of ye County aforesaid in ye Sum of One Hundred pounds Sterling to which payment well & truly to be made to ye sd Justices their heirs and Successors or

some of them we bind our Selves and every of us our heirs Exectrs & Admins Joyntly and Severally firmly by these presents Sealed with our Seals and dated this 19th day of March 1721

The condition of this Obligation is such that if ye above bounden Robt Cobbs adm with ye will annexed of all Goods Chattels and Credits of Richd Page decd do make or Cause to be made a true and perfect Inventory of all and Singular ye Goods Chattels and Credits of ye said decd which have or shall Come to ye hands or possessions of any other person or persons of him or ye same so made do Exhibit or cause to be exhibited into ye County Court of York at such time as he shall be thereunto required by ye said Court and by ye same goods Chattels and Credits and all other Goods Chattels & Credits of him ye sd decd at ye time of his death which at any time after Shall Come to ye hands or possessions of him ye d Exectr or into ye hands or possessions of any person or persons for him to well and truly administer according to law and further do make a true and Just Their heirs and successors account of his actings and doings therein when thereto required by ye said Court abd also well and truly pay and deliver all ye Legacys contained and specified in ye said testament as far as ye said Goods Chattels or Credits thereunto . . . . . end according to ye value thereof and ye Law . . . . . this Obligation to be void or else remain in full force and virtue. Robt Cobbs Jun, Matt Peirce, Wm Stone.
This bond was presented in Court and acknowledged by ye partys and is admitted into Record test Phi Lightfoot ClCur

. . . . . these presents that we Frances Mallicote Thomas Tomer & Jno. Drewery .
. . . . are held and firmly bound to ye worshipfull ye Justices of York County...
hundred pounds Sterling to ye which payment well and truly to be made . . . their heirs and Successors or some of them we bind ourselves and
every... . . . and every of our heirs Exectrs and adms jointly and Severally firmly
. . . . . . Sealed with our Seals and dated this 19th day of March 1721
. . . this obligation is such that the above bounden Frances Mallicote
. . . of Wm . . (*missing*) te decd do make or cause to be made
. . . knowledge of her ye sd
. . . . persons for her and ye same so
. . . . . to ye County Court of York at such time as she
. . . . and ye same Goods Chattels and Credits
. . . . . at ye time of his death which at any time
. . . . . possessions of her ye said Admin or into ye Hands of
. . . . (Much of rest of page is incomplete. No names until signature. (margin says (Mallincote's bond Adm)) Fra (X) Mallincote, Thos Tomer, John Drewery.

Page 114

An Inventory and appraisement of ye estate of John Steward decd
£ 14. 10. 5 ¾
These things that follow are Se. . . . . left by will of George Brown & John Steward and Jos. . . . . White decd to George White -
To Peter Cordery . . . . . cloathes
To John Haythorn Ditto
To Math Peirce Riding Coat and Black Stockings
To Wm Peirce a Sorrel Horse
. . . . . obedience to an order of York Court . . . . . febry We ye Subscribers being first sworn before Mr Henry Tyler our. . (*missing*) Justices for ye sd County . . . . . . appraised all ye estate of John Stewart decd. . . Wm Peirce his executor . . (*missing*) Druet . . . Matt Pierce . . . mes Blackhurst, Robt Crawley, Thos Cobbs
March 1721 . . (*missing.*) estate of Jon Steward. . . . admitted to record. test Phi Lightfoot ClCur

Know all me by theses presents. . (*missing*) Lawr Smith& Phi Lightfoot
Of ye County of York. . (*missing*) to ye Worshipfull ye Justices of
Ye said County in ye . . . . and Sterling by which payment
Well and truly to be made...... their heirs and successors or
Some of them Wee bind ... ... of us our and every of our
Heirs Exectrs and Admnrs....... ...firmly by these presents sealed
With our Seals and dat. . . ch 1721
The condition of this O. . . . . bounden Thos. Nelson
(margin says Nelsons bond admon Butler)

Page 115
ye goods Chattels and Credits of ye said decd which have or shall Come to ye hands possession or knowledge of him ye said Adm or into ye hands or possessions of any other person or persons for him and ye same so made to exhibit or cause to be exhibited into ye County Court of York at such time as he shall thereunto required by ye said court and ye Same Goods Chattles and Credits and all other Goods Chattels and Credits of ye said decd at ye time of his death which at anytime after shall come to ye hands or possessions of him ye sd Admin or unto ye hands or possession of any other person or persons for him Do well and truly administer according to Law and further do make a true and Just Account of his actings & Doings therein when thereto required by ye sd Court and all ye rest and Residue of ye sd Goods Chattles and Credits which shall be found remaining upon ye administrators acct. ye same being first examined by ye Justices of ye said Court for ye time being shall deliver and pay unto such persons or persons as ye said justices by their order or judgement shall direct pursuant to y Law in Such Case made and provided and it shall hereafter appear that any last will & Testament was made by ye sd decd and ye Exrs or Execrs therein named do exhibit ye same unto ye sd admin being thereto required do

render upon his letters of admon approbation of such . . (*missing*) being first had in ye said Court Then this Obligation to be void otherwise remain in full force and virtue. . (*missing*) 1721. Thos Nelson, Lawr. Smith, Phi Lightfoot. ... . . . presented in Court & Admitted to record. test Phi Lightfoot ClCur

. . . . . presents that we Robt La. . (*missing*) Robert Ballard & Wm Levingston of ye . . (*missing*held and firmly bound . . Sovereign Lord ye King in ye Sum of . . . pounds of Tobacco Convenient in ye County of York to which . . . truly be made to our Sovereign Lord . . . bind ourselves and every of us . . . of our heirs Execrs and admin jointly and Severally firmly by these . . . with our Seals & Dated this 19th day of March 1721

The Condition of this Obligation is such that whereas ye above bounden Robt Laughton has this day granted him a lycense to keep an ordinary at his now dwelling in Williamsburgh for the year next Ensuing if therefore ye sd . . . . . constantly provide Good wholesome and Cleanly lodging . . . for travellors and stableage or provender or pasturage and provender {as the season shall require) for their horses ye date of these presents for and during . . . . . . any unlawful gaming in his said house nor suffer . . . to tipple or drink more than is necessary than this Obligation . . . remain in full force and virtue Robt Laughton Will Levinston, Robt Ballard . . . . . . and acknowledged . . admitted to record. test Phi Lightfoot ClCur

. . . . . that we Robt Wills Wm Gordon & Henry Bowcock of ye County . . . . . bound to our Sovereign Lord ye kind in ye Sum of ten Thousand (Tobacco) . . . County of York to which payment well and truly be made . . . bind ourselves and-

Page 116

and every of us our and every of our heirs Execrs and admins Joyntly and Severally firmly by these presents Sealed with our Seals and dated this 19 day of March 1721

The condition of this Obligation is such that whereas ye above bounden Robt Wills hath and order this day granted him for a Lycense to keep an Ordinary at his now dwelling house in York Town for ye year next ensuing If therefore ye said Robt doth constantly provide food and provender in his ordinary Good wholesome and Cleanly lodging and. . . . . and Stableage and provender or pasturage and provender as ye season shall require for their horses from ye date of these presents for and during the term of one year and shall not suffer any unlawful gaming in his said house nor on ye Sabath day Suffer any person to tipple or drink more than is necessary Then this obligation to be void or else

remain in full force and virtue. Robt Wills, Wm Gordon, H Bowcock 19 March 1721
This bond was presented in Court and acknowledged by ye persons thereto and is admitted to record. Test Phi Lightfoot ClCur

In ye name of God Amen ye 20 day of Janry 1721 I Richd Page being sick and weak but of perfect sence Sense and memory praised be almighty God do make and ordain this to be my last Will and testament in manner following first revoking all other wills and testaments made and for all such estate as it hath pleased God to bless me with First my debts and funeral charges paid I bestow as followeth Vizt Imprimis . . bequesth to my son Richd page . . . . . of Land to him and his heirs for ever and my wi. . . . . is that all ye rest of . . . . . be equally divided between my said son Richard and . . . . . Winifred Page and to their heirs forever And lastly I . . . . . my two friends Thomas Dickson and Matt . . (*missing*) Execrs of this my last will and testament In witness whereof I have set my hand and Seal ye day and year first written. Richd (P) Page. Signed Sealed and Published in presence. . (*mis.*) Dav ... ton. . (*missing*) Court held for York County 19 Feb 1721. . . . . was presented in Court
. . . . . proved by ye Oaths of... (*miss*) Winifred Ashby is admitted to record... test Phi Lightfoot ClCur

At a Court for York County this 14 day of March 1721. Wm Sheldon, Thos Chisman

The Governours Conc. . . . . ye Justices for ye County Aforesaid or any four. . . . . and determine all reasons Felonys Murders or. . . . or done by Guy a Negro Slave belonging to . . . and ye sd Justices Having taken ye Oaths . . . ye test pro= (Lansfords negro tried)

Page 117

Guy a Slave belonging to . . . . . and arraigned For that he ye said Guy on ye said. . . . Febry last about ye 7th hour in the night of ye same day at ye parish of York Hampton in ye County of York wth force and arms ye Mansion house of one Matthew Morland feloniously did break and enter and two bushels of Indian Corn of ye value of 5 s lawfull money of England of ye Goods and Chattles of ye sd Matthew Morland then and there did feloniously Steal take and Carry away and ye sd Guy on his arraignment having pleaded not guilty ye court having heard ye evidence were of opinion that ye said Guy is guilty of ye stands accused from but for as much value of ye goods stole doth not amount to more than 12 d Sterling therefore it is adjudged and accordingly ordered that he receive 39 lashes at ye common whipping post well laid on and thence be continued in prison until ye 19th instant and then receive 20 lashes more and afterward discharged. Truly entered by Phi Lightfoot ClCur

At a court held for York County 19th March 1721. Present John Holloway Thos Nelson, Henr Tyler, Thos Chisman, Lawr Smith, Wm Sheldon, Graves Pack, Gent.

The . . . . . rates of . . . . . only adding English Cider at 1 s bottle
. . . . . Virgin. . . . (Rates of Liquors set)
. . . . . assembly . . Court do nominate and recommend
. . . . . Governour...Smith Thomas Nelson and Willm Sheldon Gent Justices as person . (. *missing*) and capable to execute ye office of Sheriff...County for ye coming year (Sheriffs Recommended)

Ordered that ye Sheriff Summon 2. . (*missing*) holders of ye County to appear at the next Court . . (*missing*) Grand Jury

Henry Bryan is appointed Constable in ye City of Williamsburgh in this County. . . (*missing*) that he repair to some Justice of ye County & take ye usual Oath
On ye. . . . . of Christopher Jackson against John Mundal setting. . . . . together with Mongo Ingles stood bound together with Sarah Godwin Executrix of Jacob Godwin decd for her administration of . . . . . Sarah having since intermarried . . (*missing*) ye sd estate of ye said Mundell . . . . . failing to appear it is therefore of ye opinion of ye . . . . . ordered that ys sd Mundall Surrender up . . . . . Godwin decd appraised by ye former appr. Als Exo. . . . . Balir Exr of ye last Will and testament of Mongo Inglis decd. . . . . together with Christopher Jackson because Security for Sarah . . . . . tion of Jacob Godwins estate who hath since intermarried . . . . . ye sum and praying that . . (*missing)* Joyntly with ye said Jackson
. . . . . Christopher Jackson having already obtained an . . . . . for ye sd Surrender of ye whole estate of. . . . .
(margin says Jackson Mundall pet & then Blair Mundall pet) . . *both notations probably related)*

Page 118
. . . . . as being Security with ye said Sarah Godwin for ye sd Jacobs Estate . . (*missing* upon ye sd Jackson doth hereby assign over his sd order agt.
Ye sd Mundall. . . . . ye sd Jacob's Estate to ye petitioner

On ye petition setting forth that Mary ye relict of Jno. West decd has recd Diverse Considerable Sums of mony since ye said death which are not inserted in ye Invtry of his estate exhibited by ye said Mary to ye prejudice of Mary an orphan of ye sd John's under ye case of her said Mother & praying that Mary ye mother may give a true account of her admon that it may appear how much ye sd orphan is entitled to it is ordered that ye Sheriff Summon ye said Mary ye Mother to appear and answer ye sd petition at ye next Court (margin says Davis West pet)

Thomas Nelson Came into Court and made oath that Walter Butler decd died without making any will so far as he knows or believes and Mary relict of ye decd having relinquished her right of dower on ye sd decds estate ye said Thomas Nelson together with Phi Lightfoot and Law Smith his Securities entered into and acknowledged their bond to the Court for his Just and faithfull admon of ye said Estate which bond is admitted to record and on his motion Certficate is granted for obtaining letters of admon in due form

A Commission of Peace & dedireus from ye Honr. Ye Lieut Governor being read as Usual John Holloway Henry Tyler Law Smith Thos Nelson & Archibald Blair gent having taken ye Oaths and . . . . . by ye said dedirius Henry Tyler & Thomas Nelson administered ye said Oaths and test to Thomas Chisman Graves Pack Wm Sheldon Wm Stark and Edw Tabb Gent & then took their places on ye Bench. Jno. Hollway Henry Tyler Lawr Smith Thos Nelson . . . . . . Thos Chisman Graves Pack Wm Sheldon . . . . . . Edw Tabb

The last Will and Testament of . (*missing*) presented in Court and being proved by the Oaths of David . . . . . was admitted to record & Matlik. . . . . and Thomas Dickson . . . . . having refused to undertake *ye* . . . . . of ye execution of sd testament Robt Cobbs came into Court and made Oath that he know. . . . . other than ye above mentioned will made by ye decd Richd Page and having together with Math Pierce & Wm Stone his Securitys enetered into and acknowledged their bond in Court for his Just and faithfull administration of ye said estate which bond is admitted to record On his Motion Certificate is granted him for obtaining letters of admon with ye will annext on ye decedents . . . . due form

Wm Cross . . (*missing*) Gibbons Jno. Potter . . (*missing*) ston or any three of them being Sworn are appointed to appraise . . (*missing*) Butler decd and make report thereof at Court

John Chapman Benj. . (*missing*) or any three of them being sworn . . (*missing*) of Jane Cully decd & Make report to ye next Court

Jn Daniel & Jno. Davis . . (*missing*) or any three of them being Sworn are appoint to appr ye estate of Richd Page . . . . . rep thereof to ye next Court

An Inventry and app. . . . . Tavernor decd was exhibited in Court and admitted to record

(Sharp's ordinary Lycence rejected)

(Steward's Inv returned)

Page 119
In ye Suit in Chancery between J. . (*missing*) of James Godwin decd Compl and Mary Read respond ye Court having fully heard ye arguments ordere that ye demurrer dismist . . Compl bill

In ye action upon ye case between . . (*missing*) Goodwin plt & Lawr Smith & Mildred his wife late Mildred Goodwin deft Consent of both parties ye cause is referred to Joseph Walker Thos Nelson and Richd Ambler former auditors to Audit estate and Settle all matters relating to the . . *missing.*

The action upon the Case between Sa. . (*missing*) (poss Cobbs) plt & Rob Fannock is dismist

The action upon the case between . . w. . Thomas plt & Jno. Jones adm of ye Goods Chattels of Thomas Hubbard decd neither part appearing is dismist

The action of Case between Jno. Hansford plt & Jno. Jones admr of ye Goods & Chattels of Thomas Hubbard decd is dismist

The action of debt between Jno. Hansford plt and John Jones admr of ye Goods and Chattels of Thomas Hubbard decd deft is dismist

The action of Case between . . (*missing*) Brown plt and Wm Biggs and Mary his wife adminr of John Brown decd deft is dismist

The action of debt between . . . . . Powers plt & James Filler deft is dismist

The action of debt between . . . . . & James Filler & Antho Tite defts is dismist

The action of . . . . . Richd Baker deft is dismist (Gordon- Baker)

The action of. . . . . Wm Downs is dismist (Swinnock- Downs)

The action between. . . . . Read deft is dismist (Martin - Read)

In ye . . . . . Hansford deft ye deft appear. . . . . three pounds . . (*missing*) Shillings Ordered that . . . . . Costs als Exo (Welch - Hansford Judgement)

. . . . . Welch plt and Richd Turner deft for five pounds. . . . . being called and not appearing on plts mon . . . . . Geo Fuller Secry for ye sd Sum and Costs

In ye action . . . . . plt & Wm Levingston deft for forty pounds due by . . (*missing*) Joseph Walker becoming Security for ye plt . . . . . called and not appearing on ye plts mon . . . . . Fran Tyler Sheriff for ye said Sum and . . . . . like defaul (Winter-Levingston)

. . . . . Brooks plt and Wm Levingston deft for . . (*missing*) Lightfoot became Security for payment of Costs . . . . . appearing on ye plt motion Judgement is granted . . (*missing*) agt Fra Tyler Sheriff Confirmable at ye next Court on. . . (Brooks - Levingston)

In ye action . . . . . Mary West plt & John Davis deft for Seven pounds fourteen Shil. . (*missing*) half penny on ye defts mon an Imparlance is granted him until……

The action. . . . . Bates plt & Anna Maria Timson deft is dismist

The action of. . . . . Bates plt & Saml Millington deft is dismist

. . . . . between Benj Weldon plt & Wm Long deft is dismist

. . . . . plt and James Minzie deft for two . . . . . deft ebing called and not appearing . . . . . him agt Fra Tyler Sheriff for ye sd (Lightfoot - Minzie)

Page 120
. . . . . Lycence ot keep and ordinary is rejected (Margin appears to say Smith)

. . . . . wife of Wm Atkinson hath further time allowed her to exhibit an Inv of Eliza Moody's estate & To give Security for her admon thereon and on Phi's. . (*missing*) Estate

Mary West . . . . . by ye Grand Jury for having a Mullatto bastard having been taken into Custody and not appearing It is ordered that the Sheriff pay her fine unless ye said West appears and answers ye presentment aforesaid at ye next Court

Richd King presented by ye grand Jury for not going to Church is fined five shillings and ordered thus to ye Same to ye Churchwardens of Bruton Parish at their next levy . . . . .

Wm Rogers presented by ye grand Jury for not going to Church on his appearance is discharged paying fees

Joseph Frith presented by ye Grand Jury for not going to church on his pet is discharged paying fees

Ezekiel Gilbert presented by ye G Jury for Swearing is fined five Shillings ord. that he pay same to ye Churchwardens of Yorkhampton at their next levy with costs als Exo

The former order . . . . . Eliz Griffin into Custody is continued

Jane Pain presented . . . . . for having a bastard Child failing to appear ordered that ye said Pain . . . . . her Security pay ye to ye Churchwardens of ye . . . . . next Levy with Costs als Exo

In ye action . . . . . Allen plt and Fra Sharpe deft for £1. 15 . . . . . desired ye Court to take upon them ye . . . . . ye evidences and plts oath were . . . . . pay unto ye plt ye said Sum of one pound . . (*miss*) fee & costs als exo

The att. . . . . is Cont. for Examination of Ness's. . . . . to pay what he is Chad. therein (Gilbert - Ness)

The accon. . . . . Powers deft is Cont until next Court. (Jones - Powers)

The Accon. . . . . Wm Biggs def is dismist. (Clifton - Biggs)

In ye ac. . . . . Armiger Parson & Eliza his wife Compltss and J. . . . . ye rept of ye Auditors is ordered to be referred. . . . . (Parsons - Hay Cont.)

The action. . . . . Bell deft is cont until next Court. (Lightfoot - Bell)

In ye pet. . . . . & Wm Palmer on hearing ye parties. . . . . (Stringer - Palmer)

Richd Bellamie. . . . . agt ye pet of Edw Stringer having attended . . . . . pay him forty pounds of tobacco for. . . . .

John Southerland . . . . . having attended 4 days ordered that. . . . . Hundre & Sixty pounds of Tobacco for ye same and. . . . .

Edwd Clark on Evidence . . . . . agt Wm Palmer having attended 4 days ord ye sd Stringer . . . . . tobacco and costs als Exo

The pet of Jno. Hay. . . . . is dismist deft having given fresh Security (Hay - Mallieste)

On ye pet of Sam Hyde. . . . . may be released fm being Security for Elinor Thebos admon . . . . . it is ordered that ye sd estate be surrendered . . . . . fresh Security at ye next Court

John Wills. . . . . deeds of. . . . . (Hayward from Will deed ack)

Page 121
Jn Wills presented and acknowledged . . . . . which at her motion is admitted . . . . . (Hayward fm Wills bond)

The action of trespass of ass. & battry between . . . . . plt & Wm Ferguson is dismist (Power - Ferguson)

An atta. being granted Henry Bowcock against ye estate of Joseph Freeman for three pounds was retern'd executed on a Cow Claimed by Fran Young By Consent the determination was submitted to ye Court who upon hearing ye evidence were of opinion that ye cow is ye property of ye said Fran Young whereupon it is ordered that ye attachment be continued and ye Cow delivered to ye said Young paying two shillings . . . . for her keeping

The action of debt between. (*mis.*) Turner & Law Wilson neither party appearing is dismist

The aacon of debt between Lawr Smith plt & Eliza Hansford deft on Apper. [*appeal*?] is dismist

The action of case between Jms Lewis plt & Arch Blair deft is dismist

The action of case between Jams Lewis plt & Wm Spruce deft is dismist no appear.

The action of Case between Eliza Hansford plt & Law Smith deft is dismist

In ye action of debt between . . . . . Pratt Gent plt & Rich King deft for three pounds one Shilling. . . . . is granted ye plt for ye sd sum and ordered that ye deft . . . costs als Exo

On ye acc. . . . . Pratt Gentl plt & Wm Levingston deft for ten pounds . . . . . due on balance of accounts Judgement is granted ye plt for . . . . . that ye deft pay ye same with costs als Exo

In ye accon. . . . . Gntl plt & Fran Sharp deft for four pounds seven shillings. . . . . ye deft came personally into Court and confessed . . (*whereupon*) it is ordered that ye deft pay ye same . . . . . (Pratt -Sharp)

In ye ... Pratt Gentl plt and Robt Clark deft for two pounds one. . . . . by note ye deft came into Court & Confessed Judgement to ye plt . . . . . ordered that he pay ye same to ye plt wth. Costs als Exo

In ye accon ... Pratt gentl plt and Jno. Hubbard deft for four pounds thirteen ... due by note ye deft come into court & confessed Judgement to ye plt for ye sd Sum ... (*missing*) its ordered that ye deft pay ye same to ye deft with Cost als Exo
. . . . . & Hugh Norvel deft is dismist (Pratt-Norvel)
. . . . . Ferguson plt & Jno. Power deft is dismist
. . . . . Gibbs adm of Edwd. Loftis decd plt & Barth Burcher deft on ye ... imparlance is granted him until next Court

In ye suit in. . . . . between Archibald Blair Complt & Jno. Mundall respond ye respond ... failing to appear at ye Complt mon an att is . . . . . returnable to ye next Court

The action of. . . . . Mattock plt & Jos Thomas deft is dismist

In ye action . . . . . Sampson plt & Danl. Mackentosh and Martha his wife . . . . . last will and testament of Cha Haines decd for . . . . . both parties Submitted ye difference to ye Courts. . . . . ye Sum of two pounds and Costs

Page 122
In ye accon of debt between Robt Cross plt & Mary Reynolds deft is dismist

In ye case between Andrew Laprade plt & Jno Mundal deft is dismist

In ye accon of debt between John Daniel plt and Jno. Bates Excr of ye last will and testament of Jno. Bates decd at ye mon of ye deft an Imparlance is granted him until next Court

In ye pet of James Bates praying that Jno Bates may give an acct of his admin on ye Estate of Jno Bates decd by Consent Archbd Blair Mich Archer & Saml Cobbs or any two of them are appointed to examine and Settle ye accounts of ye said estate and make reply thereof to ye next Court

In ye suit of Chancery ensuing between Justinian Love, Elias Love and Eliza Love by Justinian Love their Guardian and next friend Complts and John Fosset

& Eliza his wife Respondt at ye respondts mon ye att agt their bodys is further Cont until next Court

In ye action of debt between James Faison plt and David Taylor brother and heir of Henry Taylor late of . . (*missing*) parish decd deft for thirty pounds current mony ye deft having had time. . (*missing*) him to plead and being called failed to do ye same Judgement is therefore ... Confirmable at ye next Court on ye like default

In ye action of de. . . . . plt & Jno Battles deft for One pound two shillings due . . . . . called and failing to appear ye Judgement of ye last Court ag. ... his Security is Confirmed and ordered that they pay ... with Cost als Exo (Delony - Battles)

In ye action ... and Jno. Mundall & Susa Sebrell Excetrs &c ... pounds One shilling & Six pence due on balance ... allowed him to plead and being Called failed to ... granted by ye plt by Nihil Dicit Confirmable ... (Stoner - Mundal)

In ye action of debt . . . . . plt and Andr. Leprade deft for five pounds agt ye ye deft . . . . . him to plead & being called failed to do ye Same Judgement is therefore granted . . . . . at ye next Court on ye like default (Cormack - Leprade)

In ye action of Case between . . . . . & Joseph Stacy deft for one pound due for prosec. . . . . deft agt Rob Ross in York County Court ye deft Cause per. . . . . Confessed Judgement to ye plt for ye sd Sum Wherefore it is . . . . . same to ye plt wth. Costs als Exo (Randolph - Stacey)

The pet of Robert Roberts . . . . . Wm Atkinson is cont. until next Court

The action of debt . . . . . is cont. (Weller - Ives)

The action of debt . . . . . (Levingston - Weller)

In ye action of Case between. . . . . plt & Saml Sweny Excr &c of Saml Harkin decd def ye def . . . . . to Consider ye plts reply till next Court. (Shield - Sweny)

The att obtained by Jams. . . . . of Jno. Bates for fifty five pounds two Shill & ten pence & ye ordr for app. . . . . Cont until next Court. Bacchus - Bates)

Jn Mundall and Sus. . . . . to exhibit an Invry of Nath Sebrell Est

In ye action of debt. . . . . Executor &c. (Charles - Jacqueline)

Page 123

In ye att ... rry deft ye deft with ... his last plea ... for trial. (Sparks - Berry)

In ye action of debt between James Shield . . . . . Robertson def y def hath time allowed to Consider ye plt reply

The att of Joseph Walker Gent agt ye estate of Joseph Sutton is Cont until next court

The action of Case between Phi Lightfoot plt & Lawr Smith deft is cont until next Court

In ye action of trespass on ye Case between Richd Needham plt and Saml Read deft issue being Joyned ye Cause is referred for trial at ye next Court

In ye action of case between Thos Toomer plt & Edw Tabb & Eliza Hayward Excrs &c of Henry Hayward decd def Issue being Joyned ye Cause is referred for trial at ye next Court

In ye action of debt between Saml Sweny plt & Lewis Delony deft by Consent of both parties Mich. Archer Saml Cobbs and Christopher Jackson or any two of them are appointed to audit and settle all matters between them & Make rept thereof to ye next Court

The Suit in chancery depending between JW Hay & Mary his wife Complts and Thos Toomer Surviving Exctr &c of Jno. Toomer decd repond is continued until next Court

The action of debt between Thos Toomer plt & Saml Tompkins deft is dismist

The action of. . . . . between Wm Cross plt and Mary Reynolds deft is dismist

In ye action. . . . between John Sharp plt & Wm Lake deft for one pound Eight shillings & Six pence deft being called and not appearing nor any Security being returned for him at ye plts motion an. . (*missing*) is granted him a. . (*missing*) estate returnable to ye next Couret for Judgement

In ye action . . (*missing*) between Danl . . (*missing*) and Jno. Mundall and Susa. Sebrell Exctrs &c of Nath Sebrell decd is dismist

The action . . (*missing*) between Law Smith plt & Jno Wooldom deft is dismist

. . . . . plt and Jno. Robertson def for one pound Six Shillings by att . . . . . nor any Security retd for him on ye plts motion Judgement . . . . . Costs agt Fra Tyler Sheriff unless ye deft appears. . . . . (Fannock - Robertson)

The . . . . . battry between . . . Fannock plt & Jno. Brooks deft is dismist

The . . . . . between George Butler plt & Joseph Frith deft is dismist

The ac. . . . . Jno Brown plt & Jno. Crawley deft is dismist

In ye. . . . . between Sarah Sebrell by Jno. Hudson her Guardian & next friend plt & and Jno. . . . . . &c of Math Sebrell decd deft ye deft agrees to deliver ye plt a plea before . . . . . Cause is Cont

. . . . . between . . (*mis.*) Sebrell by Danl Stoner her guardian and next friend . . . . . of Matt Sebrell decd def is Contd until next Court

. . . . . Thomas Philips by Jno. Gibbons his next friend plt and Jane Rogers. . . . .

. . . . . Wm Morris and Ann his wife plt and Wm Tavernor deft . . . . . Thomas Nelson & Lawr Smith genl or either of them are . . . . . between them and make repl thereof to ye next Court

. . . . . Security hath an order granted him for a Lycence to keep
. . . . . ye ensuing year

. . . . . until ye Court in Course
Signd John Hollowell

Page 124
At a Court for York County 16 April 1722. Present: Lawr Smith, Archb Blair, Thos Chisman, Thos Nelson, Wm Sheldon, Edw Tabb

Wm Buckner genl in ye Commission of peace named having taken ye oath Appointed by ye dedunius & subserved ye test took his place on ye bench
Present: Wm Buckner Wm Stark

Wm Lark is appointed Surveyer of ye highways of ye middle precincts of York Hampton parish in ye Room of Charles Hansford Ordered that he keep ye Roads and bridges in ye said precincts in repair accordingly

Mary Mornpaice on her pet and giving Security hath an order granted her for a Lycence to keep an ordry at Wmburgh in this County for ye ensuing year

Edw Tabb on his pet and giving Security hath an Order granted him for a Lycence to keep an ordry at his dwelling house in ye County for ye year ensuing

Wm Biggs a prisoner his pet to be released from Gaol is rejected

Ordered that ye Court is adjourned until ye Court in Course. Signed Lawr Smith. Truly entered by Phi Lightfoot Cl Cur

Know all men by theses presents that we . . . . . Anthony Robinson Jan. & Phi Lightfoot of ye County . . . . . to our Sovereign Lord ye King in ye Sum of ten thousand pounds of tobacco. . . . . said County to which payment well And truly to be made . . . . . heirs and successors we bind ourselves and every of us our Said. . . . . heirs Excrs and admins jointly & Severally firmly to these presents well. . . . . Seals and dated this 16day of April 1722

The condition of this Obligation is such . . . . . ye above bounden Edw Tabb hath an Order this day granted him to keep an ordry at his house in York County for ye year ensuing . . . . . said Edw Tabb doth constantly find and provide for his ordry good . . . . . Cleanly lodging and diet for travellors and stableage and provender . . . . . as ye Season shall require for . . . . . for and during ye term of one year and shall not suffer . . . . . in his said house nor on ye Sabath day suffer and person to tiple nor drink more than is necessary then this obligation shall be. . . . . full force and virtue
At a Court held for York County . . . . . Edw Tabb
This bond was presented in. . . . . . Anth Robinson
Ye parties thereto and is adm. . . . . Phi Lightfoot . . . . . ClCur
At a Court held for York County 16 April 1722

Page 125
The Act concerning . . . . . the court precinct to Receive and Certify . . . . .

Wm Gordon preferred a Claim . . . . . Court for two Thousand one hundred twenty & nine pounds of Tobacco for publick services done & he having made Oath that all & every the services . . . . . in the acct Exhibited were really & Bona fide done & performed & That no Satisfaccon hath been received for the Same the sd acct is therefore . . . . . to be certified to the assembly for all allance

John Trotter preferred A Claim to this Court for twenty five pounds of Tobacco for publick services done & he having made Oath that ye sd Services mentioned in ye acc exhibited was really and bona fide done & performed & That no Satisfaction hath been recd for ye same it is therefore ordered to be certified to ye assembly for allowance

John Gibbons preferred a Claim to this Court for one hundred pounds of Tobacco for publick Service done If he having made Oath that ye sd Service mentioned in ye acct exhibited was really and bona fide . . . . . performed that no

Satisfaction hath been recd for ye same it is therefore ordered to be certified to ye assembly for allowance

James Mackindo preferred a Claim to this Court for two hundred & ninety pounds of tobacco for publick service done and made . . . . . that all and every ye Service mentioned in ye acc exhibited were . . . . . bona fide and performed and that no satisfaction hath been received for ye same Its therefore ordered to be certified to ye assembly for allowance

Robt Ballard preferred a Claim to the Court for one hundred and five pounds of tobacco for publick Services done and made oath that all and every ye Services mentioned in ye acct exhibited were really and bona fide & performed & That no satisfaction hath been recd for ye Same It is therefore ordered to be certified to ye Assembly for allowance

John Gower preferred a claim to this court for forty pounds of tobacco for publick Service done and made oath that ye sd Service mentioned in ye acc exhibited was really & bona fide done & performed & That no satisfaction hath been recd ye Same it is therefore ordrd to be certified to yd assembly

Jona Druett . . . . . to this court for forty pounds of tobacco for publick Services done & Made oath ye sd Service. . . . . exhibited was really and bona fide done & performed & ye no Satisfaction hath been . . . . . orderd to be certified to ye assembly for allowance

Fra Elinor . . . . . for forty pounds of tobacco for publick Service & Made oath ye ye sd Services. . . . . was really and bona fide done & Performed ye no satisfaction hath been . . (*missed*) Certified to ye assembly for allowance

Wm Keith. . . . . of tobacco for publick service done & Made Oath yt ye sd Service . . . . . bona fide done & performed & yt no satisfaction . . . . . Certified to ye assembly for allowance

. . . . . a negro slave named Duke belonging . . . . . above ten miles distance from his sd Masters re. . . . .
. . . . . de oath that she never recd any Satisfaction . . . . . be Certified to ye Assembly for allowance (Dozwells Claim proved)

. . . . . Court for taking up Jno. Dillit a runaway Servant belonging . . . . . a Slave Redin near Hampton in James River above ten m. . . . . appears by Certificate & Made oath yt he never recd any satisfaction . . . . . ordered to be Certified to ye assembly for allowance (Belvins Claim proved)

Robert Kerby. . . . . Court for taking up James Dun a runaway Servant belonging . . . . . above ten miles distant fm ye sd Jones's Residence as appears by. . . . . never recd any satisfaction for yd same. It is therefore ord... . . . for allowance (Kerby's claim proved)

Joseph Stacy . . . . . taking up Geo Blair a runaway servant belonging . . . . . ye sd Gordon's residence as approved by certificate . . . . . for ye same it is ordered. (Stacey's claim proved)

Page 126
. . . . . Court for taking up Wm Hamilton a Runaway
. . . . . Gloucester County above ten miles fm ye sd Buckner's Residence
. . . . by certificate . . made Oath that he never recd any Satisfaction
for *ye* sd . . . . . ordered to be certified to ye Assembly for allowance

Richd Ballarius. . . . . Wm Hildsman preferred a Claim to this Court for taking up Jas Pricket a runaway Servant belonging to Thos Chamberlane of New Kent County above ten miles distant for his sd Master residence as appr by certificate and made Oath that they never received any satisfaction for the same it is therefore ordrd to be certified by ye sd Assembly for allowance

Gerard Roberts preferred a Claim to this Court for taking up Allomonboe a runaway Negroe belonging to George Winter Commander of ye Mary Gally above ten miles distant from ye said vessel as appears by Certificate and made Oath that he took ye sd slave up at ye place mentioned in ye Certificate and that he never recd any Satisfaction for ye same it is therefore ordered to be certified to ye assembly for allowance

Edward Curtis preferred a claim to this Court for taking up a runaway negro Slave belonging to Wm Wise of York County above five miles distant from his sd Master's residence as appears by certificate and made Oath that he never recd any Satisfaction for ye same it is therefore ordrd to be certified to ye sd assembly for allowance

Fras Meloy preferred a Claim to this Court for taking up a runaway negro slave named Denbo belonging to Jno. Frayser of . . (*mis.*) City County above five miles distant fm his sd Master's residence as appears by Certificate & Made oath that he never recd any Satisfaction for ye same it is ordered to be certified to ye sd assembly for allowance

Davd Pegrun Edw Jones preferred claim to this Court for Jno. Jones a runaway servant belonging to Dr Burbr. . (*mis.*) New Kent County above ten miles distant fm his sd Masters residence as appears by Certificate and made oath that they never recd any Satisfaction for ye Same it is therefore ordered to be certified to ye sd assembly for allowance

Fr Bryan preferred a Claim to this Court for taking up Mary Dring a runaway Mullatto Woman belonging to Dorothy Price York County above ten miles distant from her Mistresses residence as appears by Certificate and made oath yt he never rec'd any Satisfaction for ye Same it is therefore ordered to be certified to ye sd assembly for allowance

Edw Woodhouse preferred a Claim to this Court for taking up Moll (Mell?) a runaway negro woman belonging to Jno. Powers . . (*missing*) miles distant from her master's residence as appears by certificate . . . . . never recd any Satisfaction for ye same it is therefore ordered to be certified to ye sd Assembly for allowance

At a Court 1722
. . . . . Chisman
. . . . . obb Gent

At a Comm. . . . . Majesty's Lieut Governor
Appointing S. . . . . Nelson together with
Thos Chisman . . . . . unto & Acknowledged
Their bond . . . . . his charge of ye sd office
Which is ad. . . . . accordingly Sworn high Sheriff

Fra. Tyler . . . . . by Thos Nelson Gentl Sheriff were
Sworn Under... . . . (Tyler & Gibbons Sworn UnderSheriffs)

A Power of . . . . . Richd Rawlinson & others was proved
In Court by. . . . . Cant & it is ordered to be certified (Fitzhugh Power of Att. Fm Collit)

Deed of Lease . . . . . thereon from Jno. Collit Richd Rawlinson And others. . . . . this day proved in Court be ye affirmation... of Cou ... to be Cert

Page 127
James Selator made . . . . . Satisfaction on a Certificate Obtained by him. . . . . belonging to Fra Willis It is therefore ordered to be certified

The Inventory and . . . . . ye estate of Jane Cully was presented in Court and Admitted to record

Robt Tucker. . . . . being sworn at ye motion of James Bacchus

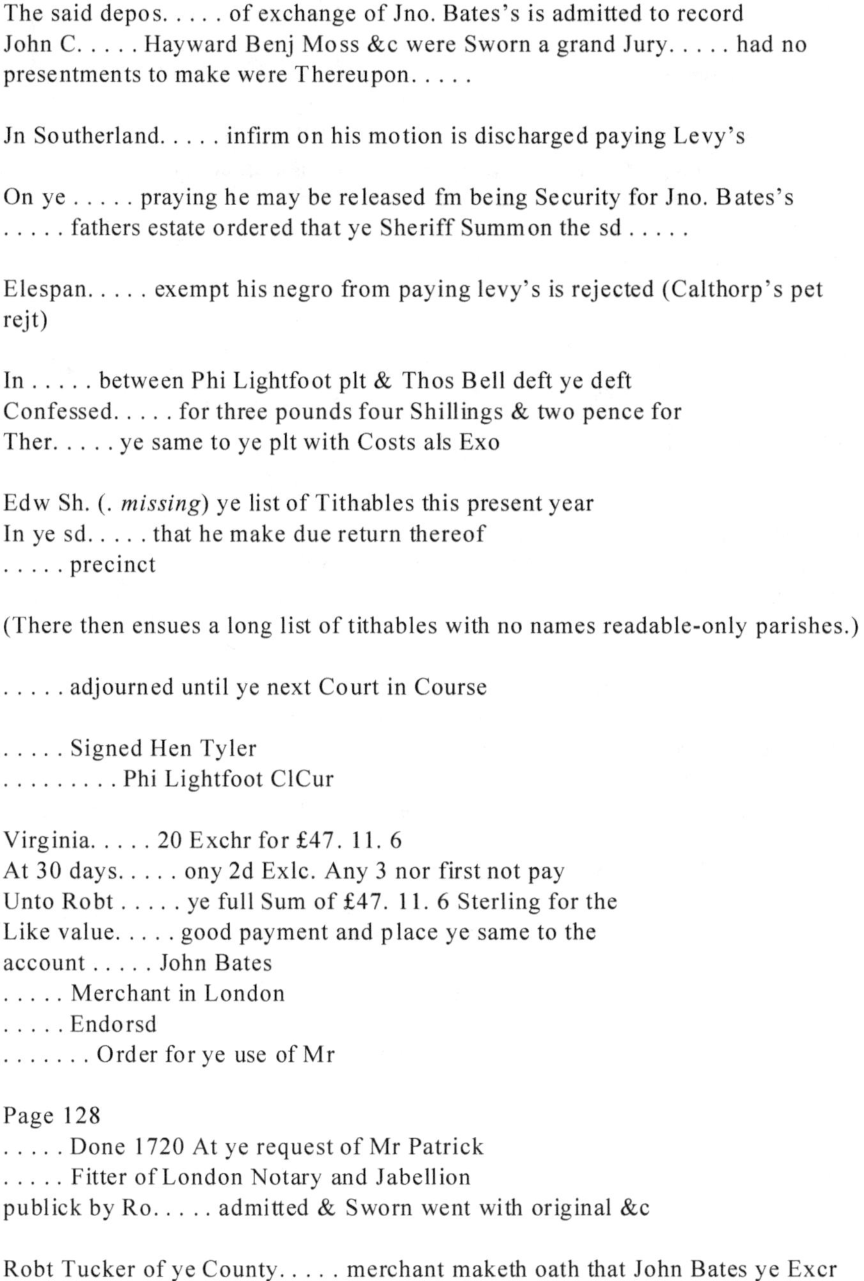

The said depos. . . . . of exchange of Jno. Bates's is admitted to record
John C. . . . . Hayward Benj Moss &c were Sworn a grand Jury. . . . . had no presentments to make were Thereupon. . . . .

Jn Southerland. . . . . infirm on his motion is discharged paying Levy's

On ye . . . . . praying he may be released fm being Security for Jno. Bates's . . . . . fathers estate ordered that ye Sheriff Summon the sd . . . . .

Elespan. . . . . exempt his negro from paying levy's is rejected (Calthorp's pet rejt)

In . . . . . between Phi Lightfoot plt & Thos Bell deft ye deft
Confessed. . . . . for three pounds four Shillings & two pence for
Ther. . . . . ye same to ye plt with Costs als Exo

Edw Sh. (. *missing*) ye list of Tithables this present year
In ye sd. . . . . that he make due return thereof
. . . . . precinct

(There then ensues a long list of tithables with no names readable-only parishes.)

. . . . . adjourned until ye next Court in Course

. . . . . Signed Hen Tyler
. . . . Phi Lightfoot ClCur

Virginia. . . . . 20 Exchr for £47. 11. 6
At 30 days. . . . . ony 2d Exlc. Any 3 nor first not pay
Unto Robt . . . . . ye full Sum of £47. 11. 6 Sterling for the
Like value. . . . . good payment and place ye same to the
account . . . . . John Bates
. . . . . Merchant in London
. . . . . Endorsd
. . . . Order for ye use of Mr

Page 128
. . . . . Done 1720 At ye request of Mr Patrick
. . . . . Fitter of London Notary and Jabellion
publick by Ro. . . . . admitted & Sworn went with original &c

Robt Tucker of ye County. . . . . merchant maketh oath that John Bates ye Excr decd Stood justly . . . . . at ye time of his death the Sum

of £11. Sterling for that debt drawn on . . . . . death of ye said John his Son Jno. Bates
Ye younger gave th. . . . . for that debt drawn on Mr In. . (*missing*)
Danson which bills. . . . . protest and act of Honour here to
Annext may appear An. . . . . protest this deponent brought suit
And recovered judgement agt . . . . . ye younger and Jan. Bacchus
His security for fifty five p. . . . . and ten pence Sterling And
This deponent further sa. . . . . bill was as above said for the
Proper debt of John Bat. . . . . no other
. . (*missing*) Robt Tucker

At a Court held for 1722

. . . . . we at ye motion of Jans Bacchus
. . . . . bill of exchange . . . Phi Lightfoot ClCur

Know all men by these. . . . . Thos Chisman & Phi Lightfoot of ye County of York are held. . . . . our Soverign Lord ye King In ye Sum of One thousand. . . . . payment well and truly to be Made to our Sd Lord ye. . . . . sors we bind ourselves and Every of us our and every . . . . . Joyntly and Severally Firmly by these presents. . . . . and date this 21 May 1722

The Condition of this whereas y hon Alex Spotswood Esq his Majesties L. . . . . authorized deputed & appoints Ye above bounden Thos... . . . York County for ye year next ensuing Know ye therefore . . . . . do well and truly perform ye office Duty and place of Sheriff . . . . . York faithfully and Justly Ordered in to ye oath of. . . . . as may be o ye Laws of England And Laws and Customes . . . . . all due process of Law and Diligently to Serve . . . . . things relating to his sd office And render to his Maj. . . . . as are appointed to receive Ye same as part. . . . . his Majestys revenues And dues in . . . . . tally and due Payment make of . . . . . shall be levied on ye afores. County of York unto ye Ser. . . . . to received ye Same & full performance Make of all things . . . . . office of Sheriff and duly and truly Execute all warrant. . . . . and precepts which have or shall Come to his hand for. . . . . in Chief for ye time being & also Diligently Enquire and . . . . . of Land held in ye sd County By any person or persons. . . . . & return a true & perfect list of rent Rolls of ye same. . . . . ong upon oath at Such time and. . . . . to be given . . . *missing*) perform . . . of this

Page 129
Court then this obligation to be void or else remain in full force & virtue

At a Court held for York County ye 21 May 1722 Thos Nelson
This bond was presented in Court and acknowledged Thos Chisman

By ye partys and admitted to record . Phi Lightfoot. Test Phi Lightfoot ClCur

An Inventory of ye estate of Jane Culley decd
To Cash of . . (*missing*) Chisman for Schooling - £0. 13. 4
To Cash of. . . . . - £2. 00. 1
To Cash of. . (*missing*) Shields Junier for Schooling - £1. 11. 10
To Cash of. . . . . p. Do. - £1. 10. 0
To Cash . . . . . . Wright for Schooling - £0. 5. 0
To Cash. . . . . iam Bond for Do. - £0. 6. 3
To. . . . . to Robert Innis - £0. 2. 7
To he. . . . . sold to Henry Barradale - £2. 10. 0
To Cash . . . . . nn Hopkins for Schooling - £0. 15. 0
To Cash of John Chisman for Do. - £0. 15. 0
To Cash of Thos Nelson for Schooling - £0. 7. 6
To Cash of A. (*missing*) Wright for Do. - £ 0. 10. 6
To Cash of . (*missing*) Tabb for Do - £0. 13. 6
To Cash of . . (*missing*) Robinson for Do. - £0. 13. 6
To Cash of. . (*missing*) Burton for Do. - £0. 2. 6
To Cash of . . (*missing*) Kerby Jun. for Do. - £1. 4. 9
. . . . Barradale for Schooling - £0. 15. 0
. . . . . . Goodwin for Do. - £0. 6. 0
. . . . . Curtis Do. - £1. 10. 0
. . . . White Do. - £0. 5. 3

(all the rest of the names have been obliterated.)
... . . . Court dated March 19 1721 we ye Subscribers
being first. . . . . Lawr Smith did meet and appraise all ye
estate of Jane Cully. . . . . brought before us by Capt Thos Chisman. Jno
Chisman, Jno. Wright, Benj Moss, . . . Lightfoot ClCur

Page 130
At a Court held for York County ye 18th June 1722
Present: John Holloway, Arch Blair, Graves Pack & Wm Stark Gentl

In ye pet . . . . . that Jno. Bates may give an acct of his admon on
Ye estate of Jno. Bates decd . . . . . former order is cont until next Court

On ye pet of John Fleming . . . . . that ye estate of Jno. Bates decd may Be delivered into his hands as . . . . said John Surrender all ye estate of ye said deceds in his hands. . . . . Fleming accordingly appraised by Saml Cobbs Henry Powers and Matt Pierce or any three of them being Sworn and its . . . . . ordered that due return be made to ye office of such appraisement

In ye action of trespass on ye. . . . . Richd Needham plt And Saml Read deft for £20 due. . . . . means of ye defendt Chasing Beating burning and wounding a . . . . . of ye plts of ye price of Ten pounds Sterling Issue being joined a Jury to wit - John Chapman RC Ballard &c were sworn who having heard ye evidence went out And being agreed retuned their verdict in these words we find for ye . . plt five pounds damage which at ye plts motion is recorded and its Considered that ye . . . . . agt ye deft ye aforesaid Sum of five pounds his damages by. . . . . in manner aforesaid as is dw th Lawyers fees and costs als Exo

Jn Atkinson and Mary his wife. . . . . further time allowed to give Security for their admon on ye estate. . . . . Eliza Moody decd

The Inv of ye estate of Richd Page decd is presented in Court & ent in record

The action upon ye case between . . . . . Goodwin & Lawr Smith & Mildred his wife late Mildred Goodwin is cont till next Court for yd audrs rept

In ye action upon ye case between Jno. Welch plt & Richd Turner deft the plt Having proved his acc for three pounds five shillings the judgement of ye last Court Agt y sd deft and Geo Fuller his security is confirmed and ordered that they Pay y d Sum to sd plt with costs als exo

Eliza Marston on her pet and giving Security hath an order granted Her for a Lycence to keep an Ordinary in Wmsburgh ye ensuing year.

In ye action of De. . . . ter (Poss. Winter) plt & Wm Levingston def for twenty three Pounds Sixteen . . . . . and eleven pounds two shillings and two . . . . . last court agt ye deft is confirmed and. . . . . with Costs als Exo

In ye action of . . . . . Levingston deft for fifteen pounds ye deft . . . . . ye Judgement of Last Court is confirmed agt . . . . . pounds and ordered that he pay ye Same to ye plt with costs als Exo

In ye Suit in Chancery . . . . . between Justinian Love Elias Love & Eliza Love by Justinian . . . . . Guardian and next friend Compltt And John Fosset & Eliza. . . . . ye responrs being called and failing To appear at ye Cou. . . . . atta is granted them ag ye bodys of ye sd respondts . . . . . Court

Page 131

On ye petition of Hannah Hay pra. . . . . appointed Guardian to Nathl. And Mary Hay Orphans of her decd . . . . . Hay It is ordered that John Hay deliver ye sd orphans and . . . . . unto ye hands of ye sd Hannah who is accordingly appointed their Guardian. . . . . giving Security as ye Law directs

The action of debt between Phi Lightfoot plt & Jas Minzie deft is dismist

The former order for taking . . . . . Prissen into custody until next Court

On ye petition of Wm Davis . . . . . ordred that Mary West state and exhibit an acc of her admon on ye estate . . . . . decd husband Jno. West to ye next Court

In ye suit of partition depending between Lucy Hill by Wm Cross her Guardian plt and Thomas Vines . . . . . Bartlett Moreland deft for 50 £ Sterling damage by means of ye dep. . . . . to permit to be divided in three equal parts five. . . . . nine hundred and thirty acres of Land with ye appurtenances in each of YorkHampton in this County of ye inheritance which . . . . . Hill father of ye said Lucy and Mary late ye wife of ye said Vines and Eliza late ye wife of ye said Bartlett Moreland . . . . . doth appertain to ye sd Lucy and her heirs in for and ye. . . . . to ye sd Thos and Bartlett by ye Curtesy &c as in. . . . . fully espressed and ye sd Thomas Vines and Bart. . . . . in their proper persons and say that they . . . . . hold ye messuages and Lands in ye declaration . . . . . and undivided & nor that partition ought to . . . . . hath declared therefore it is commanded. . . . . and law for men of his Balywick who are ... . . . consanguinity to ye partys or Lyable to any . . . . . pany with ye Surveyor of ye County he cause . . . . . nage and laws aforesaid between ye sd plt and the. . . . . and value thereof and that he make return

... . . . Mary West plt and Jno. Davis deft for Seven
. . . . . four pence halfpenny ye def having had time allowed
. . . . failed to do ye same Judgement is therefore granted
. . . ye plt Confirmable at the next Court on ye like default

. . . . . against Rob Innis for for three pounds ten shillings
. . . . . by ye plt oath an att being Servd on divers
. . . . Wise and John Welch judgement is granted ye plt
. . . . that Edm Sweny Thos Kerby and Saml Leweling
. . . . appr ye sd Goods & make report thereof by next Court
. . . . . Jones plt & Eliza Powers deft is Cont

The suit in . . . . . Armiger Parsons & Eliza his wife compl
And John Hay . . . . . is cont until next Court

In ye pet . . . . . release from being Security for
Elinor Thebo . . . . . ordered that ye sd Elinor
. . . . . husband's estate. Hyde -Thebo)

(Blair- Mundall) . . . . . John Mundall

Page 132

. . . . . Debt between Henry Gibbs adm &c of Edw Loftus decd plt and Bartl Burcher deft for 26£ or 35 lbs of Tobacco upon ye defts oath and deposition of . . . . . ye sum is dismist with costs

In ye action . . . . . between Jno. Daniel plt and John Bates Excr of ye last will and testament . . . . . Bates decd deft for Seventy two pounds Current mony the deft having . . . . . allowed him to plead and being called failed to do ye Same Judgement is therefore . . . . . ye plaintif by Nihil Dicit Confirmable at ye next Court on ye like default

Thos Nelson . . . . . exhibited an inventory &c of ye estate of Walter Butler decd mon is admitted to record

Isaac Collier. . . . . of Charles Collier decd having to choose a Guardian made Choice of Edward Baptist who upon giving Security was admitted to ye Court wherefore it is ordered . . . . . sd orphan and his estate committed to ye care of ye sd Edw.

The pet . . . . . Brooks agt Phi Lightfoot Exr &c Matt Ballard decd is rejected

Jn Fleming . . . . . with Thos Nelson and Joseph Walker his Security enterd into and acknowledged. . . . . bond to ye Court for ye estate of John Bates decd Committed to ye care of. . . . . which bond is admitted to Record

The accon . . . . . between Jams Faison plt and Dan Taylor brother . . . . . Tyler late of Charles parish decd def is dismist

In ye action . . . . . Danl Stoner plt and John Mundal and Susa Sebrell . . . . . Sebrell decd the deft hath Oyer of ye plts acc until next Court

The action. . . . . (possibly Comack) plt & And Laprade deft is dismist

Petition of Robert Atkinson . . . . . of ye estate of Jno. Williams decd
In ye hands of Mary . . . . . delivered to him by consent Saml Cobbs Jos Dab. . . . . or any two of them are appointed to audit State & Settle. . . . . make rept thereof to ye next Court

The action of debt between . . . . . (margin says... Weller& Ives) is dismist

The action of debt between . . . . . &c plt Essex Weller deft is dismist. (Levingston)

Ann Williams Orphan. . . . . on her petition had liberty to Choose a Guradian who the. . . . . Roberts ordered that ye sd orphan and her estate . . . . . are of ye sd Robert he having given Secty

In ye action upon ye . . . . . plt and Saml Sweny Exr &c of Sam Harlie decd deft Issue is referred for trial at ye next Court

The att of Jams Bacchus. . . . . Bates for £4. 2. 10is cont until next Court

The att of JamesBacchus . . . . . Bates for £35. 2. 10 is discontinued

Jn Mundall and Su. . . . . allowed them to extend an Invry &c of ye estate. . . . . Court

The att of Edw. Sparks . . . . . next Court. (Sparks- Berry Cont)

The action upon . . . . . Charles plt &c . . . . . Jacqueline Excr &c of Harwood Car. . . . . deft to bring in ye acc of ye decd Estate Settled in . . . . .

In ye action. . . . . Shields plt &c Wm Robt Robertson deft the pt having . . . . . deft ye Cause is referred till next Court for trial

In ye. . . . . Jos Sutton is discont (Walker - Sutton)

The . . . . . Lightfoot plt & Lawr Smith deft is Cont

. . . . . Toomer plt & Edw. Tabb deft is Cont at. . . . . .

(Hay - Toomer) Complts

Page 133
In ye action of Debt between Saml Sweeny. . . . . pounds five shillings Current mony . . . . . that ye Sum of fifty four pounds Seven Shillings and . . . . . due to ye plt ye said report is admitted to record and . . . . . for ye said Sum of fifty four pounds Seven Shillings and five pence and ordered that ye deft and Thos Jones his Security pay ye same to ye plt with costs als exo

The action upon ye case between Robt Fannock plt & Jno. Robertson decd is dismist

In ye action upon ye case between Sarah Sebrell by W Hudson her Guardian & next friend plt and Jno. Mundell Execr &c of Nath Sebrell deft . The deft Confessed Judgement to ye plt . . (*missing*) it being ye fifth part of two Negros belonging to ye estate of Nath Sebrell decd Wherefore its ordered that ye deft pay ye said Sum to ye plt out of ye decd estate with costs als Exo

The action upon ye Case between Fra Sharp plt & Wm Lake deft is dismist

Mich Archer Sam Cobbs and Joseph Davenport or any two of them are appointed to State & Settle ye account of ye estate of Jacob Godwin decd & Make reply to ye next Court

In ye action of Detinue between . . . . . his wife plt &c Wm Tavernor deft ye deft being called and not appearing nor any Security retd for him On the plts motion Judgement is granted him agt ye deft and Wm Gordon Sheriff for ye said Sum & Costs unless ye deft appears at ye next Court & Answers ye said action

Robt Cobb is appointed surveyor of ye highways in ye upper precincts of Bruton parish . . . . . ordered that he keep ye same in repair accordingly

Wm Gordon is appointed surveyor of ye Streets and Landings in YorkTown on ye room . . . . . Lightfoot ordered that he keep ye same in repair accordingly

Richd Steward is appt Surveyor of ye Highways in ye upper precincts of York Hampton . . . . . in ye Room of Robt Jackson ordrd that he keep them in repair

In. . . . . between Richd Houghton plt and John Rhodes & Robt Roberts deft . . . . . Shillings Robt Roberts appd and Confessed Judgement to
. . . . . Roberts motion an atta is granted him agt ye sd Rhodes for ye sd Sum and costs als exo

In ye . . . . . Arch Blair Assignee of Cath Craig plt & Jno. Mundal
And . . . . . ye deft confessd Judgement to ye plt for twenty eight pounds
. . . . . that they pay ye sd Sum to ye plt with costs als Exo

. . . . . between Hugh Allen plt & Wm Gilchrist deft is dismist

. . . . . between Wm Robertson plt & Jno. Mundal deft is dismist

. . . . . Phi Lightfoot plt & Thos Nelson admr &c of Walter Butler decd . . . . . his acct for three pounds one Shilling & two pence ordered that he pay ye same to y eplt out of ye decds estate with costs als Exo

The action between Jno. Butterworth plt & George Trust deft is dismist

In ye action of. . . . . between Mary Dun plt & Hen Irwin is dismist

In ye action of . . . . . Theo Pinket Assignee &c plt Jno. Swinock deft at ye defts motion an imparlance is granted him until next Court

In ye act . . . . . Danl Taylor plt & Jno Bates Excr &c Jno. Bates decd . . . . . him until ye next Court

. . . . . Bates deft is dismist (Jones - Bates)

. . . . . Bates deft is dismist (Swan-Bates)

. . . . . Fannock deft is dismist (Thomas)

Page 134
Debt between Jer Turner plt and Wm Levingston deft Hen . . . . . of ye plt Assumes to pay what costs and damages Shall be awarded . . . . . Suit at ye deft motion an Imparlance is granted him until next Court

The action . . . . . Phi Lightfoot plt & Richd Turner deft is dismist

Mary West having been presented by ye Grand Jury for having had a Mullatto Bastard Wm Robertson atto of our Sovereign Lord ye King is desired to exhibit an Information agt her at ye next Court to which ye said Mary agrees to plead not guilty (*illegible legal term*) ye sd presentment is Continued

In ye action of Debt between Ann Hearman plt and Thos Nelson Exr &c of Waltr Butler decd deft for four pounds due by note Judgement is granted ye plt for ye said Sum and ordered that ye deft pay ye same with cost als Exo

In ye action upon ye case between Wm Mainyard plt & Thos Nelson adm &c of Walter Butler decd deft for two pounds and five shillings and five pence by acct proved by ye plts poath Judgement is granted ye plt for ye said Sum and ordered that ye deft pay ye same to ye plt out of ye decds estate in his hands with Costs als Exo

In ye action upon ye case between Eliza Hansford plt and Lawr Smith deft at the defts motion and imparlance is granted him until next Court

In ye action of debt between Edw Miller plt & Thos Nelson adm &c Waltr Butler decd deft for three pounds ten Shillings due by note proved by ye plts Oath Judgemnt is granted for ye Sum & orderd. that ye deft pay ye same to ye plt out of ye decds est with Costs als Exo

In ye action of ye case between Wm Anthony plt & Rd Turner deft is dismist

In ye action of ye case between Wm Stark plt & Thos Nelson admin &c Waltr Butler decd deft for five pounds five shillings and five pence by acct proved by ye plts Oath Judgemnt is granted for ye said Sum and ordered that ye deft pay ye same to ye plt out of the decds estate in his hands with costs als Exo

In ye action upon the case between Ba. . . Moorland plt & Thos Nelson adm 7c of Waltr Butler decd deft an Imparlance is granted him untilo next Court

In ye action of Detinue between . . . . . plt (Toomer) & Saml Tomkins deft ye deft not appearing to prosecute. . . . . that he be non suited and that he pay ye deft damage accordingly . . . . . with costs als Exo

In ye action of Debt between . . . . . plt (Beddoes) and Wm Harwood deft ye deft Confessd Judgement . . . . . pounds six shillings and a farthing ordered that he . . . . . with Costs als Exo

The suit in Chancery between . . . . . Barradale and Judith his wife Complts and John Merry Sur. . . . . Merry decd is dismist

The action of debt between . . . . . Welch & Davd. Hollway defs is dismist (Stacy -Welch)

The action of debt between . . . . . Laprade deft is dismist (Sharp-Laprade)

The action of debt between . . . . . deft is dismist (Bowcock-Swan)

The action upon ye case between . . . . . Crawley deft for three pounds ten shillings . . . . . called and not appearing nor any Security ret for him. . . . . Judgement is granted for ye sd Sum and costs agt ye deft and Fra Tyler Sheriff unless ye deft appeasr at ye next Court & Answers ye sd Action (Brown - Crawley)

The action of Case between . . . . . Thompson plt & Charles Prince deft is dismist

The action of debt between . . . . . Power plt & Thos Swan deft is dismist

The action of case between . . . . . plt & Peter Wilson Deft is dismist (Huny or Henry)

In ye action of debt between. . . . . Sharp plt & Andr Laprade deft at ye defts motion an imparlance is granted him until next Court

In ye action of. . . . . Joseph BanisterExcrs &c of Wm Smelt plts . . . . . at ye defts motion (Banister -Holdcraft &c)

(Romer-King)

Page 135
In ye action of Case between Jno. Mattocke... . . . and Imparlance is granted him until next Court (Mattocke - Smith)

The action of debt between. . . . . Curtis plt & . . . . . rt Innis deft

The action upon the Case between Rich Needham plt and Randall Smith plt is dismist

The action between Wm Palmer plt & Jos Sled & Wm Sled Defts is dismist

The action of Debt between Phi Lightfoot plt & Wm Barber and Saml Timson deft is cont until next Court

In ye action of Case between Thos Jones gent plt & Eliza Ives deft for thirty pounds Seventeen Shillings and a farthing Sterling ye deft being called and not appearing Judgement is granted agt ye sd deft and Wm Blakely her Security for ye said Sum and costs unless ye deft appears at ye next court and answers ye said action

In ye petition of George Gilbert against ye estate of Jno. Ness it appears by ye said Ness books that there is due in ye heirs of George Allen ye Sum of two pounds Seven Shillings and five pence Wherefore its ordered that he pay ye said Sum to ye petr wth Costs als Exo

Wm Dun Servant to Joseph Thomas having runaway from his sd Master thirty one days ordered that he serve his sd Master or assigne Sixty two days for ye same after his time by Indenture custome or further order of Court is expired Ordered that Court be adjourned until ye next Court in Course. Signed JW Holloway. Truly entered by Phi Lightfoot ClCur

Know all men by these presents that we Eliza Marston Dan Stoner & Jos Davenport of ye County of York are held and firmly bound unto our Sovereign Lord ye King on ye Sum of ten thousand pounds of tobacco convenient in ye sd County to which payment well and truly to be made to our said Lord ye King his heirs and Successors We bind ourselves and every of us our an every of our heirs Execrs and Admns Joyntly and Severally firmly by these presents Sealed with our Seals and dated this 18 day of June 1722

. . . . . Obligation is such that the above bounden . . . . . order this day granted her for a Lycence to keep. . . . . dwelling house in Wmsburgh for ye year next

ensuing
. . . . . order this day granted her for a Lycence to keep . . . . . dwelling house in Wmsburgh for ye year next . . . . . said Eliza doth Constantly find and provide in . . . . . some and cleanly Lodging and Diet for Travellors and
. . . . . pasturage and provender as ye Season shall require . . . . . theses presents and during ye term of one year . . . . . unlawfull gaming in her said house nor on the Sabbath day Suffer . . . . . to tipple or drink more than is necessary then this Obligation . . . . . to remain in full force & Virture

At a Court held for. . . . . 18 June 1722 Eliza. Marston.
This bond was presen. . . . . Danl Stoner.
By ye partys Jos Davenport.

(Butler's Inv)
. . . . . Lightfoot Cl Cur
. . . . . Walter Butler decd produced

Page 136
Inventory followed (Total valuation £ 54. 11. 11)
John Potter, John Gibbons, Wm Cross

At a court held for York County . . . . . June 1722 Thos Nelson Adm
This Inv & Appr of ye estate of Waltr Butler decd was presented in Court
By Thos Nelson Adm and is admitted to record

In Obedience to an order of Court . . . . . day of March 1721 we ye Subscribers being first sworn have an Inventory & Appr ye est of Richd Page decd as follows:
One negro man named. . . . . £ 28 (Total valuation: £ 55. 18. 2)
ye above Goods appr . . . . . Subscribers. this 7day April 1722. . . . . . . Daniel, ... Blackhurst, ... Linton, Robt Cobbs Junr.
18 day June 1722. . . . . . ClCur

Page 137
Know all men by these presents . . . . . Patrick Ogleby of ye County of York. . . . . Lord ye King in ye Sum of ten. . . . . Ye said County to which . . . Lord ye King his heirs and Suucess... Our and every of us our heirs Excrs and... ... By these presents sealed with our seals . . . The condition of this obligation is such that whereas ye above . . . Mary Mompain hath an order this day granted her for a lycence to keep an ordinary ather now dwelling house in WmsBurgh in this County for ye year next ensuing if therefore ye said Mary Mompain doth Constantly find and provide in her ordry good wholesome and Cleanly Lodgings and diet for travellors and Stableage & provender or pastureage And provender

as ye season shall require for their horses from Ye date of these presents for and during ye term of one year shall Not Suffer any unlawful gaming in her said ordinary nor on the Sabath day Suffer any person to tipple or drink more than is necessary Then that obligation to be void or else to remain in full force & Virtue

At a Court held for York County 16 April 1722.
Mary Mompain, Patrick Ogleby, John Pasture.
This bond was presented in Court and Acknowledged by ye partys and admitted to record. Test Phi Lightfoot ClCur

Know all men by these presents that we Robt Roberts Wm Barbar & Samuel Hyde Are held and truly bound unto ye Worshipfull ye Justices of York County In ye Sum of twenty pounds Sterling payable to ye said Justices their heirs and Successors or some of them to which payment well & Truly to be made we bind Our Selves and every of us our and every of our heirs Excrs Admins Joyntly and Severally firmly by these presents Sealed with our Seals and dated this 18 June 1722

The Condition of this obligation is such that ye above bounden Robert Roberts shall well and truly . . . . . or cause to be paid unto Ann Williams Orphan of Jno. Williams decd
. . . . . or estates belonging to ye said as is or heretofore shall come
. . . . . possession of him ye said Robt Roberts or into ye hands and
. . . . . person or persons for him when or as soons as ye said orphan
. . . . or when thereunto required by ye said Court and
. . . . harmless ye said Court from all trouble and damage that
. . . . about or concerning ye said estate Then this said obligation
. . . in full force and vertue
. . . County 18 June 1722. Robt Roberts. . . . in court & Acknowledged Wm Barbar, Saml Hyde. . . . Admitted to record . . . Test Phi Lightfoot ClCur

Know all men by these presents that we Edwd Baptist Saml Hyde & Edwd Miller of ye County of York . . . . . firmly bound unto ye Worshipfull ye Justices of ye sd County aforesaid . . . . . one hundred pounds Sterling payable to ye said Justices Their heirs and Successors or Some of them to which payment well and truly to be made We bind ourselves and every of us and every of our Heirs Excrs and admins or Some of them Joyntly and Severally firmly by these presents Sealed with our Seals and dated this . . . . . bounden Edwd Baptist &c . . . . . . relating to Isaac Collier orphan of . . . Cause to be paid his full dues. . . . obtain to Lawfull age

Page 138
. . . . . Shall think fit and also from time to time and at all times

. . . . . save harmless and keep indemnified ye said Justices their heirs
. . . . . damages that shall or may accrew to any of them concerning
. . . . things enjoyed by law and orders of this Court
. . . . this obligation to be void or else to remain in full force & virtue

. . . . . Court held for York County 18 June 1722. Edw Baptist.
. . . . . This Bond was presented in Court & Acknowledged Lawr Hyde.
...... by ye partys thereto & Admitted to record. Edw Miller. test Phi Lightfoot ClCur

Know all men by theses presents We John Fleming Joseph Walker and Thomas Nelson are held and firmly bound unto ye worshipfull ye Justices of York County in ye Sum of fifteen hundred pounds to which payment well and truly to be made to ye said Justices their Sucessors or Some of them We bind ourselves our heirs Execrs Admins Joyntly and Severally Firmly by theses presents sealed with our Seals & dated this 18 day of June 1722

The Condition of this obligation is Such that whereas ye above bounden Jno. Fleming is appointed to take care of ye estate of John Bates decd taken out of ye hands of John Bates ye younger Excr of ye said Jno Bates decd & therefore Ye said John Fleming shall well and truly adm on ye sd estate according to law and shall render a true and Just account thereof when thereunto required by ye Justices of ye said Court for ye time being and deliver ye Same to such person or persons as ye said Courts shall appoint & Deliver then this obligation to be void or else to be remain in full force and virtue

At a Court held for York County 18 June 1722. Jno. Fleming.
This Cond was presented in Court & Acknowledged. Jos Walker. By ye partys and admitted to record. T Nelson. Test Phi Lightfoot ClCur

Know all men by these presents . . . . . Hannah Hay Thomas Hynd & Joseph Mountfort of ye County of York are held and firmly bound unto ye Worshipfull ye Justices of ye County aforesaid in the Sum of Three Hundred pounds Sterling payable to ye said Justices their heirs and Successors or Some of them to Which payment well & Truly to be made We bind ourselves and every of us our and every of our heirs Execrs & admins Joyntly & Severally firmly by these presents & Dated this 18 day of June 1722

The Condition of this obligation . . . . . ye above bounden Hannah Hay do well and truly . . . . . undertaken relating to Nath and Mary Hay . . . . . their estate and pay or cause to be paid . . . . . and custom when they shall attain . . . . . shall think fit and also from time to time and at all times hereafter shall Save harmless and keep ye said justices their heirs and Successors from all damages then this obligation to be void or else to remain in full force & Virtue

At a court held for York county 18 June 1722. Hannah Hay. This cond was presented in Court & Acknowledged Thos Hinds. By ye partys & admitted to Record. Test Phi Lightfoot ClCur

(Bowcock's ordry bond) . . . . . Joseph Druit

Page 139
And John Gibbons of ye County of York . . . . . our Sovereign Lord ye King in ye Sum of Ten thousand pounds of tobacco convenient in ye said County to which payment well and truly to be made to our Lord ye King his heirs Successors we bind ourselves and every of our heirs Excrs and admins Joyntly & Severally . . . . . these presents Sealed with our Seals this 16 day of July 1722

The Condition of this obligation is such that whereas ye above bounden Henry Bowcock hath an Order granted this day for a Lycence to keep an ordinary at his now dwelling house in Williamsburgh for ye year next ensuing If therefore ye said Henry doth Constantly find and provide in his ordinary Good Wholesome and Cleanly Lodging and diet for travellors and Stableage and provender or pasturage and provender for their horses as ye Season shall require from ye date of these presents for and during ye term of one year and shall not Suffer any unlawfull Gaming in his said house nor on ye Sabath day Suffer Any person to tiple or drink more than is necessary than this obligation to be void or else to remain in full force & Virtue

At a Court held for York County 16 July 1722.
Henry Bowcock. This bond was presented in Court & Acknowleded Jos Druet. By ye partys and is admitted to record. John Gibbons. Test Phi Lightfoot ClCur

Know all me by theses presents that we Mary Collier Wm Lee and Thos Vines of ye County of York are held and firmly bound unto ye Worshipfull ye Justices of York County in ye Sum of four hundred pounds Sterling to which payment well and truly to be made to ye said Justices their Sucessors or Some of them we bind ourselves and every of us our and every of our heirs Excrs and Admins Joyntly & Severally firmly bye these presents Sealed with our Seals and dated this 16th day of July 1722

The Condition of this obligation is such that if ye above bounden Mary Collier Admintrx of all Goods Chattels and Credits of Charles Collier decd do make or cause to be made a true and just Inventory of all and singular ye Goods Chattles and Credits of ye said decd Such have or shall come to ye hands possessions or

knowledge of her the said Mary Collier or into ye hands or possessions of any other person or persons for her and ye same so made exhibite or cause to be exhibited in ye County Court of York at such time as she shall be thereunto required by ye said Court and ye same Goods Chattels and Credits or any other Goods Chattels and Credits of the said decd made by him at any time after shall come to the . . . . . Collier or into ye hands or possession
. . . . . well and truly administer according
. . . . . account of her actings and doings
. . . . . Court and all ye rest and residue of
. . . . found remaining upon the
. . . . examined by ye Justices of ye said Court
. . . unto Such person or persons as ye
said Justices by their . . . . . direct pursuant to ye Law in
that Case made and provide. . . . . shall hereafter appear that any last
will and testament was (Made) by ye said decd and ye Excr or Excrxs therin
named do exhibit ye same . . . Court making request to have it allowed
and approved according . . . . . approbation os such testament
do render . . . . . to be void or else to reamin in full force & Virtue. Mary Collier, Wm Lee, Thos Vines.

Page 140
Presented in Court and acknowledged by ye partys and is admitted to record. Test Phi Lightfoot Cl Cur

Ye estate of Walter Butler Deceased Settled
To Phi Lightfoot Judgment- £ 3. 1. 4
To Ann Heaman Do - 4. 0. 0
To Wm Mainyard Do - 2. 12. 5
To Edwd Miller Do - 3. 10. 0
To Wm Stark Do - 5. 5. 5.
========

By ye appraisement of his estate - £51. 11. 11
By Balance Due - 2. 10. 32
Executed July 16 1722 Thos Nelson adms
================================

£54. 2. 3

At a Court held for York County 16 July 1722
This settlementof ye Estate of Walter Butler decd was presented in Court by Thos Nelson ye adms and is admitted to record. Test Phi Lightfoot ClCur

The acct of ye estate of Jacob Godwin decd
to his debt to Dr Blair - 7. 9. 8

pd D Harris - 0. 10. 0
pd Jno Gras (Grace?) - 2. 0. 0
pd Wm Philuis - 0. 12. 1
pd WmWaler - 0. 19. 3
pd D Stoner acct Mary & Susa. Sebrel - 9. 14. 0
Funeral charges of ye decd - 2. 0
pd Patrick Oglesby acct - 0. 9
pd Andrew Laprade as guardian Dav. Sebrell - 4. 17. 5
due to D Brown - 0. 15. 6
due to J Hudson Guardian Sar. Sebrell - 4. 17. 5
. . . ==========
Each child's part is £9. 17. 44 £ 37. 3. 22

By Inv & appraisement £80. 18. 5

(Much of below this is missing. . names *to Mary ... To Sarah... to ye wid. ...* can be seen. Apparently as dispersals.)

In obedience . . . . . of York County Court dated ye 18th June 1722
We ye Subscribers . . . . . stated and settled ye account of ye estate
. . . . . Mich Archer
. . (*missing*) Cobbs
. . (*missing*) Davenport

Page 141
Know all me by these presents that . . . . . Sarah Atkinson of ye county of York are held and firmly bound unto ye justices of ye sd county in ye Sum of three hundred pounds Sterling. . . . . to bemade to ye said Just. . . . .
(Margin says Atkinson's Bond admon. Moody)

The Condition of this obligation is such that if ye. . . . . Atkinson adm of all ye Goods Chattels and Credits. . . . . Decd do make or cause to be made or cause to be made a true and perfect inventory Ye said Goods Chattels and Credits of ye said decds which have or shall come to ye hands possession or knowledge of her ye said Mary or into ye hands or possessions of any other person or persons for her and ye same so made do exhibit or cause to be exhibited into ye county Court at such time as she shall be thereunto required by ye said Court and ye same Goods Chattels and Credits and all other ye Goods chattels and Credits of ye said decds at ye time of their deaths which at any time after shall come to ye hands and possessions of her ye said Mary or into ye hands or possessions of any other person or persons for her do well and truly administer according to Law and further do make a true and just account of her acting and doing therein when thereto required by ye said Court and all ye rest and residue of ye said Goods

Chattels and Credits shall be found remaining upon ye admon acct ye same being first examined by ye Justices of ye said Court for ye time being hath deliver and pay unto such persons or persons as ye said Justices by their order or Judgement shall appoint pursuant to ye Law in that Case made and provided and if it shall hereafter appear that any last will and testament was made by ye said deceds and ye execr or Execrs ... do exhibit ye same in ye said court making request to have . . . . . and approved accordingly if therefore ye said Mary being ... . . . render and deliver up her letters of admon approbation . . . . . being first had in ye said Court Then this Obligation to be void or else to remain in full force and virtue.
At a court held for York County 16 July 1722 Wm Atkinson.
This bond was presented in Court and acknowledged. Sarah Atkinson.
By ye . . . . . admitted to record. Test Phi Lightfoot ClCur

Know all me by these presents that we Thos Robins Richd Baker & Robt Ballard of ye County of York are held and firmly bound unto our Sovereign Lord ye King in ye Sum of. . . . . of Tobacco convenient in ye said County to which payment well and truly to be made to ye said Lord ye King his heirs and successors we bind ourselves And every of us and every of our heirs Excrs and admrs. Joyntly and Severally Sealed with our Seals and dated this 16th day of July 1722

The Condition of this obligation is such that whereas ye above bounden Thos RobinsHas an order this day granted for a Lycence to keep an ordinary at his now dwelling For the year next ensuing if therefore Thos doth Constantly find and provide good wholesome and Cleanly Lodging & diet for travelors and parturage and provender or stableage and provender as ye season shall require for their horses . . . . . gaming in his sd ordry nor on ye Sabath. . . . . drink more than is necessary then this . . . . . in full force & Virtue. Thos Robins, Rd Baker, Robt Ballard. . (*missing* Phi Lightfoot ClCur

Page 142
In obedience to an order of York court dated May Ye 18 1722 wherein it is ordered that a jury together with . . . . . Surveyer go to Survey and Lay out into three equal parts five . . . . . and nine hundred and thirty acres of land with ye appurtenances in ye parishes of York Hampton in this County We ye Subscribers have accordingly met together on ye day Appointed and on ye land in Controversie and there being first Sworn before Capt William Sheldon one of his Majestys Justices of ye peace for ye said County and having had regard to all papers &c brought before us did then and there agree to begin and Lay out as followeth Vizt beginning for ye . . . . . part at a Stake in Momfords Line thence running South 500 West onew hundred thirty six poles to a markt ash in ye branch thence S 55 & down ye branch thirty Six poles to a ash a Corner tree, thence S 33 W eighty poles to a stake in the old field thence S 55 W two hundred

and forty poles to Do Phillipsons dividing line for ye. . . . . for ye second part we begin at a marked ash tree . . . . . Corner tree thence up ye branch N 65 W . . . . . Mulbery up ye branch thence N70 W forty poles to . . . . . thence S 44 W two hundred forty Six poles to an oak . . . . . Line for ye third part ye remainder Vizt beginning . . . . . Stake in Momfords Line thence NW to ye road thence. . . . . Road to an Oak a Corner tree Eaton's Land and. . . . . Land thence S 15W to an Oak a corner tree . . . . . as witness our hands & Seals this fifth day of . . . . . Peter Goodwin . . . . . John Chapman . . . . . Benj . . . . Potter Thos ... Thomas Harris . . . . . . Ian (Dan?) MacIntosh

(another line of names completely missing)

Page 143
At a court held for York County . . . . . The aforesaid Survey and . . . . . Court and is admitted to Record. Test Phi Lightfoot ClCur

In obedience to an order of York county dated ye 18 June 1722
I have Cause partition to be made as to. . . . . Commanded and by good and lawfull men of my Baliwick have caused ye Lands & Messuages to be Laid out by Meets and bounds according to ye verdict hereunto annexed and have assigned ye first part to Thomas Vines ye Second to ye plt Lucy Hill and ye third to Bartlett Moorland of which I do hereby make report to ye Court given under my hand this fifth day of Jul 1722. John Gibbons DS

At a Court held for York County 16th July 1722
This report was presented in Court by John Gibbons Sheriff and is admitted to record. Test Phi Lightfoot ClCur

Know all me by these presents that we John Cooke Robert Ballard and John Gibbons of (blank) and of ye County of York are held and firmly bound unto our Sovereign Lord ye King in ye Sum of ten thousand pounds of Tobacco convenient in ye said county to which payment well and truly to be made to our said Lord ye King his heirs and Successors we bind our Selves and every of us our and every of our heirs Execrs and adminrs Joyntly and Severally firmly by these presents Sealed with our seals and dated this 16 day July 1722.
The condition of this Obligation is such that whereas ye above bounden John Cooke hath an order this day granted him for a Lycence to keep an Ordnry in his now dwelling house in York Town for ye year next ensuing and if John Cooke doth Constantly find and provide Wholesome and cleanly Lodging & Diet for Travellors and pasturage and provender or stableage and provender as ye season shall require of him for and during the term of one year nor Suffer unlawful

gaming in his ordinary or on the Sabath permit any peron to tipple or drink more than is necessary then this Obligation shall be void or selse to remain in full force & Virtue. John Cooke, John Gibbons, Robt Ballard. Test Phi Lightfoot ClCur

Page 144
(Magary's estate)
Martin Magary Dec'd
. . . . . Blair ----- 4. 1. 7 By what she made use of out of yeChge Sold Mr Jones - 7. 8. 9
. . . . . Rogers------0. 7. 10 by a Judgemt obtaind - Jas. Morris 13. 16. 0
To Monpain's acct-----0. 8. 0 by ye Invry negores being deducted 65. 18. 3
To Charles Pains acct—1. 18. 2 =====
To Andr Laprade ------- 0. 19. 0 £87. 3. 0
To John Seward----------1. 7. 9
To Funeral Charges------2. 0. ½
. . . . . Browns Jdgmnt 1/13/6
To wido Johnson -------- 1. 0. 0
To wid Craig---------------0. 7. 1
To George Gilbert---------0. 3. 0
To Saml Cobbs-------------0. 17. 1
To Do Exr of Sue Allen---0. 15. 8
To Giles Moody------------0. 14. 10
To ye widows part ---------18. 4. 8
To Martin Magarys part--- 18. 4. 8
To Jos Magarys part--------18. 4. 8
=====
54. 14. 2
Wm Bayley, Theod Bayley
At a Court held for York County ye 16 July 1722. This settlement of ye estate of Martin Magary was presented in Court and is admitted to Record. test Phi Lightfoot ClCur

The estate of Robt Tunis is appraised by ye Subscribers according to and order of the Court this date 16 June 1722
A list of supplies including Pitch, Manna, Cremor Tarter, Fine Oyl, Sal Vitro, Castor, Crocus, ... Suollin . . . . . . Sweny

Page 145
At a court held for York County. . . . . Present John Holloway, Henry Tyler . . . . . . Justices

An account of ye Settlement of ye estate of (Godwin's Est settled) . . . . . .

court and admitted to record

On ye petition of Wm Levingston Guardian and . . . . . Mary Eliza Lucy and Frances Hurlstone orphans of Nich. Hurlstone late of this County decd it is ordered that ye Sherif Sumon Mary Hurlstone Extrx of ye last will and testament of Nich Hulston decd to render a Just account of ye last Will and testament of ye sd decd and of ye sale thereof at ye next Court

In ye action upon ye Case between Jno. Goodwin and Lawr Smith & Mildred his wife late Mildred Goodwin deft by Consent Case is Cont at ye plt Joseph Walker Thos Nelson & Richd Ambler ye foremer auditors to audit state & Settle all matters relateing thereto at ye next Court

Mary ye wife of Wm Atkinson hath furthur time allowed to exhibit an Invry of ye estate of Phi & Eliza Moody it is ordered that Wm Howit and Charles Hansford be added to ye Grand Jurors being Sworn

Wm and Sarah Atkinson . . . . . acknowledged their bond to ye Court for Mary ye wife Willm Atkinson on ye estates of Phi and Eliza Moody decd which bond is admitted to record

The former ordr. for taking (Griffin) upon ye G Jurys presentation is Contd.

Issue being joyned upon . . . . . exhibited by Wm Robertson att for and in behalf of our Sovereign Lord ye King plt agt MAry West deft ye Cause is referred for tryal at ye next Court

In ye action upon ye case between John Mattocke plt and Lawr Smith deft for two pounds . . . . . pence due by acct proved by ye plts oath Judgement is granted ye. . . . . sd Sum and ordered that ye deft pay ye sd Same cost als Exo (margin says Exo. executed & Satis. recd 21 July 1722)

(Remainder of page mostly illegible. Margin says Daniel - Bates Judgement)

(Toomer - Tabb) . . . Hayward estate

Page 146

. . . . . Robert Lawson decd in his hands ordered that ye Sheriff
. . . . . Thomas & Mary his wife to give fresh Security or Surrender ye sd estate
. . . . . court
. . . . . attacmt. of James Bacchus against ye estate of John Bates
. . . . . Sheriff having ret ye sd atta. executed in ye hands of Anthony Metcalf
. . . Jno Jude amounting to ten pounds one Shilling ordered that ye

. . . . Summoned to give an account of ye said Bates's estate in his hands at ye next Court

In ye petition of Wm Davis praying that Mary West may give an acct of her decd husbands estate Math Peirce Robt Cobbs & Ralph Graves or any two of them are appointed to state and settle ye accounta of John Wests estate and ordered that they make report at ye next Court

In action upon ye case between Mary West plt and Jno. Davis deft issue being Joyned ye Cause is referd for tryal at ye next Court

In action of case between Thos Jones plt & Eliza Powers deft is dismist

In case in Chancery depending between Armiger Parsons & Eliza his wife . . . . . Hay admin &c Rob Hay decd respndr is Cont till next Court

. . . . . of Saml Hyde praying that he amy be released from being Security . . . . . Thebo's admon on her decd husbands's estate ordered that . . . . . appear at ye next Court and give good Security accordingly

Jno Cook . . . . . giving Security hath an order granted for a Lycence to keep and Ordnry on ye ensuing year in York Town

Thomas Robins petition and giving Security hath an order granted him to keep an ordnry in York town ye ensuing year

John Powers petition for his wifes Dower of ye estate of Jno. Ferguson decd is rejected

In ye petiton of (James?) Bates praying that John Bates may give an acct of his admin of ye estate of Jno. Bates decd the deft failing to Settle ye aforesaid estate ... ing to order ordered that he be taken into ... is performed or gives reason for not doing ... be cont.

(Love - Fossett) In ye suit . . . . . Justinian Love & Elias Love and Eliza . . . . . Guardian & next friend Complt and John . . . . . responrs it is decreed that the Responds . . . . . two thirds of ye estate of Elias Love . . . . . Costs als Exo

. . . . . (Butler's estate settled)

.(Stoner - Mundall) . . . . estate in his hands with Costs.

. . . . . Jno. Conner for runing away . . . . . assigns ye remainder of his

. . . . . abridged that ye petr . . . . . lashes on his (margin Smith's servant to Serve)

Page 147
Mary Collier came into court and made Oath that . . . . . without making any will so far as sh. . . . . giving Security Certificate is granted. . . . .
on ye sd decds estate . . . . . (margin Collier admon Collier)
Mary Collier Wm Lee and Thos Vines . . . . . to ye court for ye said Mary Colliers Just & Fa. . . . . estate which bond is admitted to record

On ye petition of Robert Roberts praying that his part of ye estate of. . . . . decd in ye hands of Mary ye wife of William Atkinson may be delivered to him Ordered that ye former auditor state and Settle ye account in difference & Make report thereof for payment

The action upon the case between Dan Shield plt & Saml Sweny Excr &c Saml Harkie decd deft is Continued till next Court

Wm Stark Gent Wm Cross Matt Langston and John Potter or any three of them being Sworn are appointed to appraise ye estate of Charles Collier decd and make report thereof to ye next Court

The Suit depending between Rob Sparks plt and Joseph Berry def is dismist

The motion of Wm Robertson for admon on ye estate of Joseph Barry decd in behalf of Edw Sparks is overruled

John Mundall and Susa Sebrell . . . . . decd hath an furthur time allowed to bring in an Invry. . . . . estate of ye sd decd

In the action upon ye case . . . . . plt and Edw Jacqueline excr &c Harwood Cary decd . . . . . Cause is referred for tryal at next Court (margin - Charles)

Henry Bowcock on his petition . . . . . hath an order granted for a Lycence to keep an ordry. . . . . ensuig year

An account of ye Settlement of . . . . . Magary was presented in Court and admitted to record

In ye action of Debt betw. . . . . assignee of Wm Daniel plt and John Swinnock decd . . . . . Shillings and eleven pence due by note the . . . . . allowed him to plead and being Called failed . . . . . therefore granted ye plt by Nihil Dicit. . . . . Court on ye like default

The action between Phi Lightfoot plt and Lawr Smith deft is cont till next Court

In ye action . . . . . and Ann his wife plt & Wm Tavernor . . . . . wife is referred for tryal at next Court. (Harris-Tavernor)

An ac. . . . . Jno Rhodes is discontinued. (Roberts - Rhodes)

. . . . . Lightfoot plt & Wm Barbar and Saml Timson . . . . . Shillings and three pence due by a protested . . . . . and time allowed him to plead and being . . . . . is therefore granted ye plt by Nihil Dicit . . . . . on like default

. . . . . nl Taylor plt & Jno Bates Excr &c of Jno . . . . . Sterling due by bond ye deft . . . . . being called failed to do ye same . . . . . next Court of ye like default

. . . . . Laprade deft for five pounds . . . . . and being called failed to do ye same . . . . . returnable at ye next Court on ye like default

. . . . . Wm Levingston deft for Seven . . . . . the deft Confessed Judgement . . . . . that ye plt recover of ye deft . . . . . and four pence w cost als Exo (Turner-Levingston)

. . . . . plt & Thos Nelson adm (Moorland)

Page 148
. . . . . ye Case between Eliza Hansford plt and Lawr Smith deft issue . . . . . . Cause is referred for tryal at ye next Court

. . . . . ye case between John Brown plt & John Crowley deft for three . . . . . by act prov'd by ye plt Oath ye deft being called and not appearing . . . . . ye Judgement of ye nst Court agt ye deft and Fran Tyler his security ... and ordered that they pay ye sd Sum of three pounds ten shillings ... plt with cost als Exo

In action upon ye case between Joseph Banister and Wm Smelt Excr of ... (*missing*) and testament of Wm Smelt plts and Henry Holdcraft Excr of ye last will & test of Randle Platts decd deft by Complt Thos Jones and Thos Nelson gentl are appointed to State & Settle all matters in difference & Make rept thereof to ye next Court

The action in Chancery depending between John Hay & Mary his wife complts and Thos Tomer Surviving Excr &c Jno. Tomer decd is Cont till next Court

In ye suit of partition between Lucy Hill by Wm Cross her Guardian & next friend plt and Thos Vines and Bartlett Morland deft ye Jurys verdct and Sheriffs return is ordered to be recorded

The att obtained by Wm Wise agt ye estate of Robe. Innes is order'd to be discontinued and ye appraisers rept admitted to record

In ye Suit on Chancery depending between John Brooke plt Complt and Phi Lightfoot Excr &c Matt Ballard decd y Complt having agreed to stay . . . . . Christmas next by Consent Thos Nelson Wm. Stark Gentl & . . . . . any two of them are appointed to audit state & settle . . . . . Brooks decd according to ye bill exhibited and make . . . . . next Court

. . . . . between Danl Fisher plt and Lawr Smith Gent . . . . . by means of ye defts menaceing beating & Wounding . . . . . A jury to wit Thos Vines Robe. Ballard xc . . . . . who having heard ye evidence went out and being . . . . . verdict in these words to wit we find for ye plt Six pence agt . . . . . motion is recorded and its Considered that ye plt . . . . . ence being his damages by ye Jurors in mannor . . . . .

. . . . . us Shields plt & Wm Robertson Gent . . . . . due by bond the 13th day of April . . . . . Arguments on the deft demurrer were . . . . . considered that the plt recover agt the deft . . . . . together with twelve pounds . . . . . mony for Interest thereupon & cost als Exo

From . . . . . to the 7th day of ... (Roberston - Shields appl)

. . . . . (*The following words can be seen:* "Jones, gent. . . . . Wm Blakely her Security")
(margin Turner - Ives writt of Eng)

Page 149
At a Court held for York . . . . . Present Lawr. (*missing*) Justices Arc. .

Martha Wood Sin... of felony in taking. ... Currt mony ... upon hearing ... that She ... and from the ... ordered for a tryal ... ye genl Court whereupon it is ordered (margin ... be Convey'd Publick Gaol)

Nath Brettenham ordered to ye prison of ye County in custody of ye . . Sheriff Lord ye King to be conveyed . . . . . publick gaol at Williamsburgh and Teneminal at ye genl Court on fourth day theref as ye Law directs an ye fourth day day before y Court acknowledged him els indented to our Sovereign evidence in ye Sum of forty pounds to be levy'd on his Goods Chattels Laws stands. . . . . conditions that if he shall appear at ye next genl Court on be void. . . . . and attend from time to time then and there to give. . . . . (Brittinghams &c Recognizance)

Fra S . . . . . of our Sovereign Lord ye King agt Martha Wood who themselv. . . . . Suspicion of felony these ye above recognizance to their . . . . . remain in full force and virtue (these all appear to be recogizance for individuals appearing at trial of Martha Wood)

(Collier's will) (*to be seen are:* "Son Thos Collier. . . Land from. . . plantation that I least to John Hilliard with all my lands from the. . . daughter Eliza Collierone negro Girl named Peg ...").
Page 150
. . . . . and testament of Charles Collier decd was presented in Court . . . . . last will by ye Oath of Ephraim Cockett & Wm Waugh . . . . . furthur declared that he Saw Wicklitt . . . . witnesses thereto & That it was signed by the . . . . . to record. Test Phi Lightfoot ClCur

. . . . . Charles Collier deced Colliers appr Invry Recd
Includes:
Gelding - £6. 15. . .
Pistols Holsters & Sword - 3. . . . Negro Man Jeffery   24. --
Negro woman Nanny & her child Frank - £30. --
Negro woman Hannah - 18. --
Negro man called Ned - 30. --
Negro Man Jack - 20. --
1 Negro. . . . . W ,,, -20. --
Negro Boy Sam - 20. --
Negro Boy Harry - 16. —
Wm Cross, Wm Stark, John Potter

(Love's estate) . . . . *words seen are. . . July 1722. . Love that was brought . . Steers £4. 0*

Page 151
Love estate cont.

Ren. . . . . Roberts Thos. Hand

At a court held for York County 20 Aug 1722
This app. . . . Ellis (Ellins) Love decd was presented in Court & is admitted to record. Test Phi Lightfoot ClCur

Know all men by these presents that we Wm Robertson and Wm Gordon of ye County of York are held adn firmly bound unto James Shields or his certain Attorney their heirs Excrs . . . . . in ye Sum of two hundred pounds Sterling to which payment well & truly to be made We bind our Selves and each of us our

& each of our heirs and Sealed with our Seals dated Aug. . 1722

This . . . . . Obligation is Such that whereas in a difference tryed in July Court last . . . . . Robertson deft Judgement passed agt ye sd deft from . . . . . Robertson appealeth to ye 7th day of next Genl Court . . . . . sd Sum appeal with effect and perform ye Judgement. . . . . . in case ye Judgement of ye County Court be assigned . . . . . Wm Robertson, Wm Gordon

(West's estate settled)
. . . . . Invry & appr retd. - £55. 18. 6
. . . . . Cash recd ofMr Lews. Holland - 8. -
. . . . . Jno Bates Senr - £7. -
. . . . . my fathers estate - 5. -
. . . Graves - 3.
. . . . Livingston - 2. -
. . . . . Hubbard - 1. -
. . . . . . Bates junr - 10. -

Page 152
At a court held for York County 20 Augt 1722. Present John Holloway Esq Arch Blair, Henry Tyler, Graves Pack, Lawr Smith, Thos Chisman

In ye action of Charles Hansford agt Mary Collier admrx Charles Collier decd concerning Dowlings estate is rejected it appearing ye effects of his sd p. . (*missing*) is already answered

On ye motion of Charles Hansford and by Consent of Mary Collier Jos . . (*missing*) Gent is appt to State and Settle ye est of Jas. Dowlings est & make repthereof to next Court

The action of trespass between Robt Shield plt & Jno. Degernit deft is dismist

In ye action of Detinue between Thos Tomer plt & Saml Tompkins deft for two Negro Slaves of ye price of fifty five pounds ye deft being called and not appearing nor any Security ret for him Judgement is therefore granted ye plt agt ye deft and John Gibbons Sheriff for what Shall appear due at ye next Court with cost unless ye sd deft appears then to answer ye same

The action of case between Mary Cook plt & Sam Sealy deft is dismist

In ye action of Seire faccia between Thos Jones plt & John Battles deft for eighteen pounds. . . . Shillings and costs of Suit On ye plts motion ordered that a new . . . . . agt ye sd Battles returnable to ye next Court

In ye action upon ye . . . . . n Cormack Excrx &c Cornelius Cormack decd plt Andr Laprade . . . . . and Impl. is granted him until next Court

The action of Case . . . . . Gibbons plt & Rd Needham deft is dismist

The action of. . . . . Butterworth plt & Jno. Bartlett deft is dismist

The action of case between . . . . . Shield plt & Edw. Worley deft is dismist The action of trespass between . . . . . plt & Wm Wise &c deft is dismist (Wills - Wise)

The action of Debt between W. Houghton plt & Dan. Roberts deft is dismist

In ye action of case between Geo Allen plt & Eliza Powers deft at ye defts motion an Imparl. is granted her untill ye next Court

In ye action of Case between Geo Allen plt & . . . s Platts deft is dismist

On ye action of Case between . . . . . (James Faison) plt and Daniel Taylor Excr &c Henry Taylor . . . . . deft for thirty pounds due by note ye deft being called. . . . . nor any Security ret for him on ye plt motion. . . . . him agt John Gibbons Sheriff of this County . . . . . ye deft appears at ye next Court. . . . .

Judgemt . . . . . Jas. Faison agt Jno Gibbons
Sheriff of . . . . . means of ye nonappearance ... Jams. Faison
. . . . . him agt

(Archer-R...) . . . . . is dismist

(Archer-Butter) Butter deft is dismist

(Philips- ...) . . . . . Gibbons his next friend . . . . . tion for ye return of Mr Randolph . . . . . Hurlstone Excr &c is . . . . . Randolph . . . . . h & Mildred

Page 153
In ye action upon ye case. . . . . for eleven pounds fourteen Shillings . . . . . both partys Submitted ye Cause to ye . . . . . hearing ye evidence and partys . . . . . ordered that ye plt recover of ye deft Six pounds five. . . . . and Cost als Exo (West-Davis) Exo is 18 Feb 1722)

In ye petn. of James Bacchus agt ye estate of Rob Bates for £54. 2. 8 Sterling Costs Anthony Metcalf appeared according to S. . . . . & acknowledged £10.1.9 of ye defts effects in his hands ordered . . . . . ame to ye plt als Exo

Mary Atkinson wife of Wm Atkinson . . . . . time allowed to exhibit an Invry of of ye estate of Eliza and P. . . . .

Joseph Walker . . . . . nominated in ye Couns. . . . . of peace this day took ye Oaths appointed by ye dedirnus and then took his place on ye bench
Present Joseph Walker Wm Stark, Wm Sheldon

In ye information exhibited in behalf of our Sovereign Lord ye Kind agt Mary West ordered that a dedirnus Horie directed to Jno. Holloway Esq and Henry Tyler gent for them or either of them to take ye exa. of all witnesses relating to ye cause and that notice be given to ye deft of ye time and place of Exa. & its furthur ordered that ye information be continued till next court

In ye pet of Wm Davis - Mary West an acc of Jno Wests estate being this day lodged in ye office by ye deft ye plt on his motion hath time allow'd till next Court to Consider ye same

The suit in Chancery depending between Armiger Parsons &c Complts and Jno Stacy Respondts is continued untill next Court at ye defts motion and Charge

The pet of Saml Hyde agt Elinor Thebo is dismist neither party appearing

On ye pet of Wm Holsman & Thos Wooten praying that they may be released from being Security for Jos Thomas's admon on ye estate of Rob Lawson ye deft being Summoned and failing to appear ordered that ye Sheriff take and keep him in Custody untill hs gives Security for his appearance at ye next Court

The last will and testament of Chas Collier decd was presented in Court and prov'd to be his last will by ye Oaths of Eliza Cockitt and Wm Waugh witnesses thereto and ye sd Cockit further declared that he Saw Wicklif (s) Dowling Subscribe ye same will as a itness thereto and it was signed in the year 1717 and Waugh ye other witness declared that is was signed about 4 years ago which testament is admitted to record and on ye motion of Mary Collier and her former Security Certificate is granted her for obtaining a Commision of admin on ye sd Collier exc. Oath. ye will annext in due form
. . . . . Cockit on evidence toChas Colliers will having attended on day . . . . . Collier Adm &c . . . . . 40 tobo. for ye same al Eso

(Smith pet Ordry rejd)

. . . . . to answer ye petn of Jams Purvas
. . . . . &c is Cont till next Court for Settling

(Roberts -Atkinson) is cont

(Shield -Sweny)

. . . . . of Sebrels estate according . . . . . ody untill he gives Security (Collier's est ret)

Page 154
. . . . . Thos Charles plt & Rd Jacqueline Excr &c . . . . . decd deft is Cont at ye plt . . . . . return

. . . . . upon ye case between Phi Lightfoot plt & Lawr Smith deft is cont

. . . . . action of Detinue between Wm Morris & Ann his wife and . . . . . . Wm Tavernor deft is Cont by ye deft Costs agt Mr Randolphs ser. . . . .

Thos Jones Genl presented & acknowledged his deeds of Lease & Release to Chas Degrafenried wth. rect. thereon for on e Lott lying in Williamsburgh Which deeds are admitted to record

In ye action of Debt between Fs. Pinkett assignee &c plt & Jno. Swinnock for ye Sum of £ 2. 11. 11 ye Suit is cont for Wm Daniels oath to ye particulars of . . . . . if he is out of ye County his oath before Some Justice of ye peace to ye same will be received as proof

In ye action of debt between Phi Lightfoot plt and Wm Barbar and Saml Timson defts. for thirty three pounds twelve shillings & Three pence Sterling dued upon a protested bill of exchange ye deft being Called and not appearing ye judgement of ye last Court is confirmed and ordered that teh said deft pay ye said Sum of £ 33. 12. 3 to ye plt with Costs als Exo

On ye action of Debt between Wm Clark plt & Dyer Colston Read deft for £47. 12. 6 Sterling due by means of a protested of Exchange ye deft being called and not appearing ye Judgemnt of ye last Court is confirmed agt ye said deft & Jno. Jones genl his Security and ordrd that they pay ye said sum of forty Seven pounds twelve Shillings & Sixpence Sterling to ye plt with costs als Exo

In ye action of debt between Danl Taylor plt and Jno. Bates Excr &c Jno Bates decd deft is Cont at ye defts charge for ye ret of Mr Randolph

In ye action of debt between Thos Jones plt & Eliza Ives deft on ye plt oath Judgement is granted him for thirty pounds Seventeen Shillings & A farthing Sterling deducting thereout fifteen pounds Seventten Shillings & Six pence half penny Current mony and ordered that ye deft and Wm Blaikley her Security pay ye Same to ye plt with Costs als Exo

The action upon ye Case between Eliza Hansford plt and Lawr Smith deft is Cont untill next Court for tryal

In ye action of debt between Fra Sharp plt and Andr Laprade deft ye deft on his motion hath liberty to make Sevrl plea's ye Cause is Contd. till next Court

In ye action upon ye case between Jno. Banister & Wm Smelt Excrs &c of Wm. . . . . decd plts and Henry Holdcraft Excr &c of Rand. Platts decd decd defts y former ordr for Settlement is Cont untill next Court

The Suit in Chancery between Jno. Hay & Martha his wife Complts and Tho Toomer Surviving Excr &c of Jno Toomer decd Respondr in Contind for the Return of Mr Randolph at ye Complt Costs

In ye Suit in Chancery between Jno. Brooke Compl and Phi Lightfoot Excr &c Matt Ballard decd respondt . . . . . Report was this day Lodged in Court & Ye Suit Cont untill the return of mr Randolph

In ye action . . . . . Flower deft for £2. 6. 0 ye deft . . . . . agt ye sd deft and . . . . . appears at ye next Court (trotter or Potter -Flower)

(Vaughn-Tabb) . . . . . plt & Edw Tabb & Eliza Haywood . . . . . this County defts on ye defts . . . . . next Court

(Cole. . . . -Moorland) . . . . . plt and David Moreland . . . . . Judgement is granted

(Park- Moorland)

Page 155
The action of debt between Graves Pack plt & Robt Hubbard deft . . . . .

The action of debt between Wm Ritche. . . . . Warrington . . . . . *(margin reads Gilchrist)*

(Cook- Snowdon) The action of Case between Jno Cooke plt & Rand. . . . .

(Cook-Swinnock) The action of Case between Jno Cooke plt & Jno. . . . .

(Gilchrist - Warrington) The action of Case between Wm Gilchr. . . . .

The action upon ye case between Richd Turner plt & Wm Smith deft is dismist

The action upon ye Case between Jno Cook plt & Rob Hastings deft is dismist

The action of case between (Ives-Levingston) & Wm Levingston deft is dismist

The action of debt between . . . . . ye King plt Eliza Powers deft is continued at ye defts charge. . . . . of mr Randolph

In ye . . . . . our Lord ye King plt & Marg Burk deft . . . . . joyned ye Cause is refr'd for Tryal at ye next court. (Pack-Burk)

In ye action . . . . . Debt between Robt Laughton in behalf of our Lord ye King plt & Fra Sharp . . . . . Issue being joyned ye Cause is referred for tryal at ye next Court

In ye action of Case between Cole Diggs Esc plt &c & Phi Lightfoot Exctr & Matt Bal. . . . . deft for one hundred & ten pounds two Shillings & Six pence due by act. proved Judgemt. is granted ye plt for yd said Sum and ordered that ye deft pay ye same to ye plt out of ye decd estate in his hands wth Costs als Exo

In ye action of debt between Thos Bell and Mary his wife plt and Wm Ferguson otherwise called Wm Ferguson of Charles Parish in ye County of York Blacksmith
at ye defts motion an imparlance is granted untill next Court

In ye action of trespass between Robt Wills plt and Zephaniah Martin deft at at ye defts motion an Imparlance is granted untill next court

In ye action of debt between James Price plt and Richd Baker deft neither part appearing ye suit is dismist

In ye action upon ye case between Mich Archer plt and Mary Butler deft ye deft . . . . . to ye plt for Two pounds twelve Shillings and two pence ordered . . . . . ye same to ye plt with costs als Exo

. . . . . Case between Jno. Bush plt and Dyer Colston Read deft for . . . . . appear an order's granted ye plt agt ye deft and Jno. Gibbons Sheriff . . . . . appears at ye next Court & answers ye sd action On ye Sheriff. . . . . ton Gent hath liberty to appear in his behalf and to make . . . . . deft might have done if he had appeared

In ye . . . . . of Robt Innis for £4. 10. 0 an atta. being being retd Exe. . . . . Moss appearing by Consent ye atta. is furthur (Welch-Innis)

. . . . . Patrick Christie agt ye estate of Dyer . . . . . atta being ret /executed in ye hands . . . . . es be summoned to render an acct . . . . . next Court

(Main. . . . Constable) . . . . . York Town in ye Room of . . . . .

(Love's Est appraised)

Page 156

At a Court held for York County 17 Nov 1722. Present . . . . . Holloway Esqr, Graves Park, Lawr Smith, Wm Sheldon, Arch Blair, Wm Stark Gentl

Ordered that ye Sheriff Summon 24 freeholders of ye County to app at ye November Court to be of ye grand Jury

. . . . . William Robertson Gentl made Oath that Robt Innis departed this life without making any last will & testament so far as he knows or believes On his motion and Giving Security Certificate is granted him for obtaining Commission of admon on ye sd Innis's estate in due form

On ye pet . . . . . Gibbons agt his servant Lewis Davis for runningaway Considering that the sd Davis hath been absent three months . . . . . and expended Seven hundred twenty eight pounds tobacco ordered that he serve his sd Master eighteen months one week and four days for ye same after his time by former order or Indenture Custom is expired

Present Edw Tabb Genl

On ye pet of James Mackindo agt his runaway Serv John Connor It appearing that ye sd Connor hath been absent eight days and that five hundred thirty two pounds of tobacco hath been expended in taking him up Ordered that he serve his said Master eight months two weeks and one day after his time by Indenture Custom or former order is expired

On ye pet of Wm Rogers agt his Servant Jno. Jones for running away It appearing that ye sd Jones hath been absent . . . . . days & that y sd Rogers hath expended three hundred Seventy two pounds of tobacco in retaking of him Ordered that he Serve his sd Master Six months for the Same after his time by Indenture Custom or former order of Court is expired and that he receive . . . . . at ye publick whipping post thirty nine lashes. . . . .

In ye pet of James Bates . . . . . Bates may give an acctg of his admon on ye estate. . . . . ye former order for audit and settling ye accts or. . . . . untill next

Court

Robt Cobbs Benj We. . . . . are added to ye former apprs for appraising ye . . . . . to Jno. Fleming Orderd that they appraise ye same and give report thereof at ye next Court

An Account ... es Dowling decd was presented in Court and admitted to Record

(Pescod - Nixon) on ye pet . . . . . estate in ye hands of Thos Nixon. . . . . Sheriff Summon ye sd Thos . . . . . Court

(The King - West) . . . . . agt Mary West . . . . .

(Toomer - Tompkin)

Next entry is illegible except for a few fragments as follows:. . . *committed to ye Gaol of this. . . . . from Eliza Powers a. . . . Spanish mony or. . . . aa. Harkin and. .*

Page 157
the County . . . . . be conveyed to ye publick . . . . .

(Powers Recognizance) (... *these fragments* "... Eliza Powers. . . in ye Sum. . . if she shall. . . Chattles On. . . evidence in. . . . Zephaniah Martin. . . Ann Sawser who stands Co. . . recognizance to be void or ... "

(Wills's recognizance) Robt Wills before ye Court. . . . . Sovereign Lord ye King the Sum of 20 pounds. . . . . to be Levyed . . . . . Chattles on Condition that if his Servant Ann Backwell . . . . . Genl Court and attend from time to time and there. . . . . behalf of our Sovereign Lord the King agt Ann Sawser and ... Martin who stands Committed on Suspicion of felony the ... else remain in full force & virtue

(Weyman's Recognizance) Thos Weyman . . . . . in debted to ye Sovereign Lord ye King in ye Sum of 20. . . . . . . Goods and Chattels On Condition that he shall appear at y next . . . . . thereof and attend from time to time then and there to . . . . . our Sovereign Lord ye King agt Zephaniah Martin and Ann Sawser . . . . . Committed on Suspicion of felony then ye above Recognizance of be void . . . . . remain in full force & virtue

Theod Rinning (?) on his pet . . . . . Security hath an order granted him for a Lycence to keep an Ordnry in his now house in this County ye ensuing year

The suit. . . . . between Jno. Jones plt & Jno Battles deft is Cont for new proof

The action of Case between Ann Cormack &c plt & Andr Laprade deft is dismist

The last will and testament of Nathl Hooks decd was presented in Court by Rebecca Hooks Excrx therein named . . . . . Oath to it and being proved by ye Oaths of all ye witnesses is admitted to record and on her motion and given Security Certificate is granted her for probate thereof in due form

In ye Complaint of Lawr Smith . . . . . ence agt Ann Chapman ye court to order that she . . . . . whipping post upon her bare back 15 lashes well laid on. . . . .

On ye petition of Thomas Hansford. . . . . Hansford is appointed his Guardian having given Security . (. *missing*) take care of ye sd orphan and his estate . . . . . pounds fifteen shillings to Eliza Hansford out of. . . . . receive of ye said orphan's estate

The action of ye case between Geo Allen plt & Eliza Powers deft is Cont untill . . . . Faison plt & Danl Taylor Exctr (margin Faison-. . .) . . . . . ye defts costs for Mr Randolph's

(Philip ... - ...). . . . . by Jno. Gibbons his next . . . . . defts Charge for JRans.

. . . . . Eliza Lucy & Frans. . . . . . defts Charge
(Levinsgstone-Hu. . .)

(Atkinson to ret)

(Davis -. .)

(margin may say'Barton') and these fragments. . . *ye above bounden Chas Hansford. . . . . son of Thomas Hansford. . . . . his Care and Custody.)*

Page 158
(P. . . -Peters) . . . . . Peters is dismist on non-appearance

(Roberts-Atkinson) Roberts agt Mary ye wife of Wm Atkinson is Cont at ye . . . . . of Mr Randolph . . . . . Case between Jno. Shields plt and Saml Sweny is . (*missing*) of . . . . . deft is Cont at ye defts motion and Charge

. . . . . between Fras. Sharp plt and Andrew Laprade deft ye ... . to Consider the defts demurrer

. . . . . between Thos Pinkett Assignee &c plt & Jno. Swinnock deft is dismist

. . . . . between Jno. Trotter plt and Jef Flower deft is dismist

. . . . . between Wm Vaughan plt & Edw Tabb & Eliza
. . . . . Henry Hayward decd late Sheriff of this County
. . . . . had furthur time allowed till this Court to plead and
. . . . . Therefore its considered bye ye Court
. . . . . is Sum Sued for and Costs unless ye
. . . . . Court to answer ye said action
. . . . . (margin Vaughan -Hayward Excrs N. D.)

In ye. . . . . between Thos Bell and Mary his wife and Wm Ferguson. . . . . called Wm Ferguson of Charles Parish in ye County of York deft . . . . . Hundred pounds Current mony ye deft having had time given him. . . . . Court to plead and being called failed to do ye same Judgement. . . . . granted plt agt ye deft by Nihil Dicit for ye sd Sum and Cost als Exo

The action. . . . . between Graves Pack &c plt and Margt Burk deft is cont

In ye action . . . . . Debt between Wm Clack plt and Dyer Colston Read deft for £47. . . . . Sterling due by . . . . . of protested bill of Exchange ye deft be. . . . . called and not appearing ye Judgement of ye last Court is Cont. agt ye sd. . . . . and Jno. Jones Gentl his Security and ordered that
. . . . . said Sum of forty Seven pounds twelve shillings & Six
. . . . . plt with Costs als Exo

In ye. . . . . ye Case between Jno. Brush plt and Dyer Colston Read deft Issue being Joyned ye case is referred for tryal till ye next Court

On ye pet . . . . . Welch estate of Robert Innis for £4. 14. 0 proved to be due. . . . . atta being retd execute on 25/in ye hands of of Robt Ross . . . . . to ye petr als Exo

In ye. . . . . Charles Lucas
. . . . . not appearing
. . . . . agt ye deft
. . . . . deft appears at ye
. . . . . Thos Charles for Six
. . . . . appearance of Charles
. . . . . Charles's motion and
. . . . . for ye sd Sum and

Page 159
(margin Tyler - Lucas) In ye action. . . . . Bower plt and Charles Lucas
. . . . . tobo ye deft being called
and not app. . . . Sum and Costs agt
ye deft and. . . . . appears at ye next court
to answer. . . . .

Judgemnt . . . . . Thos Charles for two
hundred two. . . . . ye non-appearance
of Chas Lucas. . . . . Thos Charles motion
an atta is granted . . . . . to ye next
Court for. . . . .

In ye action . . . . . Damazinah Roberts
deft for four . . . . . called and not appearing
nor any Security. . . . . granted ye plt for ye said
Sum and costs. . . . . Sheriff unless ye said
deft appears. . . . . answer ye said action (Haughton-Roberts)

In ye action upon. . . . . Brodie plt & Damazinah Roberts deft is dismist

In ye action upon. . . . . Martin Gentl plt & Thos Robbins & Wm
Harwood Ferr. . . . York Town to Tindalls point defts for
ten pounds da. . . . . Robbins being called and not appearing nor any
Security retd for. . . . . granted ye plt for ye sd Sum and Cost
agt ye sd Robbins . . . . . Sheriff unless he appears at ye next
Court to answer. . . . . orderd that an als Capias iss. agt Wm Harwood

The action of. . . . . Duer plt & R Needham deft is dismist

In ye action of Jno. Hoy & Ann his wife Excrs &c . . . . . deft at ye defts motion
an Imparlance is granted (Hoy-Laprade)

Robt Ballard . . . . . Mackindo and Wm Gordon or any three of them being
appointed to appraise ye estate of Nath Hook decd and make report to ye next
court

Jno Wright is. . . . . precinct of Y Hampton pa in ye Room of . . . . . repair to
Some Justice County to take . . . . . (Wright appt Constable)

(Prison to be built) In ye representive. . . . . and according . . . . . prison a room
of 16 ft . . . . . lined with Oak plank w. di . . . . . other conveniences in each . . . . .
ye old prison

. . . . . ye Court in Course
. . . . . Holloway

(Hansford - Hansford)

Page 160
. . . . . therefore that if ye sd Charles Hansford
. . . . . relating to ye sd orphan
. . . . . paid his full dues acct . . . . . Saw and
. . . . . full age or sooner if ye . . . . . shall think
. . . . . hereafter shall save . . . . . less
. . . . . heirs &c from all damages that shall
. . . . . ye sd estate and perform all other
. . . . . Then this Obligation to be
. . . . .
Charles Hansford . acknowledged. Test Phi Lightfoot ClCur

. . . . . Edw. Ripping James Shields & Jean Pasteur. . . . . firmly bound to our Sovereign Lord ye King in ye. . . . . of tobacco convenient in this County to which payment . . . . . to our said Lord ye King his heirs and Successors . . . . . and every of us our and every of our heirs Execrs and Admins. . . . . severally firmly by theses presents sealed with our Seals and dated this 1722

The Condition of. . . . . that whereas ye above bound Edw Ripping hath an Order this. . . . . Lycence to keep an Ordinary at his now dwelling house in the . . . . . ensuing If therefore ye sd Ripping doth constantly . . . . . Ordry good wholesome and cleanly Lodging & diet for Travellors. . . . . and provender or pasturage and provender as ye Season . . . . . ye date of these presents for and during ye. . . . . Suffer any unlawful Gambling in his said . . . . . Suffer any person to tipple or drink more than is necessary. . . . . to be void or else remain in full force and virtue

At a court held for . . . . . Edw Ripping, James Shields, Jean Pasteur. Phi Lightfoot ClCur

(Dowlings estate settled)
. . . . . Walker and Cash £41. 10. 0
. . . . . . Buck. 1. 5. 0
========
£126. 19. 4
. . . . . Dowling Cr
(*unclear if this is connected but just below is* "Mary Collier admr Chas Collier")

Page 161
York County. . . . . have stated & Settled the estate. . . . .
. . . . . appears to say By Jos Walker. Test Phi Lightfoot ClCur

(Hooks Will)
In ye name given. . . . . Nathaniel Hook of ye parish of York Hampton in. . . . . and week in body but of Sound and perfect memory . . . . . And for ye uncertainty of this life I make this my. . . . . also I resign my Soul into ye hands of God that . . . . . my loving wife my Lott that I . . . . . in York Town for her natural life after her decease then I . . . . . bequeath to Thos Watkins Son of Wm Watkins Junr . . . . . John son of Humphry Faison to be share & Share alike . . . . . that my Godson Thos Watkins his . . . . . lawfully begotten of his body . . . . . and Godson . . . . . Natural life and after his decease to Wm Watkins. . . . . Son. . . . . Wm Watkins desire that ye sd Wm Watkins may take . . . . . of his. . . . . my loving wife's decease I also make my . . . . . my wife Sole Excr Signed . . . . . presence. Nath Hook. Mary P. . . . . evins. At a Court held for York County 17 7ber 1722
This . . . . . test. of Nath Hook decd was presented in Court by ye Exectrx therein named . . . . . and being proved by the Oaths of ye Witnesses is admitted to record. Test Phi Lightfoot ClCur

Know ye all men by these presents that we Reba Hook and John Gibbons & Wm Watkins of ye County of York. . . . . firmly bound unto ye Justices of ye County aforesaid in ye Sum of forty pounds Sterling to which payment well and truly to be made to ye said Justices their heirs and successors or some of them we bind our Selves and every of us our and every of our heirs Exectrs & Admins Joyntly and Severally firmly be these presents Sealed with our Seals and dated this 1722

. . . . . above bounden Reba. Hook Exctrx of
. . . . . or cause to be made a true &
. . . . . and Credits of ye sd decd which
. . . . . Same so made to exhibit or
. . . . . time after shall
. . . . . just acc
. . . . . said Court and
. . . . . ye sd testament
. . . . . to extend according to ye value
. . . . . Obligation to be void or else
. . . . . Wm Watkins

Page 162
. . . . . and is admitted to record

. . . . . Lightfoot ClCur

. . . . . York County Nov 19 1722
. . . . . ith Wm Sheldon
. . . . . Blair Wm Stark Edw Tabb Gen

. . . . . between James Selater and Eliza his wife
. . . . . and Mary Selater deft for ten
. . . . . deft refusing to permit to be divided
. . . . . house and three hundred acres of
. . . . . parish of Charles in this County of
. . . . . Selater father of ye sd Eliza wife of Jas.
Selator. . . . . Mary one third whereof doth appertain to ye sd. . . . . and ye heirs of her body begotten in fee and ye. . . . . Agnes and Mary by ye Curtes ye & as in ye decd . . . . . expressed and ye said Wm Sheldon came into Court. . . . any but that he holds the Mannor and . . . . . ye declaration . . . . for ye sd Agnes and Mary with . . . . . that partition ought to be made ye plts . . . . . therefore it is commanded to ye sheriff that twelve good and . . . . . full men of his Baliwick who are not concerned or have affinity or consanguinity to ye parties or lye adj. to any. . . . . company with ye sd Surveyor of the County he cause to. . . . . mannor and Lands aforesaid between ye . . . . . according to ye quantity and value thereof. . . . . same to ye next Court

Pat a Negro Girl belonging to. . . . . (Hawkins) was adjudged to be 12 years old

In ye pet of Ro. Pescod . . . . . estate in ye hands of Thos Nixon
may be delivered . . . . . ye Sheriff summon ye sd Nixon
to appear and . . . . . that ye next court

This Information . . . . . Sovereign ye King agt Mary West is Cont at ye plts . . . . . new dedunus Issue fr Exa. of Witnessses . . . . . . Graves Pack Gentl

In ye action . . . . . Graves Pack who as well for our Lord
ye King as . . . . . part Sues plt & Margr Burk deft
. . . . . means of ye defts refusing to pay
. . . . . by means of her retaining
. . . . . to an act of Assembly
. . . . . & ye issue being
. . . . . to wit Um.
. . . . . retired and being
. . . . . these words
. . . . . which ordr. is at ye
. . . . . recover agt ye deft two

. . . . . to our said Lord ye King
. . . . . act it is provided (margin reads Pack - Burk judgement)

(Taylor-Bates) . . . . . Bates Excr &c

Page 163
On Matt . . . . . appointed his Guardian . . . . . in whose hands ye said Hill. . . . . on thereto at ye next Court (Hills pet fr Guardian)

(Pack- Bates) . . . . . is dismist

(power of atty proved) . . . . . bbins was proved in Court

Edw Baptiste . . . . . and
having given. . . . . their estates
be committed. . . . . (Guardianship appointed)

(G Jury Sworn) Jno. Chapman . . . . . were sworn by a G Jury for ye body of. . . . . received their charge retired and being recalled. . . . . some presentments and then were . . . . . persons being presented by ye G Jury be Summoned. . . . . to answer their Sd presentments

On ye petn of. . . . . Hay praying that they may be released fm being. . . . . Thos Bells care of Jno. Ferguson an orphan . . . . . der'd that ye Bell give fresh Security or surrender . . . . . next court

In ye action. . . . . Dun Shield plt & Saml Sweney Excr &c Saml Harkie . . . . . pounds damage Issue being Joyned a Jury (to whit) . . . . . later Jno. Power Fra Hayward Jno. Pasture Thos Westton. . . . . Wm Morris Robt Roberts Jno. Potter John Brush and U. . . . . Sworn who having heard ye evidence retired and . . . . . Verdt returned ye same in these words Wee find. . . . . pounds current mony which verdict at ye plts mon . . . . . its considered that ye plt recover agt ye deft ye. . . . . pounds by ye Jurors in manner aforesaid aforsd a. . . . . cost als Exo

The action of Case between. . . . . Charles plt and Edw Jacqeline Exr &c of Har. Cary deced . . . . . motion & Charge

The action of. . . . . Lightfoot plt & Lawr Smith deft is dismist

The action of debt between Wm Morris and Ann his wife plt and Wm Tavernor . . . . . at ye plt motion and charge

The action of Case between. . . . . Hansford plt & Lawr Smith deft is Contd

In ye action upon ye case between. . . . . Joseph Bannister & Wm Smelt Excrs &c of Wm Smelt decd . . . . . Holdcrorft Excr &c Rand Platts decd deft ordered that. . . . . and Thos Nelson or either of them audit . . . . . . & Make rept thereof to ye next Court

. . . . . Dun Shield agt Saml Sweny having
. . . . . ye sd Shield pay him One hundred and
. . . . . same with costs als Exo (Salater on Evidence be fin'd.)

(Tabb to be f. . . . .)

. . . . . Eliza Ives departed
. . . . . she knows or believes
. . . . . is granted her (Ives pet. admon.)

(Hay - Toomer) . . . . . . made to ye

(Ives est) . . . . . above bounden Jno Read
. . . . . Ives decd do make or Cause

Page 164
. . . . . Toomer at ye Suit of Jno. Hay having
. . . . . ye same & Cost als Exo (Wells on evidence)

. . . . . decd was proved in Court
. . . . . to it and being proved . . . Oaths
. . . . . Record & on his motion . . having
. . . . . for obtaining a probate thereof . . . . .
. . . . . Mountfort & Robt Harris or any. . . . .
. . . . . to appraise ye estate of Mary Read
. . . . . ye next Court

. . . . . by consent's of ye Exrs. of Susanna
. . . . . One thousand One hundred and ten
. . . . . on from ye sd Allens estate at 20 s/
. . . . . accordingly (Gordon - Allens est) . . . . .
Wm. . . . . Baker and James Mackindo or any three of them. . . . . appointed to appraise ye estate of Robt Innis decd. . . . . thereof to ye next Court

Wm Gordon. . . . . approbation took ye receivers Oath directed by ye . . . . . for ye furthur improving ye staple of tobacco ordered that ye. . . . . accordingly. (Gordon & Gibbons chosen receivers)

Ordered that ye Court. . . . . untill ye Court in Course . . . . . Lawr Smith. Truly entered Phi Lightfoot ClCur

(Levy Laid)
At a Court held for York County . . . . . Xber 1722 . . . . . . Wm Stark. Edw Tabb, Gentl.
To ye Secretary - 790
To Fra Tyler - 320
To John Gibbons - 1798
To Fra Tyler - 6512
To Wm Rogers - 100
To Wm Gordon - 2050
To Wm Roberts - 864
To ye Sheriff - 1080
To Mr Buck . . . Bridge - 1080
To ye Clerk - 1080
To Phi Lightfoot - 1074
To Lawr Smith - 100
To Wm Powers - 160
To James Mac . . . - 475
To Wm Nelson. - 42
(Note that the remainder of names are too fragmented to list.)
27450 (total)

Page 165
Ordered . . . . . lists of Tithables 18do. . . . . . upon refusal of payment to Lew. . . . . for ye same to such persons as. . . . . (Gibbons & Gordon Sworn)

(Reads will)
In ye name . . . . . parish in ye County of York. . . . . Sense and memory do make my. . . . . manner and form following Imprs I give . . . . . body to ye earth from whence it came to be. . . . . discretion of my Exr hereafter to be named. . . . . Silver Tankard to my loving Son . . . . . and bequeath my Small Silver tankard and. . . . . loving on Samuel Read Item I give . . . . . Silver porringer one silver Tumbler and . . . . . Son Francis Read item I give and bequeath any. . . . . and 20s to buy a Ring to my loving daughter. . . . . item I Give and bequeath one Mullatto Boy. . . . . to my loving Son Samuel Read item I give ... Negro Boy named Will & one Negro Boy named Phil. ... James Read to him and his heirs Item I give a ... Grandaughter Mary Nelson one Negro Man named ... one Negro woman named Sarah and one Negro ...bina to her and her heirs in Case She dies with out heirs ... is that her brother John & His heirs have ye said ... and bequeath to my Grandson Wm Nelson one ... after my Just debts and funeral expenses ... part of my estate which is not already given and bequeathed .... divided among my three

sons Vizt John . . . . . but in Case either of them die without heirs . . . . dying to be equally divided among ye Survivors Item I nominate . . . . . appoint my loving Son John Read my whole . . . . . Sole Excr of the. . . . . and testament revoking all other wills . . . . . appoint and desire We Benj Read &c Mr Thomas . . . . . will in witness whereof I have Set my hand. Mary Read.
. . . . . being prov'd by ye Oaths of
(Read's Bond Excrs Read)
. . . . . Jno. Gibbons of ye County

Page 166
. . . . . and Singular ye Goods Chattles and
. . . . . possession or know
. . . . . possessions of any person or persons for
. . . . . or cause to be exhibited in ye County
. . . . . be thereunto required by ye Court
. . . . . and all other ye Goods Chattels and Credits
. . . . . which at any time hereafter
. . . . . or into ye hands or possessions of
. . . . . do make a true and just acc of
. . . . . thereto required by ye sd Court and also
. . . . . contain'd and Specified in ye sd testament
. . . . . Credits will thereunto extend according
. . . . . Charge then this obligation to be void or
Lawr Smith, Jno. Read, Robt Ballard, John Gibbins. . . . . . . acknowledged. Test Phi Lightfoot Cl Cur Nov 1722

(Ives's bond admon Ives) This bond. . . . . Alice Ives Jas Davenport 2& Wm Blackley of ye County by ye party's. . . . . worshipfull ye Justices of ye County aforesaid in ye Sum of three hundred . . . . . payment well and truly to be made to ye said Justices their heirs and . . . . . Sealed with our Seals & dated this 19th Nov 1722

The Condition of. . . . . that if ye above bounden Alice Ives adm of all ye Goods Chattles and Credits. . . . . decd to make or cause to be made a true and perfect Inventry. . . . . hands or possessions or knowledge of her ye sd Alice or into ye hands. . (*missing*) exhibited into ye County Court of York at such time as she . . . . . chattels and credits of ye said decd at ye time of her death which. . . . . of any other person or persons for her and Alice Ives or. . . . . according to Law and furthur do make a true & Just acct of her. . . . . therein when thereto required by ye sd Court all ye rest as. . . . . Chattels and Credits which Shall be found remaining. . . . . deliver and pay unto such person or persons sd Court for . . . . . Judges shall appoint pursuant to ye Law in that case . . . . . and if it shall thereafter appear that any last will and. . . . . made by ye said decd and ye Ex or

Excrs therein named to each. . . . . ye said Court and make request to have it allowed and approv'd . . . . . approbation of such testament . . . . . be void or else remain in full force . . . . . .

(Baptist's bond for Guardian)
(*Remainder of page is fragmented. These fragments can be seen:* "& John Gibbons. ... Nov 1722. . . E. Baptist shall. . . . Collier orphans. . .)
Page 167
and then: Ed Baptist, Robt Ballard, John Gibbins. At a Court. . . . . Lightfoot ClCur

. . . . . . } Gentl Justices
In ye suit in. . . . . the Compl and Phi Lightfoot
Excr &c. . . . . by ye auditors report
that ye. . . . . pounds five Shillings & four pence
half. . . . . at ye estate of Andr Elmsey
decd. . . . . decreed that ye respondt.
pay. . . . . of ye sd Elmsey if so much
he. . . . . out of ye proper estate of the
. . . . . als exo

(Bates app Guardian Bates)
On ye . . . . . James Bates may be appointed his Guardian. . . . . and his estate be committed to ye Care of. . . . . Blair Gent

Wm Ferguson. . . . . presented and acknowledged their deeds of Lease and. . . . . performance of Covenants for Land lying in. . . . . County to Benj Clifton which at ye said Clifton's motion . . . . . record and ye said Hope being privately Examined . . . . . her right of Dower in ye sd Lands

(Lightfoot app Guardian Philips)
Thos Philips. . . . . permitted by ye court to choose a Guardian made choice of Phi Lightfoot who is appointed to take care of him and his estate

An Inventory . . . . . of ye estate of Nath Hook decd was presented in Court and admitted to record

(Lightfoot fm Dolliss Deeds ack)
A deed of. . . . . performance of Covenants for Lands lying in . . . . . from Mary Doliss to Fra Lightfoot was proved in court. . . . . which is ordered to be certified

The last Will and testament . . . . . of R Harrison decd was presented in Court by

Jno. H. . . . . who made Oath thereto (ye other Excr having relinquished . . . . . Excrs.) and being proved by ye Oaths of all witnesses . . . . . Record On his motion and having given Security Certificate . . . . . him for obtaining prob. therof in due form

(Cross's will prov'd) ... was presented in Court ... being proved by ye Oaths ... is granted for obtaining ... or any three ... Wm Cross ... or any three of them ... of Wm Harrison decd

Page 168
(Miller-Nelson) . . . . . his wife praying that their estate in . . . . . delivered to them by consent. . . . . Wm Sheldon . . . . . to Settle ye acct of ye est of ye sd Robt . . . . . thereof to ye next court

(Cole-Morce dismist) ... & David Morce deft is dismist

(The King -Powers) . . . . . Sovereign Lord ye King plt and Eliza Powers . . . . . is granted her of ye bond decl on . . . . .

. . . . . Laughton who as well as for our Sovereign
. . . . . part Sues plt and Fra Sharp deft.
. . . . . damage by means of ye defts refusing to
. . . . . forfeited by means of his refusing
. . . . . Contrary to an act of Assembly &c
. . . . . Clifton Robt Ballard &c were
. . . . . Evidence retired And being
. . . . . delivered ye same in these words
. . . . . ye King Robt Ballard foreman
. . . . . and its considered that the
. . . . . pounds of tobacco one moiety
. . . . . ye other to ye said Robert as
. . . . . with a Lawyers fee & Costs als Exo

Edw Moor. . . . . having runaway thirty one days and his said Master. . . . . hundred pounds of tobacco in retaking him Ordered . . . . . said Master or his Assigns ten months and Six days for. . . . . time by Indenture Custom or former order is expired

Andrew Laprade. . . . . Robt Laughton in behalf of our Lord ye King agt Fra Sharp. . . . . three days ordered that ye said Laughton pay him one. . . . . pounds of Tob. for ye Same with costs als Exo

Wm Hamilton. . . . . Robt Laughton in behalf &c agt Fra Sharp having attended. .

. . . that said Laughton pay him forty pounds. . . . . Same with cost als Exo

John Wilson. . . . . on evidence for Robt Laughton &c agt Fra Sharp. . . . . days Orderd that ye sd Laughton pay ye sd Pasture one hundred and. . . . . tob. for ye same with costs als Exo

The pet of. . . . . Thos Nixon is cont for ye auditors Settlement of ye estate of. . . . . (Pescod) decd

In ye action. . . . . between Thos Toomer plt &c Saml Tompkins deft Issue being Joyned. . . . . referred till next Court for tryal

In ye Suit. . . . . Jones plt and Jno Battles deft for
. . . . . pounds fifteen Shillings
. . . . . appear to make
. . . . . Court that Exo
. . . . . of ye sd Judgemt (Margin: Jones-Bates Exo issue bona 19 Febr 1722)

(Allen-Powers) (fragments visible include:Powers deft. . Dicet Confirmable. . .)

(Faison-Faylor (Taylor?)

(Philips-Rogers) . . . next friend. . . .

Page 169
(Livingston - Hurlstone) In ye pet of. . . . . at ye Court to answer. . .

(Gomer from. . .) John Matto. . . . . their deeds of Lease and Release of Lands in. . . . . they are admitted to record

Giles Moody. . . . . ias Moody orphans of Phi Moody decd. . . . . take care of ye sd orphans and their estate

Mary ye wife of . . . . . return an Inventory &c of ye estate of P. . . . . (Atkinson to ret Invry)

In ye petition of. . . . . an acct of her admon on the estate of John. . . . . John Wests estate to be referrd back. . . . . that ye deft have lawful notice (Davis-West)

In ye Suit. . . . . Parsons and Eliza his wife Complts and John Hay. . . . . respondr ye Auditors report is admitted to record on. . . . . defts discount It is adjudged and decreed that ye plts. . . . . Costs als Exo

Agnes Drowry. . . . . John Hay at ye suit of Armiger Parsons and Eliza his wife. . . . . days orderd that ye sd Hay pay her eight. . . . . with costs als Exo

Ordered that ye Court adjourn untill ye next Court in Course. Signed Jo Walker. test Phi Lightfoot ClCur

Know all men by these presents that we Eliza. Cross Edw Cross Jno. Gibbins & Jno. Potter of ye County of York. . . . . unto ye worshipfull ye Justices of ye County aforesaid in ye Sum . . . . . Sterling to which payment well and truly to be made to ye sd Justices the. . . . . or Some of them we bind our Selves our heirs Excrs and Admr. . . . . firmly by these presents Sealed with our Seals and dated. . . . .

The condition of these. . . . . that if above bounden Eliza & Edwd Cross Excrs of the last will and. . . . . Cross decd to make or cause to be made a true and perfect Inventory. . . . . singular ye Goods Chattels and Credits of ye said decd which have. . . . . ye hands possessions of any person or persons for said Excrs or into. . . . . exhibit or Cause to be exhibited into ye County Court of York at such. . . . . shall be thereunto required by ye sd Cocurt and ye same Goods. . . . . and all other Goods Chattels & Credits of ye said decd at ye time of his death which shall Come to ye hands . . . . . possessions of any other
. . . . . just and true account of
. . . . . required by ye sd Court and
. . . . . Specified in ye said testament
. . . . . thereunto extend according
. . . . . then this Obligation to be void
. . . . . ber 1722
. . . . . Cross
Edw Cross, Jno. Gibbins, Jno. Potter

Page 170
. . . . . John Hubberd Giles Moody & Wm Davis
. . . . . unto ye Worshipfull ye Justices of the
. . . . . pounds Sterling to which payment well
. . . . . their heirs and Successors or Some of them
. . . . . every of our heirs Excrs and adm Joyntly and
. . . . . our Seals and dated this 17 Xber 1722
. . . . . ye above bounden Jno Hubberd Exr of
. . . . . do make or Cause to be made a true and
. . . . . Chattels and Credits of ye sd decd which have
. . . . . knowledge of ye sd Excr or into ye hands or possession
. . . . . made to exhibite or cause to be
. (. *missing*) shall be thereunto required

. . . . Credits and all other ye Goods Chattels and
. . . . hands or possessions of any other person
. . . . a true and Just acct of his actings & Doings
. . . . said Court and also pay and deliver all the
Legacys contained. . . . . sd testament as far as ye sd Goods Chattels
and credits will there. . . . . thereof and ye Law shall charge
Then this Obligation. . . . . full force & Virtue
John Hubberd, Giles Moody, Wm Davis
. . . . . acknowledged by ye partys. Phi Lightfoot ClCur

(Brookes's est Settled)
List of dispersal. . none remarkable. . names as follows
cash to Mrs Brooks. . Bowcock. . Wm Nelson. . Seamour Powell. . Edw Wright. . Doctor Stark. . . Dr Philips. . Jn Brooks (Several times with Legacys) . . Jn Andrews. . . Robt Franer. . . Patrick Ogilby. . L Patrick. . Robt Ballard. . . Rd Hidedall. . . R Hains. . . . R Grimes. .
and except for J Brooks, Robt Ballard & Patrick Ogilby all were less than 1 pound
Total £373. 3. 12

Page 171
(Hooks Invry rec)
Nothing of note. Much of page missing.

(Cross's will recd)
(undecipherable)

Page 172
continuation of Cross.
(Please note that left side of page is missing.)
. . . . . four negroes vizt. Tomboy Sambo
. . . . . after my decease to my daughter
. . . . . lly begotten
. . . . . Cross a Negro boy named. . . . . . . to him

. . . . . personal estate to b appraised and
. . . . . Edw Cross and my daughter Mary Cross
. . . . . e Cross and my brother Edwd Cross Exctrs
. . . . . I have Set my hand and Seal this
Wm Cross
. . . . . County 17xber 1722
. . . . . in Court by ye Excrs who made Oath to
. . . . . be ye Oaths of ye Witnesses is admitted to

record
test Phi Lightfoot ClCur
. . . . . Bruton Parish in York County being
. . . . . mighty God I am of perfect Sense and memory
. . . . . in manner and form following Vizt
. . . . . and to my blessed Saviour who
. . . . . my body to be decently buried
. . . . . as to my worldly Goods which it
. . . . . in manner following
. . . . . a parcel of Land joyning upon
. . . . . Gilbert & Burnwell fifty acres more
. . . . . Mathew Hubberd & His heirs forever
. . . . . with appurtances belonging to it
. . . . . Maj John Custis Item I will
. . . . . Hubberd one feather bed and furniture
. . . . . Hubberd and ye said Mathew Hubberd my years
. . . . . them both Item I will and bequeath to my
. . . . . bed and furniture belonging to it
. . . . . item I will and bequeath all my Cattle and
. . . . . between them Geo Gilbert being
. . . . . current mony of Virginia and Arthur
. . . . . Robt Clark three pounds of
. . . . . thirty shillings of Current
. . . . . are paid I will and bequeath
. . . . . Matthew Hubberd equally
. . . . . d Steward & Jno. Hubberd
. . . . . Harrison

. . . . . of ye Excr who
. . . . . ye witnesses
. . . . . Cur

another fragment of a will begins at bottom of page. . . . *and my body to. . .*

Page 173

Shillings for. . . . . Ring I give unto my loving
brother Jam. . . . . of real and personal and do
appoint my. . . . . whole and Sole executor of this my last will and
testament. . . . . hereunto set my hand and affixed my Seal
this 8 . . ber year of our Lord . . . . .
Signed Sealed . . . . . Wm Buckner, Thos Nelson . . . . .
This will was presented in Court for York County 17 Xber 1722 and being

proven by ye oaths . . . . . admitted to Record. Test Phi Lightfoot Cl Cur

(Bates's Orphans Bond)
Know all men by these presents that We. . . . . Bates and Henry Holdcraft of ye County of York are held and firmly bound unto ye Worshipfull ye Justices of York County in ye Sum of five Hundred pounds Sterling payable to ye said Justices their heirs and Succesors or Some of them to which payment well and truly to be made We bind our Selves our heirs Excrs Admns Joyntly and Severally firmly by these presents Sealed with our Seals and dated this . . . . . xber 1722

The . . . . . of this obligation is such that the above bounden Jno. Bates do well and truly pay or cause to be payed unto Jane Bates orphan of Jno. Bates decd all such estate or estates belonging to ye sd orphan as is or hereafter shall Come to ye hands or possession of him ye sd Jo Bates or into ye hands or possession of any other person or persons for him when. . . . . soon as ye orphan shall attain to lawful age or when thereunto required by ye Court and shall also save and keep harmless ye sd Court from. . . . . damage that shall or may accrew to them about or concerning ye sd estate Than this obligation to be void or else to remain in full force and virtue. Jas Bates, Hen Holdcraft.

This bond was presented in Court . . . . . xber 1722 acknowledged by ye Oaths of ye partys and admitted to record. test Phi Lightfoot ClCur

(Lightfoots Bond Guardianship Philips)
Know all men by these presents that we Phi Lightfoot Benj Moss & Hen Wyth of ye County of York are held and firmly bound unto ye Worshipfull ye Justices of ye County in ye Sum of three hundred pounds Sterling to which payment well and truly to be made to ye said Justices their heirs and Successors or Some of them We bind ourselves and every of us our and every of our heirs Excrs and admns Joyntly and Severally sealed with our Seals and dated this 71 xber 1722

The condition of this obligation is such that if ye above bounden Phi Lightfoot well and truly . . . . . to be paid unto Thos Philips orphan of Ned
. . . . . estates belonging to ye sd orphan as is or
. . . . . him ye sd Phi Lightfoot or into
. . . . . him when or as soon as
. . . . . thereunto required by
. . . . . or concerning ye sd
. . . . . force & Virtue
Phi Lightfoot, Benj Moss, Henry Wyth,
by . . . . . Lightfoot Cl Cur

(Cross's Invery Rec)

Page 174
(Negro slaves were itemized but not named. : *Negro Girl. . Negro child. . Negro man. . woman.* . appear to be 7 for a total of £ 179.)

In obedience to an order of the Court bearing date of December 1722. . . . .
Subscribers being. . . . . before Colo. Lawr Smith one of his Majestys Justices of ye peace for York did appraise all ye
estate of Wm Cross. . . . . ye executors
witness our hands. . . . .
Edw Cross Excrs . . . . . Robt Harris, Mat Langston, John Morris . . . . . . foot
ClCur 28 Dec 1722

(Innis's est appr)

Page 175
In obedience to an order of York County Court the Subscribers have apprised ye aforementioned Goods . . . . . decd 3 Janry 1722
There is a Nine Gallon Cash of. . . . . Cpt Jones's Store marked RI it wanted . . . . . full at 3¾ p/Gallon. ... Robertson, Robt Ballard, James Mackindo, Richd Baker
At a Court held for York County 21 Janry 1722
This Invry and appraisal was presented to Court and admitted to record ...
Lightfoot ClCur

(Chisman's Will rec)
In ye name of. . . . . Charles Parish in York County being
. . . . . will and testament in manner and
. . . . . Edmd Chisman all my Land
. . . . . live in to him and his heirs forever
. . . . . appurtenances belonging to her one half
. . . . . hood and ye other half to my
. . . . . then I give all my said
. . . . . all my land in YorkTown
. . . . . my Son John Chisman
. . . . . Chisman a tract
. . . . . extending it Self to a dividing
. . . . . lands on Poplar branch
. . . . . and if not Jno. . . . .

Page 176
to him and his heirs. . . . . Item I lend my wife five Negro's named C. . . . . York Jack & after her death ye said five Negros. . . . . among five of my Children Vizt.

Ann Mil (dred) . . . . . s & Elizabeth item I give to my Son J. . . . . Matt I have named Adam to be possessed of ye. . . . . I am deceased to him & His heirs for ever Item I give . . . . . one Mullatto Slave named Hugh to be possessed of ye said Slave at ye age of eighteen years or married to her and her heirs forever item I give to my daughter Mildred Chisman one Negro Woman named Sue and ye first of her increase that shall be born after my decease to her and her heirs forever Item I give to my Son George Chisman one Negro Girl named Sarah to him and his heirs forever Item I give to my Son Thos Chisman one Negro girl named Phebe and ye second increase of ye Negro Woman Sue before mentioned to him and his heirs forever item I give to my daughter Eliza Chisman one Negro Girl named Grace and ye third increase of ye Negro woman Sue to her and her heirs forever and ye third increase of ye negro woman Sue which shall be born after ye three before mentioned I give to my daughter Ann Chisman & her heirs forever Item I give to my Son Edmd Chisman one best Feather bed and furniture and his female head of cattle out of the Stock where I now dwell Six ewes and a Ram twelve head of Sortable Hoggs One Mare named Jenny & her increase to him and his disposal Item I give to my S. . . . . Chisman Six head of female Cattle out of my Quarter Stock . . . . . ewes & a Ram twelve head of sortable Hoggs one horse named. . . . . ye first Colt of ye old Mare Bonny and all ye household stuff belonging unto my aforesaid Quarter Item I give fifty seven pounds . . . . . Shillings and ten pence being in ye hands of Micajah P. . . . . in London thirty pounds of ye said money I give to my Son. . . . . and ye remaining part of ye said mony to my Son John. . . . . All & every particular part of my Estate not already mentioned . . . . . to my wife during her natural life and after her decease to be equally divided among five of my children Vizt Ann Mildred George. . . . . Elizabeth except my Silver Hilted Sword my Long Gun and. . . . . paper trunk which I Give to my son Edmd Chisman . . . . . called Warner & Old little Gun I give to my Son George . . . . . Port Gun to my Son Thos Chisman . . . . . appoint my wife Ann Chisman Excrx & My Son Edmd. . . . . her of this my last Will and test. witnessed. . . . . November 1722 . . . . . Chisman
6 Novr 1722
. . . . . Sarah
. . . . . give y sd Negro to
. . . . . I give ye sd Negro to
. . . . . my daughter Ann Chisman
. . . . . should die without issue
. . . . . under my hand and
. . . . .

Page 177
At a Court held for York County ye 21 Janry 1722
This will was presented in Court . . . . . & Oath to it and being proved by ye oaths of ye witnesses is admitted to record. test Phi Lightfoot ClCur

Know all men by these presents that we Jno. Hansford Chas Hansford & Jno. Gibbins of ye county of York are held and firmly bound to our Sovereign Lord ye King in the Sum of ten thousand pounds of Tobacco convenient in ye sd County to which payment well and surely to be made to our said Lord ye King his heirs and Successors we bind our Selves our heirs Excrs and admins Joyntly and Severally firmly by these presents sealed with our seals and dated this 21 day of Janry 1722

The condition of this obligation is such that id ye above bounden Jno. Hansford hath an order this day granted for a lycence to keep an ordinary at his now dwelling house in York County for ye year next ensuing if therefore ye sd Handsford doth constantly find and provide . . . . . his Ordry Good wholesome & Cleanly Lodging and diet for travellers and pasturage & provender or stableage & provender as ye season shall require for one year and shall not Suffer any unlawfull Gaming in his said ordinary nor on ye Sabath day Suffer any person to tipple or drink more than is necessary then this obligation to be void or else to remain in full force and virtue. Jno. Hansford, Chas Hansford, Jno. Gibbins
At a Court held for York County 21 Janry 1722
This bond was presented in Court and acknowledged by ye partys and admitted to record. test Phi Lightfoot ClCur

In obedience to an order of York Court dated ye 19 Novr 1722 We ye Subscribers being first sworn . . . . . regard to all papers laid before us did proceed to Survey ye Land . . . . . in ye said order as followeth vizt. First we begun at a Gum tree standing by ye branch on ye west Side of ye mansion house then Southwesterly into ye woods to a Corner Chestnut Tree Secondly we begun at a branch westerly from ye first part thence Northwesterly one hundred and . . . . . Chains to a corner Gum in the head line Thirdly from ye. . . . . Gum South forty degrees west to a Gum a Corner tree thence. . . . . easterly to ye branch where we begun to . . . . . In witness whereof we have hereunto Signed Sealed and dated ye 28th day of Novr 1722
John Chapman, Anthony Robinson, Anthony Robinson Junr, John Robinson, Dav. Dison, Thos Kerby, John Wright, Wm Gordon, Edmund Sweny, Henry Wyth. Jno. Selator Surveyor.
At a Court held for York County 21 Janry 1722. This. . . . . admitted to Record. test Phi Lightfoot ClCur

. . . . . Giles Moody Saml Timson & Thos Crips
. . . . . unto ye Worshipfull ye Justices of ye County
. . . . . Sterling to which payment
. . . . . heirs and Successors or Some of
. . . . . Joyntly and Severally firmly
. . . . . 17day of Decr 1722

. . . . . bounden Giles Moody
. . . . . Guardian of Martha Wm and Josiah
. . . . . his Care and Custody ye estate
. . . . . doth well & Truly perform the
Page 178
. . . . . undertaken and pay or cause to be paid his full dues accordingly
. . . . . when they shall attain to Lawfull age or Sooner if ye Court Shall
. . . . . Save harmless and keep indemnified ye said Justices their
. . . . . damages that shall or may accrue to them concerning ye said
. . . . . perform all things enjoynd by Law and order of this Court then this
Obligation to be void or else remain in full force and virtue
(Giles Moody's bond pr Guardian Moody)
Giles Moody, Saml Timson, Thos Cripps
At a court held for York County Jan 21 1722
This bond was presented in Court and acknowledged by ye partys and admitted to record. Test Phi Lightfoot ClCur

Know all men by these presents that we Giles Moody Saml Timson & Thos Cripps of ye County of York are held and firmly bound unto our Sovereign Lord ye Kind in ye Sum of ten thousand pounds of tobo. convenient in ye said County to which payment well & Truly to be made to the said Lord ye King his heirs and Successors we bind our Selves our heirs Excrs and admns joyntly and Severally firmly by these presents Sealed with our Seals and dated this. 1722

The condition of this obligation is such that whereas if ye above bounden Giles Moody hath and order this day granted for a Lycence to keep an ordinary at his now dwelling house in York County for ye year next ensuing If therefore ye said Giles Moody doth constantly find & provide in his ordinary good wholesome and Cleanly Lodging & Diet for Travellors and Stableage and provender and pasturage and provender as ye Season shall require for their horses from ye date of these presents for and during ye term of one year and shall not Suffer any unlawfull gaming in his said house nor on ye Sabath day Suffer any person to tiple or drink more than is necessary then this obligation to be void or else remain in full force and virtue. Giles Moody, Saml Timson, Thos Crips
At a court held for York County 21 Janry 1722
This bond was presented in Court& Acknowledged by ye partys and is admitted to record. Test Phi Lightfoot ClCur

At a court held for York County 21 Janry 1722
Present Lawr Smith, Wm Sheldon Edw Tabb, Arch Blair,Wm Stark

The pet of Wm Hildsman agt Jos Thomas is dismist neither party appearing

On ye pet of Robert Roberts agt Mary ye wife of Wm Atkinson Adm &c ye former order for Settlement is continued till next Court

An inventory and appraisement of ye estate of Wm Cross decd was presented in Court and admitted to record

In ye act of debt between Fra Sharp plt & Andrew Leprade deft is Cont at ye plt s motion & Charge to amend ye declaration

In ye action of debt between Wm Vaughan plt & Edw Tabb& Eliza Hayward Excrs &c Henry Hayward decd defts Issue being joyned ye Cause is ref'd for tryal

In ye action of debt between . . . . . Bell and Mary his wife plt And Wm Ferguson &c defts . . . . .

In ye action. . . . . Colston Read deft for . . due by acct
. . . . . both partys
Submitted. . . . . ye arguments
. . . . . that ye defts
. . . . . Sum of (Brush-Read Judgement)

(Gordon on evidence to be paid)
. . (*missed*) Dyer Colston Read deft
. . (*missed*) for ye same eighty
. . (*missed*) Sheriff repay for one

(Gilbert on Evidence to be paid)

(Moody p. Ordry Lycense)

Page 179
(Falds -Aldo)
In ye Ejectionia Firma brought by. . . . . plt and R. Aldo deft for fifty pounds Sterling damage by means of ye deft with. . . . . and armes &c ejecting & expelling ye plt from his farm Scituate in ye parish of Charles and County of demified When by one Wm Ferguson for a term not yet . . . . . &c Oath being made by John Gibbins ye he delivered a Copy of ye declaration in. . . . . Cause with an Endorsement thereon to Mary Green widdow and John White tennants in possession of ye Lands in question It is therefore ordered that unless ye sd Mary White Green and John White or they or he under whom they Claim having legal notice of this order appear at next Court and make him or themselves deft or defts Confess Lease Entry & Ouster and insist only on ye title at tryal Judgemnt

will be given agt them by default and his Majts. writ of habere facius possessionem accorded to put ye plt in possession of ye premises The last will and testament of Thos Chisman decd with codicil thereto was presented in Court by Ann Chisman and Edm Chisman Excrs therein named who made oath to it and being proved by ye oaths of Jno. Chisman Wm Watkins Jno. Gibbins and Ann Lewelling witnesses thereto is admitted to Record And ye said Excrs having given Security on their motion certificate is granted them for obtaining a probate thereof in due form

Present Joseph Walker

A Power of Attorney from Wm Raymond and Robt Harper to Jeffery Flower Merelv. in Virginia was presented in Court and. . . . . Oath of Wm Whitesides wi/ is ordered to be Certified Giles Moody Sam Timson & Thi. . . . . and acknowledged their bond to ye Court for ye said Moody's Guardianship of ye Orphans of Phi Moody decd which bond is admitted to record

(Moodys Estate to be divided)
On ye motion of Sarah Atkinson . . (*missing*} for Mary ye wife of Wm Atkinsn's Admon . . . . . Moody decd that. . . . . be made thereof between Giles Moody Guardian. . . . . ye Admrx By Consent of ye parties Wm Barbar Chas. . . . . Hewit . . . . . Barbar and Arthur Dickinson or any three of them are appointed to make. . . . . of ye said estate accordingly

On ye petn. of Patrick Ogilvy praying . . . . . estate of Mat Hubberd in ye hands of John Hubberd may be delivered to him. . . . . ye Sheriff Summon ye said John to appear at ye next Court to answer ye. . . . .

In ye petn. of Jno Welch agt ye estate of. . . . . Innis for £4. 10. 0 An attachemnt being retd executed in ye hands of Patience. . . . . she appeared and Says she has none of ye estate of ye sd Robert Innis in her hands upon which and hearing the Evidence ye Court are of oppinion and it . . . . . orderd that ye att be discontd

James Mackindo on evidence for John. . . . . agt Patience Woolfend in having attended two days ordere'd that ye said . . (*missing*) him for ye Same eighty pounds of tobacco with costs als Exo

John Hansford on his petition and giving Security hath an order granted for a Lycence to keep an ordry in this County ye. . . . .

The action of debt between Jos Walker plt agt Chas Lucas deft is dismist ye deft being dead

The action of debt between Fra Tyler plt agt Chas Lucas deft is dismist

. . . . . of our Sovereign Lord ye King agt Mary West
. . . . . or Mullatto Issue being Joyned a Jury
. . . . . Sworn and they having heard ye evidence
. . . . . d and deliverd ye same in these words
. . . . . that ye deft pay to ye Churchwardens
. . . . . sum of fifteen Currt mony
. . . . . aforesaid according to Law wth Cost als Exo

. . . . . plt and Thos Robbins &c Wm Harwood
. . . . . defts issue being Joyned ye Cause is

. . . . . and Alex McClary deft is

Page 180
In ye action of detinue between Wm Morris and Ann his wife plt and Wm Tavernor deft for forty pounds Sterling damage Issue being Joyned a Jury to wit Robt Shields & Thos Toomer &c were sworn and having recd a Special Verdt agreed upon Both partys retired and after Some time returned again and delivered ye same in these words (To wit/ We find that Wm Tavernor father of ye deft ord. to tell John Welch that he had given his girl Judith ye Negro in ye declaration mentioned to his granddaughter Ann Morris and ye Girl was afterwards called her girl We find that ye said Wm Tavernor did sell ye mother of ye said Girl to Giles Tavernor ye father of ye plt Ann Morris and afterwards ye Wm Tavernor said to ye said Ann Nanny I will give you this Girl meaning ye said Girl for if she stays here she will be lost And we find that ye said Girl was carryed to Giles Tavernors and that she was at that time about nine months old We find that ye said Girl remained at Giles Tavernors till he dyed which was about 11 years afterwards and was both by ye Grandfather and ye family called ye Negro of ye plts wife And then Wm Tavernor sent for the Girl and she remained at his house till his death which was about a year and eight months and that upon ye death of ye said Wm We find ye said Negro came to ye possession of the deft who was one of ye Excrs of ye sd Wm We find ye will of . . . . . Tavernor hereunto annexed and that ye negro girl Judith in ye will . . . . . ye same girl which is mentioned in ye declar. We find by ye oath . . . . . Tavernor that she heard that ye said Wm Tavernor ye grandfather . . . . . ye Negro home to his house because she should not be taken as part of. . . . . Tavernors estates and said he should send her back after ye appraisement was on. . . . . she did not belong . . . . . but to his Grandaughter Nanny . . . . . find ye said Negro . . . . . to be of ye value of twenty five pounds . . . . . and if ye . . . . . plt we find for them ye sd negro or ye sd value. . . . . and one Shilling damages for ye detaining if not we pay for ye deft . . . . . foreman wch. Verd. at ye plts motion is recorded & by ...

the partys ye matters of Law arising there from are referr'd untill. . . . . Court to be argued

In ye action of debt between Wm Haughton plt and Damazinale Robert deft for. . . . . ten Shillings ye deft having had time allowed untill this Case and being Called failed to do ye same Judgement is therefore granted . . . . . Nihil Dicit for ye said Sum and cost confirmable at ye next Court on like default

In ye action upon ye Case between Jno Hoy and Ann his wife Excr of ye last will and testament of Cornelius Cormack decd plts and Andrew Leprade deft for . . . . . by acct ye deft having had time allowed him untill this Court to plead . . . . . called failed to do ye Same Judgement is therefore granted ye plts by N D for ye sd Sum & Costs Confirmable at ye next Court on ye like default

In ye action upon ye Case between R Ambler plt & Wm Pratt Gentl deft issue being Joyned ye cause is referred for Tryall at ye next Court

The action upon ye case between Saml Sweny plt & Jas Selator deft is dismist

The action upon ye case between. . . Jones plt and . . . Mc clary is dismt.

. . . . . Lawr Smith deft on ye ... . next Court (Welch-Smith)

The . . . . . (Welch-Wolfendine) deft is dismist

. . . . . is dismst (Diggs-Chew)

(Sweny-Gibbins)

(Morce -Smith)
. . . . . tin Goodwin decd plt

(Brooke-Holt)
. . . . . Holt & Henry Bowcock
. . . . . next Court

(Pescod-Nixon)
. . . . . next Court

Page 181
Jno Welch on Evidence for Wm Morris and Ann his wife agt Wm Tavernor having attended for three days ordered that ye Said Morris pay him one hundred and twenty pounds of tobacco for ye sd time with costs als Exo Hannah Tavernor

ye same

James Parsons on Evidence for Wm Morris and Ann his wife agt Wm Tavernor having attended two days ordered that ye sd Morris pay him Eighty pounds of Tobacco for ye same with Costs als Exo

In ye petition Chas Chiswell agt ye . . . . . of Wm Keith Sr for twenty . . . . . fifteen Shillings and a . . . . . an attachment being returned in ye hands of Capt John . . . . . ye Sheriff Summon to appear at ye next Court and render ye sd Sr Wm Keiths est. in his hands

Mary Cook presented by ye G Jury for having a bastard child Sumd & Failing to appr orderd that ye Sheriff take her into Custody till she give Security and appear at ye next Court and answer ye said presentment

Jane Pain ye Same
Mary White ye Same

Bernard Cowdert presented by ye G Jury for reading ye acct about Slaves according to Law on his Submission & Promise of amendmnt is excused

The Suit of Partition between James Selator & Eliza his wife plt & Wm Sheldon &c deft is dismist and ye Surveyors & Jurys report is admitted to Record

The action of Case between Thos Charles plt & Edw Jacqueline Ex &c Harwood Cary decd deft is dismist

The action of Case between Phi Lightfoot plt & Lawr Smith deft is cont till next Court

In ye action upon ye Case between Eliza Hansford plt & Lawr Smith deft for Shilling on hearing ye argument and evidence ye Court were of Opinion and its accordingly ordred that ye Suit be dismist

In ye action upon ye Case . . . . . Banister and Wm Smelt Excrs &c Wm Smelt decd plt and Henry Holdcraft & Randle Platts decd ye former ordr p. Settlemnt is Contd

The suit in Chancery depending between Jno. Hay and Martha his wife Complts and Thos Toomer surviving Excr of Jno Toomer decd Respond is Cont till next Court

Ordered that Court be adjurnd till tomorrow morning at 9 aClock

January . . . . 1722 Present Lawr Smith, Wm Sheldon, Jos Walker, Wm Stark, Gentl

In ye action of detinue between Thos Toomer plt & Saml Tompkins deft for £100 Sterling damage Issue being Joyned a Jury to wit Robt Ballard &c were Sworn and they having recd a Special Verd agreed upon by both partys retired and being agreed returned again and delivered ye same in these words to wit. We ffind a verdict of a Jury found at a Court held for York County. . . . . 1722 in a Suit depending between ye said partys hereunto annext W. . . . . Nemo & Judith in ye declaration mentioned in ye defts possession We . . . . . York County Court upon ye aforementioned verdt dated 20 Nov 1722 We find ye Negro's above mentioned to be now ye value of vizt. . . . . pounds and Judy fifteen pounds Currt mony. . . . . Toomer in ye above verdt mentioned
. . . . . Smith ye plt we find for him
. . . . . Shilling damage for detaining
. . . . . on p. plt

. . . . . Richd Holmes deft for three pounds
. . . . . left at ye defts house and he failing
. . . . . him agt ye estate of ye said (Braisie)

(Lightfoot-Taylor) . . . . . is cont

(Thomas-Southerland) . . . . . deft is dismist

Page 182
On ye Surety brought by Joseph Walker Gentl agt Wm Atkinson and Mary his wife admit of ye Goods and Chattles which were of Philip and Eliza Moody decd for renewing a Judgemnt of this Court dated ye 18 7ber 1721 by ye plt agt ye said Eliza Moody Exs &c of Phi Moody decd for ye Sum of £ 39. 12. 5 and costs of Suit amounting to 79 lbs of Tobo. the said def having been summoned to Shew Cause if any they have or know why he Exo for ye said debt and costs ought not to have and they failing to appear it is therefore order'd by ye Court and accordingly ordered that Exo go agt the Estate . . . . . & Eliza Moody in ye hands of ye deft for ye aforesd. Sum. . . . . nine pounds & twelve shillings & Five pence w. former & present costs
. . . . . upon ye case between Joseph Walker Gent plt and Wm Atkinson and Mary his wife Adms of ye Goods and Chattels which were of Eliza Moody decd deft for ye Sum of £ 8. 3. 11 ½ by acct prov'd by ye plts Oath A copy of ye writ having been left at ye defts house and they failing to appear on ye plts motion an atta. is granted him agt ye estate of ye said Eliza Moody in ye dects hands for ye aforesaid Sum and cost returnable to ye next Court p. Judgemnt

In ye action of Trespass between Robt Wills plt and Zephaniah Martin deft for £ 20 currt mony damage by means of ye deft entering with force and armes ye Close and house of ye said Robt and him in ye quiet use and occupation thereof to disturb and hinder &c ye deft being Called and failing to appear and ye issue being joyned ye Inquest was taken by default whereupon A Jury to wit Robt Ballard &c were Sworn and they having heard ye evidence retired and being agreed on their verdt retd again and delivere'd ye Same in these words We find for ye plt ten pounds Currt mony damage Wm Gordon foreman which verdt . . . . . tion is recorded and its Consider'd that ye plt recover agt ye deft ye. . . . . pounds being his damages by ye Jurors in manner aforesaid . . . . . Costs als Exo

In ye action upon ye Case between Thos Jones plt and Edw Blackwell deft for £ 15. 5. 0 John Jones became Special bail (?) for ye deft to pay ye Condemnation of ye Court or Surrender his body ye defts discount being allowed Judgemnt is granted ye plt for six pounds eleven shillings and a peny halfpeny and ordered that the deft pay ye same with Costs als Exo.

Jn Hubberd hath furthur time allowed him to bring in an Invry &c of the estate of Richd Harrison decd The pet of Edw Miller & Rachel his wife agt Thos Nixon is cont for Settlmnt

In ye action of debt between our Sovereign Lord ye King plt and Eliza Powers deft ye plt hath time allowed him to consider ye defts plea

. . . . . Wm Sheldon to be released as Security for Jno. Gibbins's admon
. . . . . Richd Philips decd the said John appeared in proper person
. . . . . surrender ye said estate to ye said Sheldon which is accordingly
. . . . . order'd that ye said Sheldon give Security for ye same at ye next Court

(Philips's estate to be settled)
. . . . . Philips Thos Nelson Jos Walker
. . . . . are appointed to audit
. . . . . decd and make

(Power-Bell)

(Collier -Bell)

(Hills pet dismist)

(Pescod- Nixon)

(Allen - Powers)

Page 183
In ye action of debt between James Faison plt and Danl Taylor Excr &c Hen. Taylor decd deft ye plt hath time allowed till next Court to consider ye defts plea

In ye pet of Wm Levinston in behalf. . . . . Mary Hurlstone ye plt hath time allowed to Consider ye defts answer

Mary ye wife of Wm Atkinson hath furthur time allowed to exhibit an Invry of ye estate of Phi and Eliza Moody decd

An invry. and appraisement of ye estate of Robt Innis decd was presented in Court and admitted to record

The petn of Wm Davis agt Mary West is Cont untill next Court

In ye action upon ye Case between Edwd Blackwell plt and Henry Irwin deft for one hundred pounds damage ye deft being called and not appearing nor any Security retd for him On ye plts motion Judgemnt is granted him agt ye said deft & Thos Nelson Gentl Sheriff for ye said Sum and Costs unless ye deft appears at ye next Court to answer ye said action The action upon ye case between Jos Sutton plt & Edwd Blackwell deft is dismst

The action upon ye Case between Wm Anthony plt & R Turner deft is dismist

In ye action of debt nbetween David Morce adm &c Martin Goodwin decd plt & Jos Frith deft at ye defts motion an Imparlance is granted him till next Court

In ye action upon ye Case between Thos Bell plt and Hannah Hay deft Issue being Joyn'd ye Cause is refer'd for tryal

In ye action upon ye Case between George Allen plt &c Jos Platts deft for four pounds a Copy of ye writ having been left at ye defts house and he failing to appear on ye plt motion an atta. is granted him for y said Sum & Costs agt ye defts estate returnable to ye next Court for Judgment

The action upon ye Case between Jno. Hansford plt and Nat Bell deft is dismst

The action upon ye case between Jno. Hansford plt and Mat Moreland deft is dismst

The action of debt between Eliza Powers plt and Phi Hains deft is dismist

The action upon ye case between Wm Gordon plt & Wm Stone deft dismist

In ye action upon ye ye Case Edw Stringer plt & Edmd Clark deft for £ 15 damage The Court on hearing ye partys were of opinion that Suit be dismst

R Albrittain on Evidence for for Edmd Clark agt Edw Stringer having attended two days ordered that ye said Clark pay him eighty pounds of tobacco for ye Same (and not to be repaid again by Stringer) with Cost als Exo

The action upon ye Case between Wm Palmer plt & Edw Stringer deft is dismst

John Read hath furthur time to exhibit and Invry &c of ye est of Mary Read decd

Ordered that ye Court be adjourned untill ye Court in Course. Signd Lawr Smith. Truly Entrd by Phi Lightfoot ClCur

(Williams's est settled)

Wm Atkinson and Mary his wife adm &c Eliza Moody decd

To ye ballance. . . . . Jno. Wms decd
to exhibit. . . . .
By 50/20 ye sd Robt Roberts is willing
to allow out of his bill pd £ 6 to Eliza
Moody dated 2 June 1720 as ye real
. . . . . ye sd Roberts by that bill & on 20ch
. . . . . Wm Atkinson acknowedged he
hath nor furthur demand
Ballance due to ye orphans £ 19. 8. 12
in c/ Date June 18 1722 ========
21. 18. ½

to ye sd orphans of Jno. Wms decd whereby
. . . . . halfpeny appears due to ye sd orphans
. . . . . Janry 1722
. . . . . Admitted to Record Lightfoot ClCur

Page 184
Inventory of appraisement of Negro's Household Goods belonging to ye estate of Eliza Moody. . Vizt
Negroes Finney £ 32 Bess £8 Jenny £ 15 Giles £10 £65
19 Sheep 4. 15. 0
3 horses & Saddle 5. 5. 0
19 Cows 23. 15. 0
3 Steers 8. 7. 6

(*Names noted:* Mr Jos Walker ... Mr Giles Moody ... Robt Roberts ...)

Page 185
In pursuance to an order of York County. . . . . 21 Janry 1722 We ye Subscribers being first Sworn before a Justice . . . . . have met at ye house of Eliza Moody decd and appraised such Goods as. . . . . before us as p. ye Inventory above and likewise have divided them as by ye. . . . . may more fully appear. Wm Hewit, Thos Barbar, Chas Hansford
At a Court held for York County 18 Febry 1722
Hus Invry. and apraaisemnt. of ye est of Eliza Moody decd also ye division of ye said est was presented in Court and is admitted to Record. Test Phi Lightfoot ClCur

Know all men by these presents that we Jno. Chapman Fra Minnis Wm Gordodn & Wm Wise of ye County of York and held and firmly bound unto ye worshipfull ye Justices of ye County aforesaid in ye Sum of eight hundred pounds Sterling payable to ye sd Justices their heirs and Successors or Some of them To which payment well an truly to be made as we bind our Selves & every of us our and every of our heirs Excrs and Admrs Joyntly and Severally firmly by theses presents Sealed with our Seals and dated this 18 day of Febry 1722

The condition of this obligation is Such that if ye above bounden Jno Chapman & Fra Minnis Exrs of ye last Will and testamt of Ann Callowhill decd do make or Cause to be made a true and perfect Invtry of all and Singular ye Goods Chattels and Credits of ye said decd which have or shall Come to ye hands possession or knowledge of them ye sd Excrs or into ye hands or possession of any other person or persons for them and ye same so made do exhibit or Cause to be exhibited into ye County Court of York at such time as they shall be thereunto required by ye said Court and ye same Goods Chattels and Credits and all other ye Goods Chattles& Credits of ye said decd at ye time of his death which at any time after shall come to ye hands or possession of them ye said Excrs or into ye hands or possession of any other person or persons for them do well and truly administer according to Law and further do make a true and Just accg of their acting and doing therein when thereto required be ye said Court and also pay and deliver all ye legacys Contained and Specified in ye said testamnt as far as ye Goods Chattels and Credits will thereunto extend according to ye value thereof & ye law shall Charge Then this Obligation to be void or else remain in full force & Virtue
At A Court held for York County 18 Febry 1722. Jno Chapman, This bond was presented in Court and acknowledged by Fra Minnis.
ye partys and admitted to Record. Wm Gordon, Wm Wise. Test Phi Lightfoot ClCur

Know all men by these presents that We Wm Blackley Jean Pasture & Lawr Holland of ye County of York are held and firmly bound unto ye Worshipful ye Justices of ye County aforesaid in ye Sum of two hundred and fifty pounds . . . . . paybale to ye said Justices there heirs and Successors or Some of them to which payment well & truly to be made we bind our Selves and every of us our and Every of our heirs Excrs and Addmrs Joyntly and Severally firmly by these presents Sealed with our Seals & dated ye 18 day Febry 1722

The condition of this Obligation is such that if ye above bounden Wm Blakely Excr of ye last will and test. of Alice Ives decd do make or cause to be made a true and Just Exc of all and Singular ye Goods Chattels and Credits of ye sd decd
. . . . . possession or knowledge of him ye sd Excr
. . . . . or persons for him and ye same so made
. . . . . of York at Such time as he shall
. . . . . Goods Chattels and Credits and all
. . . . . at ye time of her death which at any time
. . . . . of him ye said Excr or into ye hands
. . . . . him do well and truly administer
. . . . . Just acct. of his actings and doings
. . . . . and deliver all ye Legacys contained
. . . . . Goods Chattels and Credits will thereunto
. . . . . Charge then this Obligation to be
. . . . . Blackley , Lawr Holland, Jean Pasture

Page 186
This will was presented in Court and acknowledged by ye partys and is admitted to record. Test Phi Lightfoot ClCur

In ye name of God Amen I Alice Ives of ye city of WmBurgh in ye Colony of Virginia Widdow being Sick and weak but of perfect & Sound memory and Considering ye uncertainty of this life do make this my last will and testament in manner following first I recommend my Soul to Almighty God trusting in his Mercy for forgiving of my Sins through ye merits of Jesus Christ my Redeemer and my body to ye earth to be buried in a decent and Christian Like manner at ye discretion of my Excr hereafter named item my Will is that all my estate here in Virginia or which shall hereafter be sent in together with all ye estate of Elizabeth my daughter decd whereof I am Admr be sold in ye best manner by ye my Excr & that he therewith Satisfie such debts as are oweing from my said daughter & myself and that he transmit ye remainder to my Son Wm Ives of Oxford in Great Brittain Item I give to my daughter Needham of Plymouth in South Brittain forty pounds Sterling wch I desire my aforesaid Son Wm Ives to pay her out of my effects in his hands if he has not transmitted it hither and all ye residue of my said estate whether here or in England or

elsewhere I Give and bequeath to my said Son Wm Ives Lastly I do nominate constitute & Appoint my loving friend Wm Blaikley of this City gentl Excr of this my last will and testament In witness whereof I Have hereunto Set my hand & Seal This first Day of December Anno Dom 1722 Signed and published and declared Alice Ives in presence of us Mary Peel Ma. . (*missing*) Bainton Jos Davenport
At a court held for York County 18th Febry 1722
This last will and testament of Alice Ives decd was presented in Court by ye Excr herein named who made Oath to it And being prov'd by ye oath of Mary Peel and Jos Davenport is admitted to Record. Test Phi Lightfoot ClCur
Feb 7 1722

An Inventory of Part of ye Goods and Chattles belonging to Richd Harrison decd as they were appraised by Robt Jackson Geo Gilbert Jn Davis

=============

£ 17. 13. 0
test Phi Lightfoot ClCur

In ye (Ann Callowhill) . . . . . Charles
. . . . . but of Sound and perfect
. . . . . ye uncertainty of this
. . . . . do make this my
. . . . . My Creator

Page 187
Assured by beleiving that I shall receive full pardon the free remission of all my sins and be saved by ye precious death and merits of my Blessed Saviour & Redeemer Christ Jesus and my body to ye Earth from whence it was taken to be buried in such decent and Christian manner as to my Executors hereafter named shall be thought meet and Convenient And as touching such worthy Estate as ye Lord in mercy hath Sent me I do give order and dispose ye same in manner and form following that is to Say first I will that all these debt and dutys as I owe in right or Conscience to any manner of person or persons whatsoever Shall be well and truly contented and paid within convenient time after my decease by my Excrs hereafter named Item I give and bequeath unto my loving Grandson Peter Manson & His heirs for ever one Grey horse that he is now already in possession of item I Give and bequeath unto my loving Grandchildren to wit Peter Manson Ann Haughton Eliza Manson Jno. Manson James Manson Walker Manson Jno. Chapman Ann Trotter Walter Chapman Eliza Chapman Mary Chapman Ann Callowhill Ann Nightingale Callowhill Minnis and Ann Minnis twenty Shillings each of them to buy them a Ring Item I give and bequeath unto my loving daughter Ann Morril one of my Gold Rings and my daughter Frances Minnis ye

other Ring item I give and bequeath unto my loving Goddaughter Martha Freeman one Cow & Calf & One lined Suit Item I give and bequeath unto my four Children to wit Jno Chapman Elizabeth Manson Ann Morril and Frances Minnis and their heirs forever my four negro's to wit Walle Hannah Jack & Frank to be valued and equally divided among them And all ye rest of my estate in General that the Lord in his Mercy hath lent me I give unto my four above said Children last named and their heirs forever to be equally divided among them And as to what I have given to my daughter Eliza. Manson I give to her and her disposal And as to what I Have given to my daughter Fra Minnis abovesaid that after her decease I give unto Callowhill Minnis and his heirs forever being her child And of this my last will and testament I make ordain Constitute & appoint by beloved Son John Chapman & Fra Minnis my Son in Law whole & Sole executors revoking and disannuling all other will by me heretofore made or legacys given as witness my hand and Seal ye day & year first above written Ann (¥) Callowhill. Wit. Barnard Cowdert Timothy Bryant
At A Court for York County 18 Feb 1722
This last Will & testament of Ann Callowhill decd was presented in Court by John Chapman and Fra Minnis Excrs therein named who made oath to it being proved by ye oath of Barnard Cowdert a witness thereto is admitted to record test Phi Lightfoot ClCur

Index

www.ingramcontent.com/pod-product-compliance
Lightning Source LLC
LaVergne TN
LVHW050627100826
845148LV00011B/1769

9781680348293